A JOURNAL OF CONTEMPORARY WRITING

IRISH PAGES

IRISH PAGES is a biannual journal (May and October), edited in Belfast and publishing, in equal measure, writing from Ireland and overseas.

Its policy is to publish poetry, short fiction, essays, creative non-fiction, memoir, essay reviews, nature-writing, translated work, literary journalism, and other autobiographical, historical, religious and scientific writing of literary distinction. There are no standard reviews or narrowly academic articles. Irish language and Ulster Scots writing are published in the original, with English translations or glosses.

IRISH PAGES is a non-partisan, non-sectarian, culturally ecumenical, and wholly independent journal. It endorses no political outlook or cultural tradition, and has no editorial position on the constitutional question. Its title refers to the island of Ireland in a purely apolitical and geographic sense, in the same manner of The Church of Ireland or the Irish Sea.

The sole criteria for inclusion in the journal is the distinction of the writing and the integrity of the individual voice. Equal editorial attention will be given to established, emergent and new writers.

The views expressed in IRISH PAGES are not necessarily those of the Editors. The magazine has no editorial or financial connection to the Linen Hall Library or its Directors.

Submissions are welcome but must be accompanied by a stamped addressed envelope or an international reply coupon. Reporting time is four months. If work is accepted, a copy on disk may be requested.

Your subscription is essential to the independence and survival of the journal. Subscription rates are £16stg/E26/ $24 for one year, or £24/E39/ $36 for two years. For postage outside Ireland and Britain, add £4/E6/$5 per year for Europe, or £6/E9/$8 per year for the rest of the world. A subscription form is at the end of the magazine. Credit cards are welcome.

IRISH PAGES
The Linen Hall Library
17 Donegall Square North
Belfast BT1 5GB

Advisory Board
Jonathan Allison
John Gray
Maureen Mackin
Bernard O'Donoghue
Daniel Tobin

Legal Advice
Campbell Stafford & Co

IRISH PAGES is designed by Tonic and set in 11.5/12.5 Monotype Perpetua.
It is printed in Belfast by Nicholson & Bass.

Second impression.

ISBN 0-9544257-1-5

A JOURNAL OF CONTEMPORARY WRITING

IRISH PAGES

CHRIS AGEE, *Editor*

CATHAL Ó SEARCAIGH, *Irish Language Editor*

EDITED AT THE LINEN HALL LIBRARY IN BELFAST

SUMMER 2002

IRISH PAGES

VOLUME 1, NUMBER 1 SUMMER 2002

CONTENTS

Frontispiece by Alfonso Lopez Monreal

Disasters No. 1, by Alfonso López Monreal

THE VIEW FROM THE LINEN HALL

IRISH PAGES arrives at an auspicious time in the history of Belfast. The Troubles are winding down, a new constitutional dispensation is in place, and the civic and cultural transformation of the city after decades of comparative stagnation cannot be gainsaid. Inconceivable even four years ago, Belfast is now a strong contender to become the "European Capital of Culture," which falls to the United Kingdom in 2008. If it succeeds in its bid to be so, the prospect of a genuine cultural and social renaissance – reminiscent of Glasgow's year as Cultural Capital in 1990, as well as of Belfast's earlier periods of civic vitality, such as the moral and imaginative quickening of the late 18th century – may be more than an imagined glint in the eyes of the progressive chattering classes.

The founding premise of IRISH PAGES is that the magazine can be both a Belfast and an international journal – that it can keep faith simultaneously with the Irish (or British) and the cosmopolitan, the local and the international, the native ground and the wider horizon. It seeks to create a novel literary space in the North adequate to the unfolding cultural potential of the new political dispensation. The fact that it is an Irish journal with an equal international dimension in no way lessens, of course, its connection to the city. As the Northern poet John Hewitt (1907-87) might have put it, the magazine is cognisant of the need to reflect in its pages the various meshed levels of human relations: the local (Belfast), the regional (Ulster), the national (Britain or Ireland), the continental (the whole of Europe), and the global. Indeed, one definition of a healthy cultural life is that these various adjectives of human being function in fruitful and unfettered equilibrium. Conversely, the suppression or fetishizing of one or more of them is a sure sign of cultural pathology, existing or imminent.

If, arguably, in the great globalizing metropolises, our human energy and focus are being shifted away from the first two of those adjectives – whose vitality sustains the health of the rest – the same could hardly be said of Belfast in recent decades. Civil turmoil and its attendant cultural claustrophobia choked off some of the oxygen of a healthy equilibrium with the national (ironically), the continental and the global, making the city a byword (however unjustly, in many ways) for the insular, introverted and backwater.

A major consequence of the spatial and historical isolation that descended on the North during the Troubles was an atmosphere of aggravated cultural exceptionalism. We are more familiar with the exceptionalism of certain historically powerful peoples – the American, the Russian, the French, the Serbian – by which the national life or predominant ethnic community is invested by its members with a certain uniqueness, moral or cultural or both, when compared with other nation states. In the North, something similar is clearly in play and, as with all exceptionalism, it is especially apparent to outsiders. The Northern version of exceptionalism hinges on the uniqueness and antiquity of the communal quarrel– unique, partly, precisely because it *is* antique. It manifests itself in a clutch of interrelated outlooks: the conflict's putative intractability and surpassing complexity; its opacity to outsiders; and even (among certain groups) its unique mix of glamour, inevitability and fatalism set against the prosaic political modernity of the Republic and the rest of Britain. No doubt this powerful strand in Northern culture – predominant if not, of course, unchallenged – is conditioned heavily by its isolated geography at the rear extremity of a both archipelago and a continent. Naturally, too, many parallels can be drawn with the rest of the archipelago; but it is also the case there is no real contiguous or commonly used parallel that might serve the North as benchmark to offset, through vivifying comparison, the inertia of such exceptionalism.

Take, for instance, the use of the word *war* in the context of the Troubles, the militarized phase of which, in the minds of most, ended with the Ceasefires of 1994. For anyone familiar with a true war or its aftermath, the usage is deeply problematic. Apart from the formal military legitimacy it tends to confer on paramilitary formations, the word lacks empirical verification. The classic definition of war is open and organized military conflict between states, either in situations of occupation as defined by the Geneva Conventions or in zones of indisputable colonialism unmediated by democracy and the postwar understanding of human rights. In a basic anthropological sense, besides being a "hell", true war is the utter reign of death, the complete suspension of civil society – and that, with perhaps the exception of certain inklings in the early to mid-seventies, has never been approached in Ireland. For instance, in literary terms, there is no essential parallel to be drawn between the writers of Ireland and, say, those of the contemporary Balkans in the matter of war *per se*. The Irish writer has always addressed a large and functioning civil society in the North, not to mention those of Britain and the Republic. There has been civil violence, insurrection, bloodlust, pogroms, terrorism, counter-terrorism and so forth – but never the full antique anthropological activity evident in Homer, Wilfred Owen, or Primo Levi. Belfast was never Sarajevo.

There is then, in the above light, a real sense in which the Troubles were a conflict in search of a context – a lost context perhaps, that might illuminate by lessening the leaven of exceptionalism. Hubert Butler, who figures prominently in this inaugural issue, often wrote of his view that there is a much wider cultural pattern to which Ireland belongs and into which it is subsumed; namely, the small nations of Europe, the so-called Succession States, that emerged out of the imperial aftermath of the First World War. These dozen states created from the fragments of four empires (Russian, Austro-Hungarian, British, Ottoman) were, he commented, "formed at the same time (1918-21), and under the influence of much the same ideas"; but with the exception of Ireland, they all belonged to Eastern or Central Europe and the Balkans. Subsequently, the Baltic States were ingested by the Soviet Union, and the very recollection of the *Mitteleuropa* of the interwar period was suppressed by the division of Europe. With the remainder of the Succession States behind the Iron Curtain, it was understandable, if perhaps no less surprising, that there was so little sense on the island of Ireland of the rich parallels with the East. The oft-cited parallels – South Africa and Palestine – tend in comparison towards the atmospheric, media-driven or ideological, rather than the historical. Meanwhile, set against the stability of Western Europe, Ireland seemed the odd man out, the throwback without a context.

Yet this is surely set to change. All the old Succession States are back as independent nations, and the disintegration of the three communist federations has created a further eleven new European states. Without exception, the Succession States of the interwar period had intense minority-majority problems centring on religion, culture and loyalties (which the Nazis would soon exploit) and this is true of almost all the new states, some of which may shortly join the European Union. In the new Europe, there are strong echoes of interwar Europe in the creation of new states, the reemergence of the idea of *Mitteleuropa*, and the concurrent recrudescence of ethnic strife. Over time, the small states of the East, new and old, cannot but sense a certain affinity with the post-imperial history of both parts of Ireland in comparison with the more settled nations of the rest of Western Europe. In the Balkans, for instance, there has been more historical awareness of the Irish parallel than *vice versa*. All this should be borne in mind when reflecting on what Belfast might offer to the *whole* of Europe in 2008.

Readers who delve into this issue will soon discover a distinct Eastern flavour. There are essays from Poland and Croatia (as well as Japan), and Irish writing on Yugoslavia, Czechoslovakia, Macedonia, Germany and Russia. If there is a trope at work in such juxtapositions, it is that, like Ireland, these nations have a historical narrative which seems unfinished and troubled compared, say, to England's, where no shot has been fired in civil insurrection for three centuries. In the classic English poetry of Wordsworth, for instance, you feel that the historical roof is on; with a post-Holocaust Polish writer like Milosz, you know it is off, open to the sky. A similar "rooflessness," a need to accommodate the horizon of historical danger, can be felt in many Irish writers.

The close kin of exceptionalism is essentialism. (Together, they are a kind of clan). Once exceptionalism gets going in the body politic, it is but a short step to investing various cultural and religious traditions with near-sacramental, communal essence and uniqueness. Obviously, in the North, this is a process pertaining powerfully to the two politico-religious communities, but that does not exhaust its timbre. As the various identity-wars succeeding the Ceasefires suggest – Drumcree et al – essentialism is a no less powerful presence in the general cultural life. No one who views the North through the double light of inside and outside perspectives can fail to miss the deeply self-referential, monocultural, and homogeneous flavour of its society even in the mirror-like expressions of its sacrosanct differences. Its sense of itself is deeply rooted in nativist and autochthonous assumptions that are simply ceasing to be supportable in the rest of multicultural Britain and, increasingly, in the Republic. Freud spoke of the narcissism of small differences and, in the global frame, it does not seem unjust to speak of the Northern communal conflict in these terms.

As in so many other spheres, a kind of provincial cultural establishment grew up and was fossilized during the Troubles, and it – though no more than many Young Turks – liked a tight and cosy cultural closed-shop that funnelled outside attention in certain directions, while ignoring the actuality of a richer pattern, by mapping the scene along well-trodden essentialist paths. To speak emblematically, this strand of Northern sensibility likes to keep the cultural pond small, so as to better benefit from the exotic gaze of outside interest. They resist the introduction of non-native species to the pages of their essentialist guides. Or to mint another ecological metaphor: when it comes to questions of immigration and emigration, they prefer the salmon to the eel. The salmon, you will recall, spawns in the streambed but resides in the ocean; the eel spawns in the Saragasso doldrums but resides in the streambed. Like the historic waves of Irish immigration, the salmon (our first narrative of birth and origins) views the world as his oyster; but woe betide the eel (our adult narrative of necessity and movement) if he should presume the same with the auld sod. Yet the stream does in some ultimate sense belong to both – though, of course, in very different ways.

If it is still too early to speak of real multiculturalism in Belfast beyond the antique pluralism of "the two traditions," a good place to begin this necessary conversation would be with an awareness of past cultural contributions to the city by outsiders. A thorough account of cultural life in Belfast over the past few decades would turn up notable figures from Australia, Austria, Canada, Czechoslovakia, England, Germany, Iran, Mexico, Scotland, South Africa, the United States, Wales, Zimbabwe and, of course, the Republic. That list – like one's sudden recognition of the buried cosmopolitanism of Belfast street names – is liberating in itself because it suggests that the city's emerging potential does, in fact, have a strong pedigree. What is really at issue is not the existence of this pedigree but a new orientation – a new receptiveness – towards the outside world in the aftermath of the excruciating provincialism of the Troubles.

A third variable, fatalism, is part of the same psychic equation that factors in exceptionalism and essentialism. Once a society invests its divisions with an exceptional dynamic and unique communal essences, it sets in motion the pre-conditions of a pervasive fatalism. Nothing *will* change because nothing *can* change. Whatever one thinks of Belfast's bid to become "a capital of culture," and regardless of whether it succeeds, it will have done one thing at least: it will have dented that equation. It will have put into the collective image-bank the idea of re-imagining the city. For it is not merely the deep relevance of the city's recent history to the new Europe, but the very process by which a civil society re-imagines and recreates itself, that makes Belfast the dark horse worth watching.

THE PATH OF THE BORDERLAND

—

Krzysztof Czyzewski

—

A parable for the New Europe.

THE PATH

The earth is traced with paths.

They are like the wrinkles on an old man's face: deepened by pain, drawn taut by vigilance, cast with a quiet light from tears of bitterness and joy, with death they become overgrown.

They leave a trace. They print what is in act.

Wisps of destiny vanishing in the shadows, beyond the next bend, or when looking towards the sun. They are struck by striving; twisted, because obedient to the earth; with the pollen from flowers and the dust of the ages; always going against the wind, because they return without turning back upon themselves, different now.

No one on the Earth knows their entire map.

No one is sure whether they originate from within us, from our will and intuition, or whether it is the invisible hand of the Lord of Fate that has traced them.

Maybe the Indians knew the answer as they drew the image of the She Who Watches on the cliff rock by the Columbia River.

Perhaps. We do not know.

The traces are swept away, and the knowledge is forgotten.

It is the animal's trail a wayfarer chooses to follow.

The animal trails are the only paths left in those places where Indians were forced to live on reservations, where there were *Kristallnacht* orgies, and where transports to the Gulag set off, one after the other. They are found beyond the newcomers' horizon, in places they do not know, where the underbrush makes memory impossible.

The slender bridge, lost in the forest in Stanczyki near Sejny, seemed to be a pillar supporting the path of an ancient civilisation. Lifeless, leading nowhere. No-longer-a-path.

Because the path runs through, cutting through the undergrowth.

It requires living feet, an eye in every inch of one's body, hesitation before stepping into the unknown.

Wanderers – an animal, a man, and an angel – prepare to sleep on the path, which is why it is so full of the hope of awakening and continuing on one's way.

That is how dream comes to be practice.

No-longer-a-path perishes in nostalgia, still asleep with its dreams.

Each name goes along its own path, unique.

Each path prints that which is unique in each of us: our heart's weight, the strength of our backbone, our vision.

The path bears our name.

The path runs in different ways.

A man plants a tree, builds a house, presents an artwork, but a path he follows. Day and night. Without even being aware of it. He is not dealing with the path's practice. He comes to know the skills of different professions, which enable him to conquer new territory and erect new buildings.

He settles on specialized islands, which are drifting apart from each other, barely communicating with one another.

The path hides.

We do not have it in our civilisation, where everything is prepared for presentation and sale, put into showcases or on the stage, or sometimes just on a modest pedestal, isolated and specialized. Everything there is "about" something, and "in relation to" it.

The path is not "about" something and "in relation to" it. It just runs.

It is all in the acting, which means it is actually an uninterrupted succession of small steps.

In today's culture the path has come down off the stage and has begun tweaking the numbed feet of the audience.

It wants to be an active culture, though it has no technique for accomplishing this.

The nameless are taking their first steps.

Around them the thick overgrowth. They draw out an oddity that seems a bit silly to the rest of the audience. But they no longer escape into seclusion, to be by themselves as was once the case. They stay amid others and are active among them.

The path is a sphere, filled with the voices of other people, children, history, responsibility, and all of life's small things.

For this path, even the sky is beneath feet, where all of our day-to-day matters lie.

The path falters.

Not because it has lost its way. It is simply searching in a different way, setting that which is already prepared and familiar aside.

It sees with our closed eyes. When we will stop bowing to the audience or applauding the illusionist.

The path comes right up to the border.

This is the only way it can live.

Everything that is awakened knows the border. Day and night have their borders, as do human communities, states, and religions. They are among others, and others are other among them. They define the border and remain close, just across the way, always in the neighbourhood.

And the path goes that way, 'twixt.

The path comes right up to the Other.

Only in this way can it bear a name.

Everything that is open meets the Other.

The path that runs along the border strengthens it.

Another one crossing it becomes a path of the borderlands.

As an uninterrupted succession of small steps, it is in its own element on both sides, neither strengthening the border nor eroding it. But crossing it. It is like a bridge which continues on, but upon which one cannot build a home.

One can only be at home in a place from which it is possible to leave.

The borderland runs along the path.

THE BORDER STONE

A border stone exists since a path is printed on the earth.

A man laying down a border stone is marking where his property ends, the space of his homeland. Not only is he marking his possession of it, and his belonging to it, but also his own separateness. That is how he gives himself a name.

Borders rest deep within us all, providing support for our imaginations and locating us in our place under the sun. They should not be violated.

A border stone used to be defensive.

It fortifies. It closes us within our own, in an introverted circle.

It defines the *limes,* our civilisation's border, beyond which lurk the barbarians; or a buffer along the border, beyond which lies a different nation (since we live in nation-states); or the boundary of our farm; or our front door; or the threshold of our apartment, demarcating the point beyond which we find our neighbour – the Other.

A man who lacks the instinct of self-defence perishes.

A man who has a besieged-fortress mentality kills, and if he himself dies, a plague befalls those within the walls.

It sometimes happens that a man draws from the border stone only the defensive strength. This is how he forms his own culture, handed down from generation to generation. He feels good among his own kind. He does not like to travel much, and forgets about the code that accompanies a culture of dialogue. The Other becomes a threat. For him, it is torture every time guests must be received, and he must show a familiarity with the principles of *savoir vivre* in front of his neighbours. He begins to develop complexes. He reinforces his border. He stands guard at the entrance gate.

The culture of the nation-state is that of the gatekeeper.

Closed. This has not been brought about by a sudden slamming shut of the gate. The closing lasts over generations. It has had its inevitabilities, its triumphs and praise, as well as its heroes and geniuses. Over time, it engenders many habits, approaches, traditions, and a certain mentality … And it erases all traces of the Other, opposing and forgetting it.

A man raised in this culture erases the foreign-sounding names of old monuments, without having any sense that he is missing anything in particular by doing so.

He knows nothing about the polyphony, and is deaf to the harmony of one voice joined by others.

For him, dissonance always sounds off-key.

He strives to be self-sufficient and to encompass the *universum* within himself. The *limes* that he defines thus no longer embraces the entire civilisation, but rather his own nation – making those beyond its borders into "foreigners", and, most often, enemies.

A closed culture is created virtually imperceptibly.

Those who believe that the gates to their world remain open until they hear them slam shut are merely deluding themselves.

The culture of private property is that of the gatekeeper.

The entire space of the Western world is delineated by private property, with signs announcing: "Keep Out", "No Trespassing", "No Entry". Gatekeepers stand near these signs, on edge. They are concerned for the sake of peace and quiet, and for their own safety.

The Other appears as a threat once again, though merely keeping him at bay does not change the fact that inside the walls there is sure to be more unrest than peace and safety.

In this culture, there is no longer a servant acting as a doorman.

He was a slave yearning for his freedom.

In this culture, there is now a lord on his estate, with capital that is increasing, and it is he who is the gatekeeper now. He does not yearn for his freedom because he does not even know he is a slave.

Western culture does not yearn for its freedom.

It, too, has been in the process of closing for generations. It, too, has its lofty values, its martyrs and it great victories. And it, too, has been closing imperceptibly, without any great slamming shut of its gates.

It is natural for a man to possess something of his own, to improve his property, and to protect it like his own child. There is nothing immoral about this. Worse, however, is if the *agora* disappears along with it – that place where people can meet others, where views can be exchanged, where there is motion, a place of confrontations and polemics.

If it does, then the places where people live turn into long, straight streets, intersecting less and less, mere extensions of people's private property, with their own guarded gates. The little crooked streets disappear – those that become narrower the closer they get to the city center, bringing people together more the narrower they become, tempting them with cafés and clubs, drawing them out of their homes – at least in the evenings – and beckoning them to the market square that is everyone's to share.

Agora – that meeting place that gave rise to democracy itself – has ceased to be the center of that space.

The culture of private property has transposed the center there, to people's private possessions, which are self-sufficient, and armed with an increasingly perfect technology that enables them to communicate with the outside world. Except that they are within thick walls, with its ever-vigilant gatekeeper, always on edge.

A person who has lost his *agora* is not capable of giving or receiving gifts.

One such gift to another can take the shape of a celebration that binds the community, creating a basis for its very existence.

In the language of the Pacific Northwest Coast Indians, the potlatch was just this kind of gift, a word that Marcel Mauss has translated as "to nourish". In their material culture, a representation of the gift was "eaten" during the act of giving, and the gift was only consumed at that moment – here I am drawing on the work of Lewis Hyde, author of *The Gift* – "when it moves from one hand to another with no assurance of anything in return".

Some Indians, however, in their later ceremonies suffered the erosion of the original meaning of potlatch.

In our culture, a gift has become a present, faded and multiplied to the point of being erased completely by wealth, made into something purely material in nature, something conditional, something given without any sense of the needs of the gift's recipients.

A present makes us dependent; a gift makes us free.

A present ensnares us through possession.

A gift exists thanks to possession, but it goes beyond that, giving possession sense through the careful giving of a gift to someone else.

Maybe that is why the Haida Indians called their potlatch "killing wealth". And maybe that is why a gift hears the Other.

A present is at home in the culture of receiving, passive, in a conditional exchange.

A gift is at home only in an active culture, one of participation. It leads one onto the path.

A man who looks over his shoulder, checking to see how he can get ahead and expecting some kind of reward, is not someone on the path.

A gift is the path that takes us through the *agora*.

That path does not go back on itself, and the gift does not expect to be reciprocated.

The path learns about returning by going forward, and a gift enriches unconditionally.

A border stone abounds in ambiguities.

It influences those nearby in different ways.

And people and borders are always in close proximity, just like animals and the forest.

Man places a border stone out of his fear of infinity, of spatial limitlessness.
He places it, because to be everywhere is to be nowhere.
And "nowhere" is not a human's real name.
So he searches for his own place.

Space without a border stone is one of rootlessness.
The path goes along, searching for a place.
How the path practices is how it finds its place – there is no other that can be found.

The path and the border stone rooted us in a space that is infinite, nameless, and overgrown.
They get our bearings in the world, as do the sun and stars.
We take our bearings from them – we who have survived the cataclysms of the twentieth century, we who inhabit the landscape after the end of the world, where the "exiled and lost were at home" (Celan).
An inhabitant of these areas where orchards have grown wild, where memory has become overgrown, and where bridges have been torn down – mostly a newcomer from somewhere else, because there are few natives left now – he must place his border stone anew – in other words, he must now define himself. He must do so in a new way, working out his own technique from scratch, finding himself on the path cutting through the undergrowth.
By placing the border stone, a man identifies a new *u-topia*.
The poet Paul Celan – a poet-survivor, who juxtaposed a new word with silence – wrote this word *u-topia* down in this way to refer to a place that does not exist, but which we nevertheless aspire to: thus, it actually exists, "faraway and occupiable". He juxtaposed *u-topia* with another Greek word, *me-topia,* which describes a place that does not exist as a "non-place".

A border stone is also a striving, transcending, start of the quest.
A journey is not undertaken by men who are everywhere and nowhere.
A non-place has no path, no memory, no border, and no name.
Everything that makes the path, memory, border, and name, creates the place itself.
A man most often places a border stone where there are crossroads.
That is how he establishes a meeting place.
By marking his separateness and giving himself a name, a man gets his bearings with respect to the Other, becomes more inclined to engage in conversation, watches to see if someone is coming.

Not always so that they can shut the gates and ward off intruders.

Sometimes he does this in order to get news from the outside world, to get a taste of dialogue, and to brush up on his debating skills.

At the border stone stands not only a gatekeeper, but also a *pontifex*, the builder of the bridge.

He needs a clear edge for the span that is to raise the delicate construction of links, a border that will be crossed. That is why the *pontifex* chooses to locate the span by the same stone the gatekeeper uses to mark his property.

The construction of the span at first is like that of a tower.

The gatekeeper might believe he knows something about this field.

But bridges are not constructed alongside rivers.

A *pontifex* turns the tower into the bridge's span, something that had been closed into openness.

He transcends the bank that served as his foundation.

He bridges that which had been divided.

This cannot be accomplished overnight.

Culture sustains the bridge's builder, just as it does the gatekeeper.

A culture that transcends the bank that served as its foundation is a border-land culture.

BORDERLAND

The borderland is the shadow cast by the border on the nearest neighbour-hood.

Therefore, a life-giving buffer zone takes shape, one protecting diversity.

It differs from the usual kind of buffer zone – empty, guarded, and rife with enmity.

The borderland does not erode the borders, but rather expands the sphere that they encompass, absorbing those who live there, accepting their intermingling as a matter of course.

Borderland is an *agora*. Here, he who is not in dialogue with others simply vegetates on the periphery.

The centre of this sphere is always found in the meetings that take place there – and its circumference is found in that which remains untouched by Otherness – in other words, nowhere.

The borderland deprives the border itself of the ruthlessness inherent in a thin line that slices through open space and divides it, while at the same time rendering everything in its immediate vicinity barren.

Anyone who lives in a border zone thinks more about crossing it than about going back home.

In the animal world, the borderland plays a role similar to the one it plays in the human world. Ornithologists use the idea of an "abrupt edge" to refer to the border between two zones of vegetation, and also to the benefits of spending time in both.

> *The advantage of the edge is that it allows the bird to live in two worlds at once, and the more abrupt the more intense the advantage. From a position of height or secrecy, the bird can spy for danger or prey; it can come and go quickly, like a thief. Here the vegetation is more varied, the shade and cover thicker; the insect life rising, the tanager can sweep down from its treetop, the thrush can fly out from the gloom, and the redwing can sit on the fence post all day in the summer sun.*
>
> *The edge is a concept of a doorway, shadow and light, inside and outside, room and world's room, where the density and variety of the plants that love the sun and the open air yield to the darker, greener, cooler interior world, at the margin.*
>
> *It is no surprise, then, that the greatest number of species as well as individuals live at the edge and fly the pathways and corridors and trails at the joining of the juxtaposition. That is where the richness is, the thick, deep vegetable life — a wall of life, where the trees turn to meadows, the meadows to columnar, watchtower trees.*
>
> *A man of sense, coming to a clearing, a great open space, will always wait among the trees, in the doorway until the coast is clear.*
>
> Stanley Plumly, *The Abrupt Edge*

Space — naked, shadeless, and lacking a safe refuge — is hostile to those who happen to pass through, as well as to newcomers and outsiders. Nowhere else is their difference so noticeable.

In a place where there are no bridges, there are also no neighbours willing to help each other build the roofs over their heads.

In the borderlands, a man lives in the shadow of the Other.

He lives because he struggles with him, engages in polemic with him, profits from him (even if it is only in the form of theft).

He gains identity by emerging from the shadow.

He emerges from the shadow by gaining identity.

Only in a struggle, in that constant grappling with the Other, does he become unique, his own man. Separate traditions and religious or national affiliations are not enough. Only when one confronts, when one meets with Otherness in this place of intermingling, does one's identity appear. Here – in the borderland.

The borderland is not a promised land for those seeking peace, assuagement, and neighbourly love.

Tension and quarrels are something endemic here, just as the threat of cataclysm is implicit whenever the earth begins to quake – the order of the day in tectonically active areas. And just as distilled water is not good for the human body, any attempts to render differences sterile only poison the living tissue of the borderlands.

Otherness is the bacteria that makes it possible to live and survive in borderland.

The borderland, as a sphere for communication, also provides a place for true separateness.

Precisely because the *agora* is at its center, all around different districts can continue to exist while maintaining their own traditions.

The borderland does not know conformity, only consensus.

It knows renunciation, but not renouncement.

It witnesses reconciliation, which, although always difficult, never comes at the cost of blurring the truth, or of oblivion.

Here "shared" does not mean "homogeneous", and what is "in-encounter" does not mean "standardize".

It is the counterpoint, not the conflict that's essential here.

The borderland resounds with a dissonance that supplants the culture of the gatekeeper.

The borderland's song is inherently polyphonic, one whose harmony arises from voices sung in dissonance in relation to the main melody, which has no voice of its own, but rather emerges from many, creating one amidst them all.

The song of the borderland cannot be sung by one man alone.

It is structured on the basis of polyphony, thanks to which not even one voice will be dominated by others or obliterated. The silence of one voice makes the listener wait.

The dynamic of the borderland derives from the drama of failed encounters.

When it does come to pass in the borderland, the *Vergegnung* that was so troubling to Martin Buber incites discussion and makes us aware of our own ignorance and narrow-mindedness.

Not knowing a language when you need to communicate with someone else makes you realize the need to learn it. The same is true of the shame of not noticing differences, and the injury that can arise from someone's unfamiliarity with other people's customs.

This is the path of the borderland.

Unsuccessful encounters do not break the dialogue off. Sometimes such events actually initiate dialogue by laying bare how difficult – and sometimes even impossible – it can be.

The borderland constantly puts a man to the test with these failed attempts and guarantees their occurrence. Thus, they draw us, too, into the drama of the path they are on.

The path becomes overgrown and the space for such encounters disappears only when non-encounters take place, and when there are no situations that can put us to the test, when our isolation proves complete – often the result of an ideology characterised by hatred and threats.

It is then that the temblors and tensions inherent to the borderland can explode into a destructive cataclysm.

The following Hassidic story says much about the borderlands:

> Once Rabbi Chaim of Krosno, one of Baal Shem Tov's pupils, was watching a tightrope walker with some of his own pupils. He seemed so absorbed by the spectacle that they asked him what he found so fascinating in such a simple-minded display. "That man," said the rabbi, "is risking his life, but I wouldn't be able to tell you why he is doing it. He cannot be thinking about the fact that he is making 200 guldens by doing it, because if he were, he would certainly fall."
>
> Martin Buber

The borderlander is like that tightrope walker, going along a thin, taut line between forces that can easily annihilate him if he loses his balance. This is an art.

Most importantly, we must stop being so focused on ourselves, on our "200 guldens".

To make a step further in the borderland, a man must leave his cozy hearth, still warm from his own opinions, values, and interest, and concentrate on the Other by stepping into the shoes of that person on the opposite bank.

Otherwise he won't budge an inch.

And if you stand still on a tightrope, you lose your balance.

If a concept of tolerance does exist in borderland, it does not just mean the acceptance of others.

Understanding and respect go one step further, but always fall short.

The only way we can live up to the word "tolerance" is when we carefully reach out to others, and in so doing liberate ourselves from those "200 guldens".

This is not just a superfluous question of style or a caprice for borderlanders, it is a question of life and death, just as keeping his balance is for a tightrope walker.

I cannot say why it is that a borderlander does these things – why he wanders away from home, among different peoples, across bridges into the unknown.

I know only that if he turned back, concerned about his own possessions, he would lose the love of his life forever, whom he should betroth upon crossing to the opposite bank.

THE PLACE

We have no one to teach us which parts of our landscape were once thought to be sacred.
Gary Snyder

The path is rubbing against the border stone that gives a foundation for a bridge's span and the bridge is crossed by a borderlander.

A new beginning arises from what is closed and overgrown, from wordless conversation.

The bridegroom crosses the threshold of his own home.

A practitioner steps on to the path, which runs to the very place.

A memory being awakened knows a place, so it goes ahead, because there is no other one, only a place before us, unattainable.

Indians build their *longhouse,* different than their own homes, so they can have a place to meet.

The bride waits on the opposite bank.

She/He Who Gives ties a community.

Marriage awaits those who transcend themselves and their possessions.

Sitka, Oregon, Spring 2001

Translated, from the Polish, by the author.

Krzystof Czyzewski is the Editor of Krasnogruda, *a Central European review. He lives in Sejny, near the borders of Lithuania and the Oblast of Kaliningrad (Russia).*

AN IRISH EPILOGUE

Helen Lewis

For a survivor of Auschwitz, Belfast is home.

I

I was married to my second husband in June 1947 in Prague. Harry Lewis came from the same small town in Bohemia in Czechoslovakia that I grew up in – Trutnov (or Trautenau in German), in the Sudetenland. It was very near the German border and at the foot of the Giant Mountains. We had been at grammar school at the same time in the late 1920s. Harry, who was born in 1909, was seven years older than me, so that when he was in his last year, I was in my first.

In the mid-thirties, we had had a small romance. He must have been very fond of me – he must have loved me. (It came back to him with a vengeance, I guess, after the war!). I was in my last year at school. Harry had gone to Vienna and Florence (and Paris briefly) to study in the early thirties. His parents still lived in Trutnov, and when he returned with a doctorate in commercial science – economics now – he was Dr Lewis. The degree enabled him to obtain higher and better employment, and he soon obtained a managerial job in a handkerchief factory.

We met a dance in early 1935. It was a real romance, very deep. I finished *Realgymnasium* later in 1935 with the *Matura* exam. After that, my mother and I moved to Prague (my father had died in 1934), and I entered professional training in dance and studied philosophy at the German University of Prague. At the same time, I continued private studies in French. So I was very busy studying French, philosophy and dance, a rather funny combination in retrospect.

Harry and I broke up about a year later over my love for dance. Dance in those days was not quite recognised as a higher art, not quite seen to be up to the standard of good society. It was not considered by some totally respectable; not something a proper middle-class girl took up. Harry disliked not dance itself, but my fervour and passion for it. He was unhappy and less-than-understanding about my professional training. But I was totally devoted to it, and it was of a very high standard. My teacher, Milcá Mayerová, had studied in Germany with Rudolf Laban, the first and greatest founder of modern dance in Europe. To this day, there is a Laban school of contemporary dance in London. In dance, Laban is supreme. I was lucky enough to meet him once in postwar London on a summer course.

So a romance had blossomed between Harry and me. But because he didn't appreciate how dance was a very important artform, it remained for him a slightly dubious entertainment. We hadn't spoken of marriage, we were too young – he 26, me 19. Probably he was fed up hearing me go on endlessly about dance when we met during holidays. There was a slight element of jealousy towards dance, since I was always telling him how much I loved it. He was jealous, but also suspicious, which together amounted to the wrong attitude. Instead of happy times, we argued. I couldn't go on with the relationship, given my love of dance, and so we parted.

A short time afterwards, I met Paul Herrmann. He was a Czech of Jewish background. By chance, he lived in the same building with his parents. We met at some social occasion and our romance developed quickly. By now, I was about 20, and Paul 27 or 28. He ran a factory making leather gloves. We fell in love very swiftly. My mother was still sorry, however, that I had broken up with Harry.

Very shortly after finishing my three years of training in dance (1935-38) and just after my university exams, Paul and I married. We went on a wonderfully idyllic honeymoon to Yugoslavia, to the beautiful island of Rab in the Adriatic. It took, in all, about three weeks. But how long can you spend on honeymoon? We travelled by bus and train along the Dalmatian coast, through Rijeka, Split and Dubrovnik. A lovely honeymoon on Rab – can you imagine?

We returned to Prague. 1938 was a critical year, politically. We had a lovely modern flat in a modern building. I was teaching at Mayerová's school of dance as a kind of assistant to Milcá. But I also did some choreography with my pupils. That art takes time, however, to develop. I was still very young and a bit of a beginner.

The Munich Agreement came in the autumn. It changed everything: our whole life, our whole outlook. Nazi Germany was now the threatening neighbour. The first signs of the catastrophe were in Sudetenland where Nazi ideas spread quickly and willingly. The Germans of the Sudetenland absorbed Nazi ideology with great eagerness and enthusiasm. Difficulties emerged in the border regions. In Trutnov, Nazism became strong and viscious. The Germans in Prague became contaminated. Paul and I knew it was getting closer and closer to us – we were reading and listening to the radio day by day – we knew something very dangerous was imminent. Hitler's speeches were already orientated against Czechoslovakia. He made his demands for the Sudetenland – that it should become German geographically as well as in mind.

We were part of the Czech nation but also, as Jewish people who spoke German, aware of the fierce anti-semitism of Germany. In late 1938, the border regions were taken over. Then on the 15th of March 1939, Czechoslovakia was invaded. From that moment, everything changed utterly for us – and for everyone. The first deportations of the Jewish population came in late August 1941. From a peaceful, democratic life, we were under threat from the Nazis. President Benes had fled to England; Hacha became the puppet President. When I was a little girl, Masaryk was President in the first democratic republic. A writer, philosopher and politician, he was one of the greatest men of Central Europe. Now Czechoslovakia had been shrunk to its centre. We were deported in 1942 to Terezin, in Bohemia; and then, in 1944, to Auschwitz, where Paul and I were separated.

Helen Lewis's unforgettable memoir, A Time To Speak, *focuses on her last years in prewar Prague and the horrors of Terezin and Auschwitz. It ends with a brief Afterword on her arrival in Belfast in 1947. Of this memoir, Ian McEwan has written:"Helen Lewis survived the greatest nightmare ever dreamed by man. Her story is appalling, mesmerising, and one reads on with increasing gratitude for her clarity, honesty and courage."*

II

Paul had not survived. He died on a forced march in the spring of 1945, just before the war ended. When I returned to Prague in 1945, I didn't know, of course, that Paul wasn't alive. It was very, very hard to accept it when the news came. And my mother had also perished. But my father's sister Tilly had survived, because she was married to a German and "Aryan", according to the race laws. They were my only close relatives alive, and lived in Mladá Boleslav. I was in hospital in Mladá Boleslav and spent quite a lot of time with them. It was in hospital that Tilly brought me the first letter from Harry.

Harry had escaped to Britain from Czechoslovakia in 1939. His parents had left first, since they were British citizens. His father had previously emmigrated to South Africa and had served in the Boer War, for which he was awarded British citizenship, before returning to Europe. But Harry arrived as a refugee (as British citizenship did not extend to children), joining his parents in Belfast. They had come to the city through some previous connection to the linen industry in the Czech Lands.

Harry saw my name in Belfast on a Red Cross list of survivors. He wrote. It took a long time – some weeks – for the letter to reach me in October 1945. It was my last day in hospital when my aunt brought me the letter. I still remember how she smiled, because she knew Harry well. He was easily the last person I would have expected: it was not only a great joy but a great surprise. Harry was overjoyed that I was alive. We started to write to each other. He had never married. He must have waited for me. The correspondence became warmer and more loving. When he travelled to Prague in June 1947, we knew there was a certain purpose behind it. We still had to meet to see what the personal chemistry would be like apart from the correspondence. We married about a fortnight after his return. This is how I became a British citizen.

Harry went back to Northern Ireland before I left. I had so many things to settle. I arrived in Belfast in October 1947. I came to a new world. There were so many things to learn – the language and, indeed, everything. Ireland seemed a little, innocent land. Innocent in comparison to what we had been through in Central Europe; innocent in that, in this sense, Ireland seemed untouched. In 1947, I couldn't really understand the trouble between Catholics and Protestants (I still don't) – that was something unknown to me then. In those days, it just seemed a peaceful land. It took a very long time before I could even accept there was trouble. Compared to the Sudetenland – well, there was no comparison at all. Anything that happened here seemed childish. Remember that this was just after the War, just after the Great Evil, and everything in that light seemed innocent and almost childish.

It wasn't easy to get used to everyday life here. Language was a big problem, for my English was poor. Everything seemed very strange. For instance, the dampness of the climate compared to the dryness of Central Europe. Or the customs, in so many ways – and then so many of them, good heavens. After the War, there were numerous survivors like me in Central Europe. But here, in Belfast, I think I was the only one. No one could even begin to understand what I had been through. I never spoke of my experiences, but on the rare occasions when I felt I had to, I met complete disbelief. People were reluctant to ask questions. They didn't even want to know because it was all so painful and gruesome.

I did meet in Belfast the greatest friend of my life: the painter Alice Berger Hammerschlag, who was from Vienna. She was married to Heinz Hammerschlag whose first wife Hilde Inwald was, strangely enough, also from Trutnov. Hilde's younger brother was in the same school class as me. During the war, I had met Hilde by chance in Prague a few days before she was deported on a punishment transport. I was the last person able to tell Heinz of having spoken with her just before the transport. Heinz had escaped earlier. He and Alice met later in Belfast. Again, strangely enough, Alice's elder sister Trudy had been a girlfriend of Harry's at university in Vienna.

It wasn't easy to overcome the shadow of past suffering – to live a normal life. I didn't realize it at the time, but the fact that I was transferred to such a completely different environment was a great help. What helped enormously, too, was having children: Michael was born in 1949, and Robin in 1954.

Of course, the loss of my own family – mother and Paul, uncles, aunts – was never easy to overcome. To say you overcome loss doesn't mean you ever forget – or could ever place it outside the new life. With time you just learn to accept it. And I realized I was just one of so many who had suffered such losses, and that helped a little. To this day, I can say that the loss of my family is something I can never reconcile myself with or really get over. You always carry the sorrow. You cannot say the loss of family and friends in the camps is like losing loved ones due to a long illness or old age. To perish that way, in the camps, was a uniquely cruel fate. My mother was taken when she was healthy and still only 50: God knows what terrible way she died. She was deported before us, in early 1942, directly to Poland on a transport, probably bypassing Terezin. She died in a death camp in Poland from which no one came back. It was total destruction.

I had my dark periods, of course, but living here in a different world, with two beautiful and successful children, sustained me. And then there was dance. The time was ripe, and the place was right, for dance in Belfast. In the late fifties, there was such an eager response because, until then, modern dance was an unknown style here. Only classical ballet and Irish dancing were known and performed. And I found gradually I had a talent for teaching.

Beyond my happy marriage – wonderful and understanding husband (who didn't object to my dancing anymore!), and two lovely children – what sustained me was my very close, intimate and precious friendship with Alice. It was the sort you don't find everyday, one of those rare and unique communions – a spiritual closeness, enriching life deeply. We were as close as any two people can be. When she died in 1969, it was a terrible loss.

For both Alice and I, integration here was not so very difficult. It happened easily and naturally in a smooth way. I can't remember any difficulties on the grounds of being a foreigner. I have been very lucky in this respect. Belfast people were interested and sympathetic. I think the mental state of most people here is not adverse to outsiders. The strange thing is they have conflicts with themselves, but not with outsiders like myself. Not only strange, but perverse — and ridiculous. Our friends have always been from both groups.

Until the end of my school years, I would have considered myself German. But when we moved to Prague we stopped feeling German because Germany had become a Nazi state. I still speak, read and write German and Czech fluently. Yet I can feel no identity with Germany after what has happened. Now my language is English.

My survival still remains to me both a mystery and a miracle. That is because so many who were stronger physically and emotionally did not survive. When I came back from the camps and realized how many had not survived, I saw it had no logical explanation. Some who were tough didn't survive — some who weren't tough, like myself, did. Survival wasn't based on any particular qualities.

The Czech nation is now much more close-knit and homogeneous. I grew up in the most democratic and diverse period. Things and people have changed tremendously. I still correspond with a few distant relatives, though my last close Czech friend died a few years ago in Prague. For me, it is a strange country now.

When I visited Czechoslovakia in 1967 and again in 1990, I felt I was at home in Belfast. I loved visiting, it was the country where I had grown up and which I knew intimately; but it made me feel closer to Belfast. Home was Belfast. In the best sense of the word, this is home.

In conversation with the Editor

Helen Lewis has lived in Belfast since 1947. Her memoir of the Holocaust, A Time to Speak *(Blackstaff Press), was published in 1992.*

TWO POEMS

Harry Clifton

THE FOREST BRETHREN

They had formed a republic,
A small one, in the depths of the forest,
The Belorussian forest. Partisans,
If you like, of a lost ideal –
Their uniform, if such it could called,
A thing of rags and patches,
Battle fatigues, abandoned
In the advances, in the retreats
Of vast armies, passing away like phantoms.

Stillness. Dripping. Every sound
From the frightened chitter of birds
To the snap of a twig, invested with Greek meaning,
Hearkened to, preternaturally pure
In the presence of death
For inattention.
                    Herbs, and natural medicines –
To come back here, in lieu of family,
Hearth or village, since the very first winter
Blackened, razed. To stumble, one day,
By miracle, on the likeminded,
Pitching, striking camp,
Where women also fought, and men could cook,
And beauty was not forgotten.

By the third Spring, between the lines,
The rumbling grew much louder,
Switched direction. "What century is it out there?"
Somebody read from Pasternak.
A new sadness, deeper than liberation,

Racked everyone. It would come, alright,
The future of mankind,
Bypassing them. For the time being,
The fight was elsewhere. Then, like a second thought,
Intelligence would smoke them out.
They would be handed over.

TO THE KOREAN COMPOSER SONG-ON CHO

So tell me, please, what all this means to you –
Thirteen years in the west, the German night
Trembling the windows of your studio
As haulage thunders past, and the Hohenzollern Ring
Adazzle with traffic, the roar of Cologne,
Sex cinemas and drugstores, supermarket lights,
Dwindling, inside you, to a Buddhist drone.
Lay it all out between us, like the tea you bring

On a China service. Bass clefs, ideograms
Litter the floorspace. Peremptory, inquisitive,
Leaping from chair to chair,
Inspecting titles, "Clock, Toy Soldier and Drum
For the Leipzig Ensemble …" hardly believing my ears
At static buzz in the room,
Tinnitus, or the music of the spheres,
I ask you – Is this how an Asian woman lives,

Alone, in our midst? Instead of explanations
Listen, you bid me. "The Stronger, The Weaker Brother,"
Confucian, scored for the voice
Of an ancient woman. *Once, a bird flew south,*
Returned in the Spring, two pumpkin seeds in its mouth,
For the stronger loss, for the weaker one increase –
But please, no moral! "East and West …"
You smile as you change the spools, and give the knob a twist,

Fast-forwarding us to the twentieth century.
Silence. A drum. From the audience a cough,

Embarrassed, as it waits
And hears itself, in the terrible void between notes.
I look at you, and you look back at me.
Is this how it has to sound when the line goes dead?
Drumtap, processional shuffle
At the court of the last boy-king, long since beheaded.

Flip the switches, plunge us back into silence,
Real, contemporary. The tea goes cold
Between us, and I watch you, as night deepens,
Listening out, for the gangs on the stairs
Who crowd your lovemaking, damn you for your laughter,
Rifle your garbage, cut your electric wires
And send you hate-mail the morning after.
"Now, I can only write for the pain threshold ..."

You say, as if no one is here. "Subliminal sighs,
A waterdrop, the tick of the clock,
Or screeching kilohertz – but nothing in between."
In the corridor footsteps, detonating through the apartment block
Like an echo chamber, bring the fear to your eyes
Till they die away, and the noise of Cologne
Takes over again, the razzmatazz
In a sonic void, where each of us is alone.

Harry Clifton grew up in Dublin and now lives in Paris. His latest book is a work of non-fiction,
On the Spine of Italy *(Macmillan, 1998).*

BELFAST IN EUROPE

—

John Gray

—

Of Iceland and dragons.

It was in the early sixties that I proposed British entry to what was then the European Economic Community at the Campbell College Debating Society. Belfast's self-proclaimed schoolboy élite gave this oratorical debut short shrift. The very mention of the EEC's founding treaty, The Treaty of Rome, led to speedy and humiliating defeat.

Thus to the ever-present threat of Rome rule in Ireland was added evidence of a wider conspiracy. In large measure the architect of this simple equation was the Reverend Ian Paisley, who by the late sixties was systematically nailing his theses through the heart of the Ulster body politic. At those great Ulster Hall rallies of his, where we were sufficiently European to slip Italian lira into his collection plate, it always struck me as ironic that the mainspring of his rhetoric lay in the religious convulsions of 16th century Europe.

Other ideas came more immediately from the outside world. There was Jimmy Simmons in the first edition of *The Honest Ulsterman* calling for "revolution", a breaking of the bounds of our narrow and repressed society. More directly those democratic hands raised on the posters of Paris in May 1968 reappeared on the posters of Belfast's own radical student movement, the People's Democracy. Perhaps we could join the mainstream?

It was never going to be that simple. The smashing confrontation of our own particular forces required a re-interpretation of any ideas that came to us from afar. European ideas suffered the fate of those successive invading armies of our pre-history, cast upon rocky shores, lost in bogs and forests, pounced upon by wood-kernes, and surviving if at all only by going native.

In any case we drew in upon ourselves. It was not just the emerging Provisionals who cried "Sinn Féin" and meant it. Unionists were being betrayed by Britain itself, and were hardly going to trust in Europe. As for Europeans themselves, until our "Troubles," they were not always certain where we were. Ireland was sometimes confused with Iceland — as though those 16th century charts, the ones with bits of coastline missing which caused the Armada so much trouble, were still in use. One of those missing bits was certainly Northern Ireland. Now, as it finally appeared on the map, it was marked with dragons as the ultimate historical anchronism, an arena for the kind of medieval conflict on which the European venture had called closure. We remained "beyond the Pale".

The Gaelic chieftains held out longest in Ulster, before, as the "Wild Geese", they fled to Europe. It would be wrong to assume that the settlers of the new seventeenth-century town were any closer to the metropolis, whether that lay in London or Dublin. As John Milton furiously told the inhabitants of this "barbarous nook" in the 1640's, they were "a generation of High-land thieves and Red-shanks". A century and a half later, Sir Boyle Roche, speaking in the Irish House of Commons in February 1792, described them as a people whom "no king could govern – no God could please". Depending on circumstance, these were doughty defenders of their immediate settlement boundaries, or radicals who moved beyond known frontiers.

Their own exclusion from the Anglo-Irish body politic, and increasing commercial prosperity, were the trigger to the flowering of radical possibilities in the late 18th century. Belfast, then a town of some 20,000, briefly took upon itself twin mantles as the most revolutionary centre in the British Isles and as the "Athens of the North". It was an episode that came to a bloody end with the defeat of the Rebellion of the United Irishmen in 1798.

What should continue to haunt us is their breadth of vision – both of a Belfast that sought to transform Ireland and of a Belfast that thought internationally. They did not just celebrate the American Revolution in which Ulster Presbyterians had played no small part, or the French Revolution; they extolled the progressive regimes of Holland and Poland. Their newspapers gave as much scope to the proceedings of the French Assembly and the American Congress as to the London and Dublin Parliaments. They corresponded with George Washington and Benjamin Franklin, and thought nothing of dispatching addresses to the French Assembly, and expected and got replies. They psychologically reduced the actuality of distance and the perils of travel to nothing. They were the only Belfast generation ever to enthusiastically learn a foreign language – French – and this while seeking to revive the Irish language.

They sought too to create a civic society capable of underpinning their wider hopes. As Seamus Heaney has fondly reflected, today's Linen Hall Library is a survivor from that time. Consider the colossal enlightenment agenda that the small Reading Society founded in 1788 took upon itself: to create a library, yes; to create a museum; to provide free and universal education; to revive the Irish language and the ancient music of Ireland; and to run Belfast's first meteorological station. Its members supported immediate Catholic Emancipation, and admitted women to the Society.

Meanwhile, history interrupted. As William Drennan ruefully noted at the time of the Act of Union, change would have to come more slowly and from without, meaning the British Parliament. British dominance in the nineteenth century created commercial, trading and industrial imperatives for Belfast. This was especially the case in the last quarter of the century – Belfast's period of breakneck growth built on the twin pillars of linen and shipbuilding, which were particular beneficiaries of imperial expansion. Simultaneously, for most Protestants, the Union became a secure line of defence against the advance of Catholic and Nationalist forces.

It goes without saying that a great industrial city and port like Belfast has always had international connections. They are reflected in our street names. In the twenties, Belfast could count more than 40 named after European cities and rivers, and just under 30 deriving their names from Empire. And yet in Unionist rhetoric and argument, the European streets were silent, and all the noise was along the avenues of Empire. Belfast's Nationalist minority were not necessarily dissenters. Only a few looked to Europe – amongst them the Young Irelanders who in 1848 watched the revolutionary efforts of other small nationalities, amongst them Hungary, with warm sympathy. Arthur Griffiths was later to return to the Hungarian example, as a model case history for the new Sinn Féin. However the first foreign conflict to polarise Belfast opinion was a colonial one, the Boer War, with rival gangs named after British and Boer generals.

In the 19th century heyday of the city, there was little of the cosmopolitan about its cultural life. In 1881, Sarah Bernhardt played to half empty houses because the play was considered "immoral" and was in "a foreign language". Ten years later, a correspondent noted that Belfast had "only one theatre where there might be two" and that "there are those who would as soon visit the infernal regions".

Yet in the 20th century Belfast was massively engaged in two great European catastrophes – the World Wars. We are still regularly reminded of the losses at the Somme, or of the Blitz. Here surely lie stronger European credentials? Belfast enlistment, however, was more often a response to the call to duty to support the British cause, than a stand in the defence of small Catholic nations, or in opposition to Hitler. Republicans (remembering the old Fenian adage that "England's peril is Ireland's opportunity") matched their pragmatism in seeking German arms with an actual nihilism of international perspective. On the wider plane, the experience of great armies, whether being slaughtered in the trenches, or advancing through defeated and ravaged countries, was never a major opportunity for cultural exchange.

War provided Belfast with short-lived revivals of an otherwise collapsing industrial economy, and an opportunity to assert an overblown sense of its own importance. It spawned endless Captains and Colonels bearing their military sobriquets through decades of peacetime. Little was done to widen cultural horizons. John Hewitt, one of our few writers in this period to think simultaneously in Irish, British and European contexts, saw the lot of the writer in the interwar years as that of "the bitter gourd". After the Second World War, we rewarded him for his telling insights by quite literally sending him to Coventry.

And then came the EEC. British disbelief at the potential of the venture was more than matched in Northern Ireland. Who needed this strange alliance of former friends and foes set against the internationalism of Empire – a sunset we failed to spot? Even for those who did recognise the winds of change, Northern Ireland's relationship with Europe and later with the European Union was to be dogged by wider British uncertainty and lack of commitment; and they, after all, represented us.

For the Irish Republic, it was to prove very different. The economic failure of isolationism and protectionism suggested a new start, and an alternative focus to overwhelming dependence on the British market. All those old European links from the saints and scholars to the Wild Geese were readily polished up; and Dublin, a capital city in a way in which Belfast never was, was ready to play a major role on the European stage. There was real engagement, matched by success in securing very major funding. Nowadays, in a final irony, the EU flag with its blue ground and white stars has more than eclipsed Connolly's Starry Plough.

Belfast's divisions are no longer a unique aberration in a Europe extending to the Balkans. Our experiences have relevance to others, and theirs to us. These exchanges and interactions, the capacity to look through other eyes, can help us find better ways forward than terrorism, or the war on terrorism, with their ultimately equivalent capacities to slaughter the innocent. Better this kind of engagement than the willful co-option of every other bloody conflict to our own. (As I write, Israeli flags fly in Loyalist Tiger's Bay, matched by Palestinian ones in the Republican New Lodge.)

Where then does culture lie in all this? In a divided society, it will certainly include doing unthinkingly what we have always done traditionally, and often apart from each other; but the important aspects are those that help us undo strait-jackets – those aspects that, of necessity, are subversive of the here-and-now. Thinking of this, I am brought back to a quip by Sam Hanna Bell in the early 1980's concerning the Linen Hall Library: that it was "a breathing hole in the ice cap that is closing over us". A more optimistic scenario would be to set about widening the breathing hole. It is certainly a metaphor worth any number of corporate vision-statements and business plans for the arts. In the event, our writers and artists have already found that sufficiency of cultural space to be both true to us and to speak to the wider world.

John Gray is the Librarian of the Linen Hall Library.

COUNTRIES OF THE MIND: GROWING UP IN PORTADOWN

George Watson

England, Ireland and all that.

I

ENGLAND: A COUNTRY OF THE MIND

We all live in actual places, but we all equally inhabit, imaginatively, countries of the mind. I was born in a small town called Portadown, in County Armagh, and lived there until I was 21. I want to talk about the various ways in which I have been possessed by imaginative senses of England, a country which in some ways seemed more real to me than the Northern Ireland I grew up in. Inevitably, I will be talking about the effects of cultural imperialism on me, as an Irishman, but I hope to avoid the Hibernian tone so deftly characterized by Evelyn Waugh, when he spoke of the Irishman as "carrying everywhere with him his ancient rancor and the melancholy of the bogs". Perhaps, too, what I say may be of interest for the light it throws on the complexities of cultural arrangements and accommodations within the tiny archipelago which is called the British Isles.

Portadown is where the Orange Order was founded in the late eighteenth century, and has remained a bastion of Orange bigotry to this day. When Sir John Lavery wished to paint the strange tribal rite known as "The Twelfth", when the Orangemen parade on 12 July with their drums, bands, sashes and banners through the streets in celebration of their domination over the sullen Papists, he choose – appositely – to site his picture on Portadown's main street. I could have been one of the small boys on Lavery's canvas, standing back on the edge of a Catholic street to watch the parade from a safely discreet distance. Catholic adults stayed indoors, but even Catholic boys found it hard to resist the appeal of the bands – accordion, flute and best of all, the pipes in the "kilty" bands. And watching those parades as a very small boy was where I first encountered a sense of England. The Orange phenomenon might have been a purely indigenous growth, but its iconography asserted the might of England. The Union Jack was everywhere; the huge Lambeg drums which thundered ceaselessly the warning "Croppies lie down" proclaimed "God Save the King" on their gross swollen bellies; the banners portrayed the Crown; on them, King William of Orange urged his white charger across the Boyne to smash King James; on them, Queen Victoria, in full regalia on her throne, held out a Bible to a kneeling black African who kissed it, over the legend "The Secret of England's Greatness" – a message easily translated and understood by Northern Ireland's Negro population. The Royal Ulster Constabulary were out in force to prevent riot, revolvers in their shiny holsters and their oak-pale batons prominent, on their caps the insignia which emblematized our status – English crown above Irish harp. The Orangemen – indeed, the whole state – was "Loyalist". Loyal to England. And the Orangemen hated us. So presumably England hated us, too? I would never go to England; if it could be like this on its fringes, what must it be like at the center?

In the home, however, things became more complex, and it was difficult to identify "English Ulster" with "England". Every evening at nine, with the immutable regularity with which we said the family rosary, my father would switch on the wireless. And there would be a different England. The glorious solemnity of Big Ben filled our Irish kitchen: my first sense of drama came from that moment of complete silence between the ending of the chimes and the first of the nine reverberating gongs. Then "This is the BBC Home Service, and this is Alvar Liddell with the nine o'clock news. Today on Luneburg Heath, Field Marshal Mongomery accepted the surrender of all German forces. The war in Europe is over…". The beautifully modulated voices, the rational moderation ("so far, these reports are unconfirmed" was a phrase which ran like a leitmotiv through the news bulletins of my boyhood), the largeness of the issues, all seemed totally unrelated to the tight bigotries of Northern Ireland's streets. For me, the BBC was quintessentially English – those accents! – and provided an enormous sense of security. I remember how particularly I loved the shipping forecasts, especially on stormy nights, when the wireless would bring to the warmth of the kitchen a comforting sense of other men's danger, but danger, the smooth voice always implied, under control: "The meteorological station issued the following gale warning to shipping at 0600 hours Greenwich Mean Time: 'Gales are imminent in sea areas Dogger, Rockall, Fisher, German Bight, Lundy, Fastnet, Faroes, Finisterre …'". There was a kind of poetry in this; and also early on, I derived a strong sense of the poetry of English place names. I lived near places with beautiful names – Tandragee, Banbridge, Slieve Donard in the Mourne mountains, Slieve Gullion, Slemish (where St. Patrick fasted and prayed), Ballynahinch, Magherafelt, Magheramore – but, of course, I didn't see anything special about them. The place name is without honour in its own country. There is a wonderful moment in Brian Friel's fine play, *Translations,* which is about the imposition of English names on Irish places carried out by the Army Ordnance survey in the nineteenth century. One of the English officers falls in love with the music of Irish place names, and with an Irish girl. For her, however, his glamour is located at least in part, in *his* places:

> Winfarthing – Barton Bendish –Saxingham Nethergate – Little
> Walsingham – Norwich – Strange sounds, but nice; like Jimmy
> reciting Homer.

My response to English names originated less romantically, but in its own way, just as strongly.

Once again, it was the BBC which at 5 pm every Saturday opened a casement on a magic land: "Here are today's football results: Tottenham Hotspur 2, West Bromwich Albion 0; Wolverhampton Wanders 1, Manchester United 1; Blackburn Rovers 1, Accrington Stanley 2; Brighton and Hove Albion 3, Nottingham Forest 2." Wolves did wander, I knew, and Robin Hood lived in a forest near Nottingham, but who was Stanley? and could anything hit the ear, let alone the imagination, more finely than the tripping rhythms of "Tottenham Hotspur"? (Our local football team was called, prosaically, Portadown.)

And England was the home of cricket. My mother was born in the province of Connaught, in Connemara, on Ireland's western coast, a beautiful but barren, boggy, rocky and mountainous region, its coastline deeply fretted by the huge Atlantic breakers which take their first bites at this last output of Europe on their voyage from North America. Like most people of that area at that time, she spoke the Irish language; and I know she never saw a cricket match – perhaps not even a cricket pitch – in all her life. The game's terminology – leg before wicket, silly mid on, long leg, the slips, the gully, the covers – remained obscure to her, as to me for many years. Yet I remember our mutual raptness as the wireless transmitted commentary on the Test Matches, especially those between England and Australia, from distant Lords, or the Oval. I suppose it was something to do with the very mysteriousness of the arcane terminology. "And Bradman has swept Bedser down to fine leg for two runs." Certainly it was to do with the round gravelly tones of John Arlott, whose deliberation was a byword and who seemed to *relish* all those moments – frequent in cricket – when nothing is happening. "And Edrich just gives a little tug at his cap, while a small boy moves behind the sight screen. Probably on his way to buy a bottle of pop. It's certainly a hot enough day here at the Oval, with the famous gas-ometer shimmering faintly in the heat haze." Most of all, the appeal of cricket on the BBC was precisely due to its suggestion of a world of harmless ritual, of endless sunny afternoons, of soporific torpidity – all of which contrasted so appealingly with the tension and latent violence of our lives in the North. England, as refracted through the BBC, with its dignified voices which high-lighted the more our spiky hard-edged local accents, with its romantic names and its calm, was – most confusingly for me – the great good place.

We could also receive, of course, and did, the broadcasts of Radio Éireann, the radio service of the Irish Free State, lying a mere twenty miles south, where the famous border runs from Crossmaglen to Bessbrook and Forkhill. But Radio Éireann was a sponsored service, and even as a boy I thought that some of the dignity of its news bulletins seeped away when they were followed by advertisements for Donnelly's Pork Sausages ("is it true they're the talk of the nation, a sausage excitingly new?") or for Galtee and Mitchelstown Cheese ("keeps you slim, trim and brimful of energy"). Our relationship as a family with the Free State, which became officially the Republic in 1949, was in any case an uneasy one.

My father was born in Kilkenny in 1898, my mother in Connemara in 1900. Both Catholics. Both believed in Home Rule. Like many another southern Irishman, my father saw no incompatibility between believing in Home Rule for Ireland, and enlisting as an infantry private in the British Army during the First World War, where somehow he survived the carnage of Passchendaele. When he returned, lacking any real educational accomplishments, he joined the Royal Irish Constabulary. But the Ireland he returned to was a different place. In the aftermath of the Rising of 1916, Ireland had embraced the repub-lican doctrines of Sinn Féin, and the IRA had begun a policy of harassment, intimidation – and, indeed, shooting – of members of the RIC, as these were seen as representative of the English Crown forces in the island. His family's house was burned down, and many of his comrades shot. Coincidentally my mother's house was also burned down – her father was also a member of the RIC. And so, when the Treaty which partitioned Ireland was signed in 1921, they both came North to the new statelet, and my father made the worst mis-take of his life – though what else could he do? – and joined the Royal Ulster Constabulary. His seven children were all born in the North. Externally, the conditions of our lives were not easy. It wasn't so much that we were poor, though we were (my father had a constable's wage); but we were Catholics in a Protestant state designed, as its first prime minister put it, for a Protestant people. (Indeed, my parents gave themselves away every time they opened their

mouths, because they retained their Southern accents.) Worse, our co-reli-
gionists regarded us with deep suspicion – the RUC was unquestionably a sectarian police force. My father wore his revolver and carried his baton as if the
albatross were hung around his neck.

Internally, in terms of that imaginative sense of tradition and continuity
which all of us need, I found it equally difficult. Even had I wanted to – for
that matter, even had my father wanted me to – I could not identify with
Northern Ireland as a state or polity. The Protestant boys whom we had to
fight almost daily on our way back from primary school told us we were Fenian
scum, and in a probably unconscious echo of Cromwell's words told us to get
the hell back to Connacht. They were British, we were Irish.

Things improved slightly when I was sent to secondary school at St. Patrick's
College in Armagh, ten miles from Portadown (which did not, of course, have
a Catholic secondary school). Armagh was a Catholic, nationalist town, and
since the school served the arch-diocese of Armagh, I was surrounded by boys
from South Derry, Tyrone, Fermanagh and even from across the border, from
Dundalk and Dunleer and Ardee. For the first time in my life, I remember feeling that *we* outnumbered *them*, and that it was *our* Ireland.

But... while I learned Irish, played Gaelic football and handball and found it
easy enough to identify with nationalist Ireland, I could never go the whole
hog. Partly it was to do with differing attitudes to the Second World War.
Southern Ireland had remained neutral, and I knew Catholic boys from Belfast
whose families deliberately left lights burning in skylights during the blackout
in the hope that German bombers would spot them. As regards the war, I was
firmly pro-British and even more so after seeing those ghastly newsreels about
the relief of the concentration camps. But mostly my internal complications
about nationalism centered on feelings about my parents and their history. A
youthful idealism and a love of eloquence in me responded powerfully to the
canonical texts of the Republican tradition – to Robert Emmet's speech from
the dock in 1803 ("When my country takes her place among the nations of the
earth, then, and not till then, let my epitaph be written"); to the proclamation
of the Republic in 1916 ("Irishmen and Irishwomen, in the name of God and
of the dead generations, Ireland through us summons her children to her flag
and strikes for her freedom"); and above all to the graveside oration delivered
by Patrick Pearse in 1913 over the body of O'Donovan Rossa: "They think they
have foreseen everything. They think they have foretold everything. But the
fools, the fools, the fools! They have left us our Fenian dead, and while Ireland
holds these graves, Ireland unfree shall never be at peace!" But these texts,
learned lovingly at school, could not be uttered in my home. They would have

affronted my parents who had been driven into exile, in a very real sense, by the ideology which lay behind them. Indeed, my father never referred to Patrick Pearse without appending the bitter phrase "that squinting idiot". (Pearse had a cast in one eye.)

I think all boys hunger for heroic models. I could find nothing heroic in Ulster Protestantism, save perhaps in the memorials to those killed on the Somme and in Flanders, and I didn't see why these memorials insisted on giving the impression that only *they* had fought there. I found plenty that was heroic in the long nationalist tradition, but my access to that was hampered and thwarted by family *pietas*. Perhaps inevitably – however paradoxically – the simplest solution for me was to go for English heroic models, which were, emotionally speaking, uncomplicated. This applied particularly to one Sergeant Matt Braddock, vc, the eponymous hero of a serial story that appeared in the boy's comic, *The Rover*, every week. Strong of chin, blue of eye, Matt Braddock was co-pilot of a Lancaster bomber of the famous Tiger Squadron. Only a sergeant, note – part of the great appeal was Braddock's ordinary background. He wasn't just co-pilot – on its bombing mission into Nazi Germany, the plane was attacked usually by thousands of Messerschmitts (their pilots saying over the radio things like "Jawohl, mein Fuhrer, the English Schweinhund will be brought down before Bremen") and the flak was always most alarming. Matt therefore generally had to fly the plane single-handed – Squadron Leader Neville "Tufty" Tufnell having taken some shrapnel over the Ruhr – and navigate it, and act as rear gunner, and drop the bombs (always spot-on and always on a factory making tanks for the Waffen SS), and nurse the crippled Lancaster – G for George – back to Lincolnshire before the chip shop closed. I loved it – I had not heard of Dresden. It was all so black and white – Nazi Germany was evil, it had to be beaten – and such a relief from the complexities of the home terrain. I think it was the very simplicity of English heroicising that appealed. Even before I came to Matt Braddock, I had thrilled to the patriotic stanzas in the poems I found printed in Arthur Mee's *Children's Encyclopaedia* (a kind of handbook of empire), poems like Sir Henry Newbolt's:

> The sand of the desert is sodden red,
> Red with the wreck of a square that broke; –
> The Gatling's jammed and the Colonel's dead,
> And the regiment blind with dust and smoke.
> The river of death has brimmed its banks,
> And England's far, and Honour a name,

But the voice of a schoolboy rallies the ranks
"Play up! play up! and play the game!"

I took that imperial England for a heroic dream remote as Hollywood, I could see no connection between it and the circumstances of my boyhood life. We were not, as it seemed, threatened by British soldiers or gunboats. The treat lay in the flint-faced Calvinism of Stormont, in the Orange Bigot ranting his hatred, in the B-Special waving down your bicycle at night with his squat Sten-gun.

In his famous essay, "Boy's Weeklies", George Orwell remarks that "the worst books are often the most important because they are usually the ones that are read earliest in life". Later in life, when I read English literature at University, I was to encounter the genuine cultural wealth of one of the world's greatest literature. "The gaunt thorns all bent one way as if craving alms of the sun" in Wuthering Heights, the district where the young Wordsworth was "fostered alike by beauty and by fear", the heroic pathos of Milton's Satan – "If thou be'st he, but O; how fallen, how chang'd …", the creamy sensuousness of Hardy's Tess, the laconic effrontery of Jonson's knaves and Shakespeare's Edmund, and so much more, became part of my mental furniture forever. However, I think Orwell has a point. I was an avid reader of public school stories, my favourite being a book called *Teddy Lester and His Chums*. It was prototypical of thousands of pages I read of a similar kind. Teddy Lester himself was superb at all games, and preternaturally fair in competition, but with a disarming weakness at French irregular verbs. Conversely, Ivor ("Bat") Robinson was the school genius, absorbing vast amounts of knowledge through thick spectacles, completely unco-ordinated at Rugby football, but with one special talent, for bowling devilish googlies. Lord Edward Ponsonby was a real sport, and constantly treated the chums at the tuck shop with fivers sent him by his "pater". Need I go on?

Orwell suggests that the great attraction of the public schools lies in its snob-appeal, the overall class glamour of the thing. This was not what appealed to me, and I doubt if any Irish boy would have felt that particular attraction – the niceties of the English social register were well beyond us. Mainly I think, the appeal lay in the notion of codes and rules, especially as those applied to enmity. You might have to fight, that is, but if you did, it would be with boxing gloves in a ring, with a proper referee, and afterwards hands would be shaken. Even the cads and bounders subscribed to the notion of "fair play". In that world you would not see, with that sickening lurch of the heart, three shadowy figures detach themselves from a wall and saunter towards you, while you realized that your mental navigation – Matt Braddock where were you? – had let you down, and you had blundered into an Orange street. In Teddy Lester you would not get a half-brick on the head because you were a "Papish".

Orwell describes sardonically the mental world of the public school story.

> You are sitting down to tea in your study on the Remove passage after an exciting game of football won by an odd goal in the last half-minutes. There is a cosy fire in the study and outside the wind is whistling. The ivy clusters thickly round the old grey stones. The king is on his throne and the pound is worth a pound. Over in Europe the comic foreigners are jabbering and gesticulating, but the grim grey battle-ships of the Bristish fleet are steaming up the Channel and at the outposts of Empire the monocled Englishmen are holding the niggers at bay. Lord Mauleverer has just had another fiver and we are all settling down to a tremendous tea of sausages, sardines, crumpets, potted meat, jam and doughnuts... Everything is safe, solid and unquestionable. Everything will be the same forever and ever.

Exactly. As a boy, I would not have had worries about the comic foreigners of Europe or the black or yellow peril. But what this England of the mind offered, in its atrocious way, was an image of security so powerful that the rubs of sad experience and the much greater literature I read subsequently could never quite expunge it. Perhaps it was because the Orangeman with the half-brick was such an immediate danger; but there was also in that cosy study and that English public school world of *Teddy Lester and His Chums* a more metaphorical kind of security – a security of cultural identity. A complacency, even. Perhaps an arrogance: the English were so obviously the master race that they didn't have to argue about it; they had the effortless superiority of the Balliol man. How I envied that confidence! At a simpler level, the physical comforts were not to be sneezed at: one of the reasons why I enjoyed middle-class English children's fiction, from Enid Blyton's Famous Five series through Richmal Crompton's William stories, to the works of Arthur Ransome where the girls were called amazing names like Titty – one of the reasons, apart from the fact that William and Co. had to invent their enemies, why I enjoyed them so much was that nearly everyone had a bedroom to himself of herself. And tents. And boats. And the church clock stood at 10 to 3 and there was honey still for tea. No world is as timeless as the world of our first reading, especially if that work is itself deliberately nostalgic, as I began to see that it was when I graduated to P.G. Wodehouse, in whose work the Drones Club, Blandings Castle and Mr. Mulliner's bar are simply immortal, places out of time.

I had, then, lived quite intensely in various Englands of the mind before I arrived, aged 21 in Oxford, as a graduate student. Perhaps that almost farcically beautiful city is not the best place to begin an encounter with the real England; but so, for me, it was. The first shock to my system was to discover how completely secular a country England was, compared to my own. I remember my first Sunday walking to mass and wondering where everyone was, until I began to notice various manifestations of the most sacred English religion of today: the Worship of the Car. Everywhere machines were being washed, polished, buffed, hovered, dusted, adored. Religion in England had dwindled, I saw after a while, to what I might call secular rituals – the weekly car-wash, show-Saturdays, race-meetings, seaside outings, weddings at Whitsun: the secular rituals celebrated so beautifully, yet with such characteristic English agnosticism, in the poetry of Philip Larkin. I perceived this secularism with a kind of contempt; I was sufficiently Irish to consider the worship of material things vulgar. Further, I could see that England had not really excised intolerance: there was no religious intolerance, true, but that was only because religion was a dead duck in England; what there was was plenty of racial intolerance.

The second major shock was to encounter, even in the sacred colleges of Oxford University – or perhaps – I should say *especially* in the colleges of Oxford? – condescension and ignorance. The condescension was well meant in the sense that it was friendly, but all the more alarming for being so: one was made to feel like a monkey in the zoo. I would not have minded so much being a monkey in the zoo if I could have felt that the spectators were rather more informed about the monkeys. Precisely because I had lived imaginatively in England, I expected (unreasonably?) that the English might have devoted a little thought, a little imagination, to their oldest colony. They hadn't – as was made quite clear in the desperate flailing scramble of the editorial writers to clarify 50 years of total neglect, when the Northern Irish time-bomb finally exploded in 1968-9.

The wheel had come full circle. The trials and tribulations of life in Ireland, plus the proximity and sheer bulk of English culture, had helped to turn me into a kind of exile in my own country, who responded to versions of Englishness. Living in England, explaining myself, and watching my little province tear itself apart, I found I was driven back on my Irishness. Further, I have asked myself: What does it all mean?

There is a famous paradigmatic moment in Joyce's *Portrait of the Artist* where Stephen Dedalus experiences the shadow of imperialism falling across his conversation with an English priest:

He felt with a smart of dejection that the man to whom he was speaking was a countryman of Ben Jonson. He thought: The language in which we are speaking is his before it is mine. How different are the words *home, Christ, ale, master,* on his lips and on mine; I cannot speak or write these words without unrest of spirit. His language, so familiar and so foreign, will always be for me an acquired speech. I have not made or accepted its words. My voice holds them at bay. My soul frets in the shadow of his language.

Speaking the English language, listening to the BBC, reading English school stories, considering soccer and cricket superior to Gaelic football and hurling, more interested in the Battle of Britain than in the Battle of Clontarf, wanting to go to Oxford rather than to University College, Dublin – I might be a perfect specimen of the colonised, if the index of that condition is the degree to which the coloniser's value system is internalized. But how intensely do I feel "the smart of dejection"? Or, in general terms, how evil are the effects of cultural imperialism? To answer that question would require the best efforts of political theorists, sociologists and anthropologists. Indeed, it may not be possible to give a comprehensive answer. That would be part of my point. For it is certainly easy to dramatise, even sentimentalise, and over-generalise about, the condition of the colonised.

Thus, I can easily sympathise with, even identify with, those Irish writers who seek to restore in their art the consciousness of 'the dispossessed', the consciousness of the Gaelic civilisation of Ireland which began to die in the eighteenth century, and which received its mortal wound in the calamity of the Great Famine. My sense of deprivation is there and is real as I recall some of my mother's Irish phrases and turns of speech. But there is also the question of realism. I would agree with the Irish poet Thomas Kinsella's remarks on the vanished Gaelic world: "The inheritance is mine, but only at two enormous removes – across a century's silence, and through an exchange of worlds." The broken tradition, the fragmented culture is a reality, and it is only honest (if painful) to accept that this is so. To pretend otherwise, to imagine that the clock can be turned back, is a mistake; and the sterilities (and the dangers) of a strident assertion of the purity of the national identity – "little Irelandism" – are sufficiently obvious in the island today.

I see now all the faults in my youthful embrace of the simplified stereotypes and clichés of Englishness, which the English manufactured with such facility and export with such success, what might be called "Masterpiece Theatre England" (*Brideshead* and all that) in all its ineffable silliness. But I must ask myself: was I wrong to feel that to respond to England's involvement in the Second World War with the traditional phrase "England's difficulty is Ireland's opportunity" was to respond narrowly and myopically? Would I have received a university education if I had not had the benefits of the British university grants system? Was it a bad thing to be opened to English culture, and through it, to the culture of the Anglophone world, whether American or Australian or West Indian? Was it not useful, certainly instructive, to grow up even in Northern Ireland, where I learned early the oppression, discrimination and bigotry which is the fate (at more frightening levels) of so many people of the world? Cannot an admiration for Irish cultural traditions coexist with an admission of the relevance of the modern world? I learned many useful things from my encounter with "Englishness"; and on balance, I would say the benefits outweighed the very real drawbacks: ethnic political resentment is a fact, but so is a sense of cultural enlargement.

I understand the feelings and motivations of those who would insist on the purity, or the purification, of their own cultural traditions. The homogenization of the world – MacDonalds in Munich, Coca-Cola in Khartoum, "Dallas" in Dublin – is not a pretty sight or a pretty prospect. But I have more faith in the unquenchable, individualising diversity of cultures, despite the leveling forces at work in our modern world, than those who, even for laudable ends, would erect *cordons sanitaires* around their own ethnicities. And clearly, as the history of the twentieth century shows with depressing clarity, cultural nationalism can be a very dangerous force indeed.

II

FROM HANOVER STREET TO THE GARVAGHY ROAD

Portadown is, in Irish terms, especially those of fifty years ago, a medium sized town, and was also comparatively industrial. The town in which I was born and grew up had a population of about 17,000, nine factories making carpets and linen, and other factories making boxes and products connected to the apple industry of County Armagh, "the orchard of Erin's green Land", as the local ballad had it, along with the news that "the girls are so gay and so hearty". (Wade's, where my eldest sister worked briefly as a typist, made those small glass animals, deer, squirrels and chipmunks, which were so popular once upon a time). It had three cinemas, and was an important rail junction with lines from Belfast to Dublin, to Cavan and to south Derry all going through its four-platform Victorian station. The station was much beloved of Sir John Betjeman, who ran a campaign to preserve it, but to no avail, as the rather fine building was pulled down in the 1960s, along with much else, including many of the factories.

Portadown was also where, in a nearby townland called Loughgall, the Orange Order was created in 1795, after a particularly fierce encounter between the Catholic Defenders and the Protestant Peep O' Day Boys, at the Battle of the Diamond. Ever since then, Portadown has been seen as the Orange Citadel of Northern Ireland, a byword for loyalism, sectarianism and intransigence. In Catholic areas of the six counties, it is usually referred to, confusingly, as "Black Portadown". Though a superior, more middle-class branch of the Order wore black, rather than orange sashes, the description pointed more, I think, to a metaphysical or spiritual perception of things, than to a colour. "Portadown on a wet Sunday" was a phrase frequently used in Northern Ireland to suggest the ultimate in Beckettian *tristia*.

In her book about the Orange Order, *The Faithful Tribe* (HarperCollins, 1999), the Dublin-born writer Ruth Dudley Edwards refers to a Northern Irish Catholic friend, apparently very liberal on all other counts, who said he would never speak to her again if she wrote a book in defence of the Orange Order. She writes:

> "But they are much less bad than they seem," I protested. "In fact, lots of them are good." What I had forgotten was that George came from Portadown, which is regarded as the most sectarian place in Northern Ireland.

I did speak to her again, but only to say that she had done what I knew she would do, which was to apply her high intelligence to demonstrate that Orangeism is in fact a fruit of the Enlightenment, that it *believes* in "civil and religious liberty". She takes the Order at its ostensibly tolerant word, that it "will not admit into its brotherhood persons whom an intolerant spirit leads to persecute, injure or upbraid any man on account of his religious opinions". This, as Henry Fielding said in a different context, is a very wholesome and comfortable formulation, to which we have but one objection, namely, that it is not true. The same may be said of *The Faithful Tribe*. At the mercy of her own bright civil service rationalism, and her programmatic revisionism, Dudley Edwards completely misrepresents the malign part played by the Orange Order in the sorry history of the North of Ireland, presenting it as a kind of Mozartian Masonic Club, when it has functioned rather more frequently like the Ku Klux Klan. Its baneful effects have been especially evident in very recent years, where for the last five Julys, the Order's determination to march through the nationalist Garvaghy Road in Portadown has brought the peace process to its knees, and the attention of the world's press to the town and its little townland of Drumcree.

My title is intended to suggest the polarities inside which I was raised, as a Catholic in that town in the 40s and 50s. The Garvaghy Road stands for the Catholic/nationalist ethos (though in truth when I was a boy, Garvaghy Road was an insignificant locus of the Catholic population: the Catholic ghetto then was in a place known universally as the Tunnel, because a dip in the road took you under the main railway lines to – literally – the wrong or Catholic side of the tracks). Hanover Street stands for the dominant ethos. I was born around the corner in Thomas Street, but Hanover Street was where we played all those games that children no longer play on any street. I walked to school in a loyalist crescendo of nomenclature past Hanover, Coronation, Queen and Union Streets. At the bottom of Thomas Street, the railway line to Dublin ran over a bridge bearing the huge painted legend "Remember 1690: No Surrender". (1690 is the date of the Battle of the Boyne, when King William of Orange defeated the Catholic James II, and thereby ensured the supremacy of Protestantism in the British Isles). There was little danger of ever forgetting 1690 in Portadown, or 1688 (the Siege of Derry), or 1691 (the Battle of Aughrim).

When my family moved from Newtownhamilton in nationalist South Armagh to Portadown three years before I was born, one of my older brothers had been playing in Hanover Street on the day of the arrival for about 20 minutes before he came in to ask my mother, "Mammy, what's a Fenian bastard?" When we moved house in Portadown later – I was nine – the caretaker of the adjoining school ostentatiously hoisted the Union Jack to greet our arrival, and asked my younger brother Richard and me, "Why the hell don't youse get back to Cork, or wherever the hell youse Taigs come from?" Taigs (a corruption of the Irish name Tadg), Micks, Fenians and Papishes were our common designations, spiced with plenty of good Anglo-Saxon four-letter words. Our first elementary school, which I attended with my younger brother Richard between the ages of four and eight, was in the Convent of the Presentation Sisters, where we were taught by nuns; but to get to it and from it, we had to encounter the Protestant kids from the nearby Thomas Street school, and with these we had to fight pretty often, usually in denial of the assertion that the nuns wore their wimples because underneath they were all baldies, or in contestation of the doctrine that St Patrick was a Protestant. The second school, St Columba's Boys' Primary, was in Carleton Street, right opposite the Orange Hall. More fights. Richard and I played in Hanover Street with two Protestant lads called Bobby and Hadden Todd, but never on Sunday, when our punting of a ball outside their house, after Mass, in the hope that they might join us, was rebuked by their angry granny, who would raise a net-curtained window to tell us: "Away in out of that with your papish ball, and read your Bibles!" The sheer tedium of a Portadown Sunday is a vivid memory yet. In a wonderfully named and fiercely regimented place of recreation beside the Bann River, called The People's Pleasure Gardens, all the swings and roundabouts were firmly padlocked. All cinemas were shut; all shops; and even cigarette smoking in public was eschewed in Presbyterian rectitude.

The Papishes were always seen by Orangemen as seeking to subvert the state and turn it over to "Old Redsocks in Rome", as the Reverend Paisley calls the Pope. Our most frightening encounter with the state came on the Twelfth of July in 1954, when two RUC policemen called at the house to charge us with contravening the Flags and Emblems Act. Richard and I, with another boy called Patrick Pearse Lawlor (a heroic if suicidal name in that town) who lived beside the railway lines, had chalked a crude Irish Tricolour on a large piece of cardboard, and waved it from trackside at the enraged occupants of the numerous special trains taking the Brethren from Portadown for their annual county Orange parade, which that year was held in a small town south of us, called Bessbrook. Unfortunately, Bessbrook also had telephones. It was forbidden to display the Irish flag, even in cardboard; my father had to do a lot of talking before the police left. Then he belted us for the risk we had taken and the closeness of the shave.

The quotidian nature of the sectarianism is what I chiefly remember – how alert at all times we were about what streets and areas to avoid, how in the summer holidays boys were always in groups in the parks or the soccer pitches, circling each other warily like packs of strange dogs, marking out the territory. In those days, there were frequent encounters between Catholics and Protestants that were not violent, of course, but there was always that wariness and the possibility of trouble. It was always there in short, and when the political temperature rose in the sixties with the onset of the Troubles, the polarities widened swiftly. It was no surprise to anyone from that town that those boys would metamorphose into hardline thugs, on both sides but more spectacularly on the Orange side, that Portadown should be at the heart of what became known as the Murder Triangle, and that it should spawn the notorious loyalist killer Billy Wright, a.k.a. King Rat, the annual confrontation between Orangemen and the residents of the Garvaghy Road, the police and the British Army, and rioting and mayhem all over the North.

My purpose here, however, is not to tell you in the words of Paul Muldoon's comic Pancho Villa of "guns and drums" and "how it happened here" (see "Lunch with Pancho Villa", in *Mules*, 1977), but to try to put the tensions of Northern Ireland in a more personal context, not in autobiographical arrogance, certainly not in any pretense that I have an answer, less still *the* answer. If anything, I aim to make it even more complicated.

——

In the first place, then, I would have to say that despite the realities of what I called quotidian sectarianism there, being a boy in Portadown in the late 40s and 50s was not like being Anne Frank's brother in Nazi-occupied Amsterdam; and one of the things that everyone from Northern Ireland needs to guard against is the tendency to self-dramatization lurking in phrases like "the oppressed minority", or in glamourising for the international audience one's walking down those mean streets.

I have been thinking a lot about an essay by Pierre Nora, the French historiographer, called "Between Memory and History: *Les Lieux de Memoire*" (*Representations* 26, Spring 1989). Nora says that

> Memory and history, far from being synonymous, appear to be in fundamental opposition … Memory is a perpetually actual phenomenon, a bond tying us to the eternal present; history is a representation of the past … History is perpetually suspicious of memory, and its true mission is to suppress and destroy it…

He is pointing to the reductivism inherent in the historical method, and distinguishes between what we may call sites of history and what he calls the *milieux de memoire*, the real environments of memory. In my own words (and this is an adaptation of Nora rather than a paraphrase), he suggests that process whereby a whole environment is shrunk to a point of single significance, as for example, when the little market town of Omagh, with its fairs and markets and river and town square and the Loreto Convent where my sisters went to school, becomes in one sudden moment in August 1998 a place of atrocity and death. And this will now be for always what "Omagh" will recall, will even be. This is perhaps an extreme example, and in any case history *must* function by selection. But something very important is lost. I put beside Nora's essay a passage from Emmanuel Levinas, who writes in *Totality and Infinity: An Essay on Exteriority* (Duquesne University Press, 1969):

Interiority is the very possibility of a birth and a death that do not
derive their meaning from history. Interiority constitutes an order different from historical time, in which totality is constituted, an order
where everything is *pending*, where what is no longer possible historically remains always possible.

Denis Donoghue, who cites this in his memoir about growing up in Northern
Ireland, *Warrenpoint* (Cape, 1991), glosses it imaginatively thus:

By "history", I presume he [Levinas] means: that which produces the
future. Something comes into history by playing a part in the production of the future. If it doesn't do that, it merely enhances the moment
in which it is entertained. But Levinas is tender toward such experiences. The historian has no time for them, since they didn't come into
historical time. Levinas recovers the dignity of the inner life, so that
such experiences regain their self-respect. History is only one way of
being significant. Memory gives the unofficial sense of history.

So, for me, the Orange Citadel, the capital of the Murder Triangle, will also
and always be a *milieu de memoire*, a place of unofficial history. I cannot quite say
with Wordsworth that "fair seed time had my soul, fostered alike by beauty and
by fear"; but it wasn't bad. There was the Carnegie Library in Edward Street,
presided over by the forbidding Miss Windsor, who not only had the Queen's
family name but who even looked a bit like the Queen, though the Queen on
a diet of prunes and battery acid. When you borrowed a book (*Biggles in the
Gobi*), it was wrapped up in the library's blue dust-jackets with adverts on them
for local firms such as Bustard Brothers, Fleshers and Poulterers; and the
Easiphit Shoe Store – "let your feet breathe with Easiphit!"; and with a list of
don'ts to stop the spread of TB. Apart from the library, I will never forget my
favourite cinema, The Savoy, near that library and our home. It was always
called "The Catch", because of the local legend that nobody could go there
without catching its fleas. It had murals of the big Hollywood stars, Joan
Crawford all red lips and metallic hair, Jane Russell all big bosom and cowgirl
shirt, Humphrey Bogart eyes narrowed against the curl of his smoking cigarette, Victor Mature all slobbery mouth and soulfulness, and of course John
Wayne in that expression that ran the gamut of emotions from A to B. The
Catch had only one record which was played relentlessly before the show started and at all points during the show when there was any kind of break. It was
Slim Whitman singing "China Doll", and the swooping guitar, and that nasal

whine, and the disconcerting yodel or falsetto which lurked in every phrase, waiting for release, recalls hundreds of Saturday matinees. "Her eyes are bloooer, her lips are trooOOer, mah China doll". We went swimming where the Bann met the Cusher, at a place called the Point, on Sharkey's bog; and although Portadown will never feature in Tourist Board brochures, being flat and ugly in a "here-be-the-slums-of-Manchester" red-brick sort of way, it had, because of its flatness in the Bann valley, a stunning view of the Mountains of Mourne, which rose like a line of blue Alps about 25 miles away.

These may be just the private memories that all of us have of their childhood places, and therefore of no larger significance. However, these things happened, they went on, they took more of people's daily interest than the doctrine of transubstantiation, or the Republic's claim to the whole territory of Ireland. Even the sectarian background requires the nuances of individualised memory rather than the flattening categorisations of history. There were four Watson brothers, and we were all very keen on football (soccer), which we played regularly on a local pitch called the Fair Green. My two older brothers knew a group of Protestant lads, who often joined us. One had the resplendently Protestant name of Bothwell Vennard. Bothwell was in the notorious B Specials, much feared by all Catholics who saw the "B"s with some justice as particularly bigoted Orangemen, the more threatening because armed and in uniform. Yet Bothwell was a good natured and simple big soul. At this time, in the 1950s, he was "in the front-line defending Ulster", as the *Portadown News* had it, or at least guarding the railway bridge over the River Bann at Portadown station against the possibility of attack from the IRA, who were then waging a sporadic campaign. Given the rock-solid Orangeism of Portadown, and the relative incompetence of the IRA of that time, this could be described as an easy posting. My brother Gerry asked him one day after one of our kickabouts what he was paid, and what it was like being in the B Specials. Bothwell smiled, "Ten shillings a night". Then after a pause, and beatifically, he said: "By God, it's money from America". Years later, he was shot dead by a more efficient IRA just outside Portadown.

What stays with me most of all as a positive memory is the vigour of the local speech. I stress this for two reasons, one being that the Northerners are generally described as dour and unforthcoming, stingily Presbyterian and reflecting the Scottish inheritance in their thin dole of speech. Even Northern Catholics are seen as dour of speech, compared to people from, say, Cork. Our local speech in fact was wonderfully rich, but I have only time to illustrate how well stocked it was by taking the category of derogatory terms (at the risk of reinforcing the stereotype of the Northerner as vicious in all things, even speech). An irritating child could be a wee *blirt*, a wee *scut*, a wee *nyaff*, a wee *nyerp*; a whiner or moaner would be a wee *nyark*. If you were stupid, you were a *stumer*; and if you combined stupidity with oafishness, you were a *hallion*, or, best of all, a *gulpin*. You might say of a woman overdressed that "*she was done up like a circus horse*", or that "*she stood there like a mutton dummy*". A woman who left her house without coat or hat before high summer would be sniffed at – "*Would you look at the cut of thon one, away out in her figure*". If somebody entered house or pub really soaked on a night when it was lashing it down or bucketing, you might say that "*he came in looking like a travelling rat*". Physical misfortunes were never overlooked – "*he had a belly on him like a poisoned pup*". "*He had a hump on him like a dog shitting razor blades*". There was the wonderfully suggestive and very common phrase "*He looked like somebody let out*" – of a mental asylum? a prison? a hospital? And I have heard an infant school teacher say of an educationally challenged youngster, "*Sure the poor lad couldn't spell shite without putting a Q in it*". That energetic gusto did much to compensate for the austerities of the Presbyterian Sundays, and the pervasive sense of low-level threat.

Was this, then, a perfectly normal Northern Irish Catholic boyhood, oppressed and hounded by Orangemen, the RUC and the B Specials, cut off from my natural home in the Republic under the curse of partition, cut off from the Gaelic world which was my natural birthright but pluckily making the most of my cultural deprivations? Not really; and here, as they say, the plot thickens.

In terms of what we might call my street cred, or school cred at St Patrick's College in Armagh, having an RUC father was not good, and it was compounded by my name and by my place of origin. In the earlier part of this essay, I was trying to convey something of the texture of Protestant hostility. I want to turn now to Catholic exclusivism, which in my experience was more uncomfortable. That is to say that I was never in any doubt in Portadown what I was – a Fenian bastard, a Mick, a Taig, a Papish. But in Armagh, questions of identity became more complex.

Northern Ireland is a place where names are major signifiers. As Seamus Heaney writes in one of his poems ("Whatever You Say Say Nothing", in *North*, 1975):

> Smoke-signals are loud-mouthed compared with us:
> Manouevrings to find out name and school,
> Subtle discriminations by addresses
> With hardly an exception to the rule
> That Norman, Ken and Sidney signalled Prod

And Seamus (call me Sean) was sure-fire Pape;
O land of password, handgrip, wink and nod,
Of open minds as open as a trap ...

I was a boarder in St Patrick's, and it was the custom of the older boys to check up on the new arrivals, with a special view to estimating potential as Gaelic football players. I did not have an easy passage. "What's your name?" George. "What sort of a name is that? What's your second name?" Watson. "What? Where are you from?" Portadown. "Are you sure you're in the right school?" In Heaney's terms, George Watson from Portadown signalled sure-fire Prod, or if not, somebody whose blood did not flow the pure green, white and gold of the Republic. In the context of boys with names like Brendan Quinn, Eamonn Kelly, Seamus McConville, from Aughnacloy and Ballygawley and Dundalk, I quickly learned the realities of the conjugation "Irish – Irisher – Irishest". I was already very low down in the food chain, on name and place alone; the discovery of what my father did put me, in terms of Irishness, with the bottom feeders and invertebrates. (How we came by our surname is easily told: a Scottish Presbyterian great-grandfather came over in the nineteenth century from Ayrshire to Fermanagh to farm, but met and married a Donegal woman, a Catholic called Bridget O'Donnell, and "turned". Thus the Protestant name came down through the Catholic family. As for "George", there just is no excuse. My father said he was running out of names by the time I was born).

I had a more general problem, one going beyond names and naming. Ireland in the 1950s was still a very depressed society, disillusioned with the apparent-ly paltry returns from independence, suffering greatly from poverty, emigra-tion and tuberculosis. (This was the era when TB was endemic in Ireland – one of my sisters had it, so I read those blue dustjackets very carefully; an Ireland where the most popular radio programme was called "Hospital Requests", and where the requests themselves had a stunningly lengthy roll-call: "And now, John McCormack to sing *Panis Angelicus*; for John, Kevin, Brian, Nora, Philomena, Teresa, Madge, Gerry, Oliver, and Seamus, all in the Peamount Sanatorium, hoping to see you back home before the New Year, from all your friends in Cashel"). Ireland suffered also from a lack of confidence, a kind of colonial hangover or national inferiority complex. This was compensated for by an aggressive cultural protectionism, under the codes of which all things Gaelic and Catholic were good and to be cherished, and anything else was English, foreign, modern, and godless. The Gaelic Athletic Association did not merely encourage the playing of Gaelic football and hurling and camogie. If you played other games – rugby, soccer, or – heaven forfend – the peculiarly English game of cricket, you were automatically banned from playing Gaelic games at any kind of representative (school or county) level. This official GAA ban on foreign games was rescinded only recently. In the 50s, sporting protectionism was very strong. In my second year at St Patrick's, I was called to the office of the President, Father Sheridan (known as "Brassjaws" for his sonorous voice), and was solemnly told that, because I had started a little five-a-side soccer league, I was "corrupting the Gaelic morale of the school". I was amazed. Portadown was, as might be expected, absolutely suffused with what might be called the reference points of British popular culture, and I had grown up on Stanley Matthews and Manchester United and cricket and Wimbledon. That did not stop me being a Fenian bastard in Hanover Street; but it apparently did stop me being truly Irish in Armagh.

I found the same exclusivist attitudes, alas, in relation to the Irish language. In the nineteenth century "Ireland for the Irish" had been the politicians' promise, made, of course, in the English language which was and is the liturgical language of Irish nationalism. "Irishness for the Irish", to be achieved primarily through the restoration of the Irish language as the first language of the country, was the promise of the Gaelic League. This was founded in 1893 after a famous lecture by Dr Douglas Hyde, "On the Necessity of De-Anglicising Ireland". Irishness for the Irish was a more seductive, more all-encompassing and ultimately more damaging promise. The idea of a language revival was, of course, intensely and pleasingly idealistic, but it was asking the Irish people to change their language for the second time in a few centuries. This was always going to be difficult; in fact, it proved impossible. Yeats spoke for most Irish people when he said that "Gaelic is my national language, but it is not my mother tongue" ("A General Introduction for my Work", in *Essays and Introductions,*). The fruits of the policy of compulsory Gaelic in the new Free State were unpalatable. Most obviously, there was the hypocrisy of Government Ministers in the new Free State, who had themselves no Irish, making Gaelic compulsory in schools and for all Government jobs. What the Professor of Irish in University College Cork called "the tyranny of gaelicisation" blighted the promotion prospects and soured the lives of a generation, leaving "a heritage of resentment and hostility to the language that only time will obliterate" (R.A.Breatnach, "Revival or Survival? An Examination of the Language Policy of the State", *Studies*, vol. 45, 1956). More pervasively damaging was a kind of cultural protectionism. The Irish language became fetishised as a symbol of an essential Irishness, which defined itself not only by opposition to England, but to the modern world in general. Further, the new Free State was one in which the Catholic Church had a special position, and it promoted the language as a barrier to what it saw as the immorality of the English popular press and cheap literature. The Catholic Truth Society and the Legion of Mary lined up with the linguistic authoritarians. Father Donncha O'Floinn, for example, Professor of Irish in Maynooth College, wrote in 1949 that "if the Irish language disappears, the Irish Christian culture which has been inherited through 1500 years will be very seriously thinned out", and it was he who saw the Legion of Mary as the most effective means of spreading his message. In the North, while Irish was not compulsory, it was even more important: it was a patriotic duty to study it in the midst of the Orange state, which actively discouraged its Protestant children from studying Irish. It was not the fault of the language, but certainly in my time in Armagh, Irish became associated in my mind with an authoritarian nexus of nationalism, cultural morality and racial purity, which was extremely conservative and very hostile to any vision of Ireland not based on the rural Gaeltachts of the western sea-board. In a lecture called "Nationality and Language", delivered in Maynooth in 1946, Desmond O' Donoghue conveys the characteristic and authentic tone which I remember, when he writes: "Irish is the expression of a purely Catholic culture … even if the revival is not successful, the exercise will stem the flow of foreign influences and guard the foundations of the Catholic faith".

In a famous passage in Daniel Corkery's *Synge and Anglo-Irish Literature*, he bemoans the experience of an Irish boy forced to a diet of English reading, which alienates him from his own experience:

> What happens in the neighborhood of an Irish boy's home – the fair, the hurling match, the land grabbing, the priesting, the mission, the Mass – he never comes on in literature, that is, in such literature as he is told to respect and learn. Evidently what happens in his own fields is not stuff for the Muses!

One sympathises; but what this Irish boy found in the Irish books I had to read during my six years' study was just as alienating as the educational experiences of Corkery's hypothetical boy stuck with English books. We read and learned by heart *Scealta Johnny Sheimisin,* versions of the stories told by a famous shanachie in the Donegal Gaeltacht; we read Pierre Loti's *Pecheur d'Islande*, translated from the French as *Iascaire Inse Tuile*; we read a dreadful lugubrious novel called *Eadarbhaile*, about famine, poor land, and the sounds of water under your feet in wet fields. Incidentally, it, too, was a translation, this time from English. It was not so much that in the middle of the twentieth century

~~that~~ the Irish syllabus deemed that the century had not begun, though it was partly that. In Irish, towns did not exist, let alone trains or jet planes or World War I or II, or Little Mo Connolly or the Busby babes or Paris in the springtime.

I was no fanatic for topicality, however. Indeed, by some mystery, no doubt to do with the Northern Ireland Ministry of Education's desire to stifle any Fenian fires in our young breasts, the crucial English syllabus for entry to higher education was the literature of the Augustan Age. So we read for our Senior Examination Pope's *Epistle to Arbuthnot, The Essay on Man, The Rape of the Lock,* Johnson's *Rasselas* and his *Letter to Lord Chesterfield,* Swift's *Gulliver's Travels*, and Gibbon's *The Age of the Antonines.* We had a wonderful teacher, Jerry Hicks; but I cannot remember anything that he said to us about the literature. He just let it work on us. For me, the sheer and total foreignness of it all not only inculcated a powerful sense of the otherness of the past, but shocked me into a realisation of the strangeness of language:

> The lamb thy riot dooms to bleed today
> Had he thy reason, would he skip and play?

It took me months when I was sixteen to figure out that when Pope used that word "riot" (in *The Essay on Man*), he was not talking about the Twelfth of July in Portadown.

Why did I not get the same pleasurable sense of otherness and strangeness from Irish? Because the dread ethos of political correctness hung over it all. This was the real stuff, here was the true, the only – if hidden – Ireland; to read it, to speak it was to serve your country and your God, and keep at bay all those alien influences which might corrupt the Gaelic morale of the school, the county, the country. The really sad thing about the impact of the Irish language in my time is that, in the constricted and sectarian circumstances of the North, it functioned not to open, but to narrow the cultural arteries.

So where did all this leave me? A perfect specimen of the success of colonisation is one good answer. Well, if I am colonised, there is not much I could or can do about it, and I feel pretty bobbish about it, except for a deep regret that though I really liked languages (Latin, French, English), Irish was just a politically correct labour and not a labour of love. I did feel upset in Armagh and other nationalist venues at the Watson? George? Portadown?? treatment; later I could even play my own games with it.

As I got older, I saw that my experience of uncertain identity and confused loyalties is not aberrant, and that the world where it is healthy is healthily hybridised. There is much talk in Northern Ireland to this day about identity, and there is a real paradox at work in the ceaseless use of the word by politicians and cultural pundits. Normally, when one speaks of "a sense of identity", one might seem to be pointing to the sheer individuality of experience, its unique particularity. In Northern Ireland (though not just in Northern Ireland – one thinks of the coverage of the Balkans), alas, the phrase is employed almost always to emphasise the *common* nature of experiences, and to provide these experiences with a significance and meaning already mapped out in cultural or historical terms.

I have come to feel that it is a good thing to be loose or loosened from identity politics, and that in some ways, I was lucky to get the loosening early. Jeremy Popkin makes an interesting point about a matter of far more significance than my puny experiences. He discusses the memoirs of the Holocaust written by those – a large number of them professional historians – who had had their whole lives disrupted by Hitler and the Nazi regime. A common element in all their very different stories, whether they now live in Jerusalem or Manhattan, is a rejection of, a real distaste for, the reduction of their identity to the single word, Jew. That, after all, is what Hitler was all about.

A final point. One of the dangers of cultural nationalism is its insistence on the absolute uniqueness of the cultural experience, whether German, Japanese, Iranian or Irish. But we who are modern live increasingly in a discontinuous, polyglot world, and what is now clear to me is that the experience described in this essay, of confused loyalties and uncertain identity, is not, as I once thought, unusual. In a world often politically and culturally disrupted, it is an experience which becomes increasingly typical.

I will end with a letter I came across some years ago, which I find both amusing and consoling in all my thinking of these issues. It was written by that great spokesman for tradition, stability and continuity, T. S. Eliot, in 1928, on St George's Day (Eliot's own inscription) to the art critic Herbert Read:

> I want to write an essay about the point of view of an American who wasn't an American, because he was born in the South and went to school in New England as a small boy with a nigger drawl, but who wasn't a southerner in the South because his people were northerners in a border state and looked down on all southerners and Virginians, and who so was never anything anywhere and who therefore felt himself to be more a Frenchman than an American and more an Englishman than a Frenchman and yet felt that the USA up to a hun-

dred years ago was a family extension. It is almost too difficult even for Henry James, who for that matter wasn't an American at all, in that sense.

And I thought I had problems?

George Watson teaches in the Department of English at the University of Aberdeen, where he is also Associate Director of the Research Insitute of Irish and Scottish Studies.

THE VERNACULAR CITY

Tom Paulin

Will 2008 be Belfast's year?

In a short poem entitled "To Be Carved on a Stone at Thoor Ballylee," W.B. Yeats writes about the ancient Norman tower that figures so strongly in the poems that he wrote about the civil war:

> I, the poet William Yeats
> With old mill boards and Sea-green slates,
> And smithy work from the Gort forge
> Restored this tower for my wife George;
> And may these characters remain
> When all is ruin once again.

Yeats in this verse reminds us that the writing of poetry, like building work, is a process that recycles used materials – quotations, allusions, old bedsteads – and he also draws his inspiration from those dissonant "old mill boards and sea-green slates" – two clumps of three strongly stressed, bunched monosyllables that issue from Yeats's early love of Orange songs and popular ballads:

> My Aunt Jane has a bell on the door
> a white stone step and a clean swept floor
> candy apples hard green pears
> conversation lozengers.

The line "a white stone step and a clean swept floor" uses an identical rhythm, and of course "My Aunt Jane" is a talismanic song which expresses the great, marvellous, clattery tenderness of Belfast speech.

An early Belfast poet called Percy, who is sometimes described as "cracked", is famous for a couplet, not written in the city's vernacular, which celebrates the Long Bridge, which preceded the Queen's Bridge:

Spanning the Lagan, now we have in view,
The Great Long Bridge, with arches twenty-two.

Percy added, "It was only twenty-one arches, but as a poetical licence, and for the sake of rhyme, I had to add another arch." This reminds us with sly, apparent dopiness, that writers make things up, that adding an extra arch to a bridge is what the imagination can, and at times must, do.

The decision as to which UK city will be appointed European Capital of Culture in 2008 will be made later this year. To argue against Belfast winning the honour because it has no opera or ballet and has not produced a Belfast *Ulysses* is to deny the aspirations of present and future generations – culture pitches itself endlessly forward; culture is a debate, an argument. This is in the great Belfast poet Louis MacNeice's phrase, "the yeast of culture." Out of that fermentation – "soundlessly collateral / And incompatible," as MacNiece puts it in that wonderful early poem, "Snow," set in his father's episcopal residence on the Malone Road – there arises a classical ambition to give epic shape to a particular society's imagination, and one of the ways in which that shaping or architectonic process expresses itself is through translation. The poets who belong to Belfast have created a formidable body of translations from Irish and many European languages: Greek, Latin, French, Italian, German, Spanish, Bosnian and Russian. Just recently we have seen distinguished translations of Horace by Seamus Heaney and Paul Muldoon, and Michael Longley has translated and reworked classical texts extensively.

This body of translations, which has yet to be studied as a subject in itself, is similar to the great cultural effort made in England after the disintegration of the Commonwealth and the restoration of the monarchy. Foremost among those translators was John Dryden, the Catholic convert, who in his translation of the *Aeneid*, Virgil's epic of the founding of Rome, made a subtle rapprochement with the new Orange State that replaced James II's rule. Dryden's theme is Virgil's theme – war and peace and the founding of *civitas*, the creation of a new culture whose heart is civil and ironic, not martial, and which makes us all imaginative, peace-loving citizens. I never read these lines from the beginning of the *Aeneid* without thinking of Belfast – Belfast reformed and at peace with itself, at peace at least where arms are concerned. In these lines from the beginning of the *Aeneid*, we are all Trojans:

An age is ripening in revolving Fate,
When Troy shall overturn the Grecian State:
And sweet revenge her conqu'ring sons shall call,

To crush the People that conspir'd her fall.
Then Caesar from the Julian stock shall rise,
Whose empires ocean, and whose fame the skies
Alone shall bound, whom, fraught with Eastern spoils,
Our Heav'n, the just reward of human toils,
Securely shall repay with rites divine;
And incense shall ascend before his sacred shrine.
Then dire debate and impious war shall cease,
And the stern age be softened into peace:
Then banish'd faith shall once again return,
And vestal fires in hallowed temples burn.

Dryden's climbing lines – his heroic couplets – sing the architectonic force of culture, and they assert it as a value which is created and strengthened by a shared civic sense. It informs and shapes our lives as citizens, and it is shaped by our lives – just using that word brings back Derek Mahon's volume *Lives*, with the photograph on its cover of pre-First World War shipyard workers leaving the yard at the end of a day's work, and the Titanic rising behind them. This reminds us, as Mahon intends, of the connection between art and industry – a connection which in recent years has led to culture being described as a "creative industry." In a *New Statesman* lecture, "The Economy of the Imagination", given last year by the Labour peer Lord Evans, the argument was advanced that culture needs to be regarded as an economic resource, rather than as what used to be termed "super-structure." He pointed out that in the UK, the creative industries account for more than 5% of GDP.

In 1979, the historian F.S.L. Lyons published a collection of lectures, entitled *Culture and Anarchy in Ireland 1890–1939*. The title draws on a famous collection of four linked essays published in 1869 – *Culture and Anarchy*, by Matthew Arnold. Arnold did much to shape literary criticism over the decades that followed. His work gave rise to T.S. Eliot's *Some Notes Towards of Definition of Culture*, and Raymond Williams's *Culture and Society*. Eliot's short work is essentially an attack on the consensual climate of ideas which gave rise to the 1944 Education Act – he argues that, in order to truly appreciate culture and art, you need leisure and a private income. Williams is critical of Arnold's idea of culture; Arnold sees culture as the prerogative of those "aliens", as he terms them, who have transcended the limitations of social class and upbringing. Williams's objections are persuasive, but his work has attracted a type of socialist sentimentality, which echoes the conservative sentimentality that Eliot's work continues to attract.

What all these writers agree on is that culture and creativity are founded on the critical act – as Oscar Wilde observed, "Criticism is itself an art." For Arnold, the critic has to possess the supreme virtue of being disinterested, and his idea that the critic must be detached, impartial, above political and ideological argument, and on no side – without an axe to grind – has been very influential. It is in this idea that we can begin to trace the roots of the critical, creative and intellectual northern Irish culture that Belfast represents and embodies.

Arnold took the idea of critical disinterestedness from the 18th-century northern Irish philosopher, Francis Hutcheson, and from the critic, William Hazlitt (or *Haizlitt*, as his surname is pronounced in Belfast.) His paternal grandparents were from the North of Ireland. Hutcheson is often described as the father of the Scottish Enlightenment, but he is a neglected figure. He taught with and influenced the father of William Drennan, founder of the non-denominational reform society, the United Irishmen, and the Royal Belfast Academical Institution. Hutcheson's seminal work, *An Inquiry into the Original of our Ideas of Beauty and Virtue* (1725), is the founding text in English of the subject we now term "aesthetics". It is on his concept of natural disinterestedness that aesthetics is founded, and Hutcheson's distinctive critical address to art and society finds its most considered expression in Hazlitt's writings.

Neither Hutcheson nor Hazlitt believe in the idea of a free-floating, impartial disinterestedness, which Matthew Arnold promulgated. What they argue and represent is that the disinterested critic always has a position – is on a particular side – but that that position necessarily involves respecting and admiring the arguments offered by those writers on the opposite side. Hazlitt, for example, was a Whig radical and republican, who nevertheless believed that the Tory convert and monarchist, Edmund Burke, was a great writer. It was a test of what he termed "the sense and candour" of anyone of the opposite party to Burke's that they recognised Burke's greatness.

So in arguing and affirming that Belfast deserves the title of "city of culture", we base a central part of that argument on the fact that the culture which helped to found the modern metropolis of Belfast is disinterested, critical, aesthetic and candid. The bland, unimpassioned disinterestedness, which Arnold recommends, is not the active and engaged foundational disinterestedness with Hutcheson and Hazlitt embody.

It is the critical spirit which Hutcheson designs in his philosophical and aesthetic writings that helped to bring about the "golden age of the city", as Seamus Heaney and Michal Longley have called 18th century Belfast. There was, as we all know, an Ulster Enlightenment: the French Revolution was a major event in the history of the city. Here, I'm reminded of the story about the great Chinese leader Chou En Lai who, when asked what he thought the effect of the French Revolution on world history had been, replied, "it is too early to tell".

In William Drennan's seminal letter of 1784, which effectively founded the United Irishmen, we find that he writes of establishing "communication with the leading men of France." This central value of communication is, I think, part of the fabric of this city's culture. The foundation of *The Belfast Newsletter* by Henry Joy in 1737 – the oldest daily newspaper in these islands – exemplifies and embodies this ethic of communication. Francis Hutcheson observes in his introduction to moral philosophy that there is "scarce any cheerful or joyful communication of mind" which does not "naturally require to be diffused and communicated."

The source for this idea of communication is John Milton. We know that Milton was no friend to Belfast – his attack on Belfast as "a barbarous nook … whose obscurity til now never came to our hearing", and of that "blockish presbyters of Clandeboye" is still remembered. But in one pamphlet he praises the Athenian commonwealth, and then recommends the establishment of schools and academies, which would spread knowledge, civility and religion by "communicating the natural heat of government and culture more distributively to all extreme parts, which now lie numb and neglected." There is a direct link between Milton's argument about the necessity for communication and William Drennan's foundation of the non-sectarian Royal Belfast Academical Institution. Communication, education, the practice of journalism, all go together.

Belfast history begins with a battle between the Cruithin and the Ulaid in AD 666. The chronicler, writing in Irish, says that the "Farset here alluded to was evidently at Belfast, on the River Lagan." For many of us it begins with this Irish poem:

> The wee blackbird settles
> in a whin bush
> on the slope of the hill
> then opens
> its yolkyellow bill
> – now its fresh
> song rises up and fills
> the sky over Belfast Lough

That blackbird by Belfast Lough sings for ever innocently, like a daylight nightingale before all the history that was to come. As historians have shown, Ulster was the most Gaelic, the most impenetrable and least-known part of Ireland, and into it came a series of English adventurers, notably Sir Arthur Chichester, the true founder of the city, who was the most ruthless of the Lord-lieutenant Mountjoy's lieutenants and who was given the Castle of Belfast in 1603. He then set about turning the settlement into a model plantation town. The historical dialect which created the city has many sources – on the one hand, battle, skirmish, riot, protest; on the other, communication, education, invention, religious practice, industry. We know that this area is poor in natural stone so the city is built of clay and is founded on mud and clay. The poet Robert Johnstone observes:

> The moment of Belfast's ascendancy was entirely an act of will: the very ground on which the shipyard stands is man-made. Like the city as a whole, the industry was created by human hands, and provides the richest metaphor of the founders' idea of the world and of themselves.

The noun *ascendancy* is well chosen, because as Johnstone argues, it was the middle-class that took the lead in challenging the ascendancy.

The industrial power and creative energy of Belfast are a permanent source of pride – the Oceanic II, launched in 1899, was the world's largest ship, and the first vessel to exceed in length Brunel's Great Eastern. In the years before the First World War, Belfast had the greatest shipyard, rope works, tobacco factory, linen mills, dry dock and tea machinery works in the land. What it lacked was a poet like Walt Whitman to celebrate its enormous industrial might and the creative intelligence that designed its ships and other products. We know that it is a city of mathematicians, engineers and inventors, and we know that, as well as the Dunlop tyre, the tractor, the ejector seat and barbed wire were invented in the Province. (I know there is a view that it was the Belfast plough, not the tractor, which was invented here, and that the pneumatic tyre was developed, rather than invented; but this view is offered in support of an argument against Belfast becoming a City of Culture, and so represents that strain of negativity and lack of confidence which is such a persistent strand in the city's culture.)

If Belfast lacked a Whitman to celebrate its brain and muscle, it can be seen as the embodiment of everything that that great laureate of Empire, Rudyard Kipling, stood for. I recall a placard outside the shipyards in 1985, during the protests against the Anglo-Irish Agreement – it adapted Kipling's poem, "Ulster 1912", and read:

Before an Empire's eyes
The traitor claims her price.
What need of further lies?
We are the sacrifice.

The culture of the shipyards is celebrated in David Hammond's prize-winning documentary film "Steelchest, Nail in the Boot and the Barking Dog." The title is a series of lethal shipyard nicknames for fellow workers. It is part of the city's creativity, this genius for the exact inscape of a nickname – often a nickname with an etymology or derivation: Wire Nail was "a big tall fellow, he wore a flat cap so he got a nickname, Wire Nail".

According to one shipyard worker, quoted in a book that came out of the documentary, to launch a ship in the yards you always put tallow and black soap or "glowter", as they call it, on the slips. The workers used to use glowter as soap. "There was a plater called Lord Antrim," Charlie Witherspoon, a former shipyard worker, remembers,

> I don't know what his real name was, but he was the heart of corn, a kindly man, but a very coarse Christian, as we would say. And there was a story that one day he was walking down the Shankill Road with his wife. His wife was wheeling the pram and the pram was squealing badly. He was a very impatient man but he stuck it for a good while. Then it annoyed him that much that he burst out, "For God's sake, Aggie! Throw the bloody thing over and put a drop of glowter on her!"

That phrase, "the heart of corn", in its spontaneous, off-the-top-of-the-head immediacy, expresses something of the vernacular energy and pithy imagery of the city's speech, as well as that deep lovingkindness in the culture while the word "glowter" – the, I guess, gritty black soap – takes on the symbolic properties of the Irish word "plamass", which in English means something like "fudge" or "soft soap," and which represents the value of compromise, of blurring the hard edges of opposed positions. How to construct a spoken language adequate to this is a problem that needs facing and discussing – it is a speech which requires, perhaps, a particular kind of oily irony that stops just short of being oleaginous.

Deep in the city's cultural memory is the experience of the linen trade. As Robert Johnstone writes, "The fibres came to the hacklers retted, dried and scutched, like long, flaxen hair which would comb through metal brushes." Belfast, which may possibly come from the name *Bealafarsad*, meaning "hurdle-ford town", is expressed in the recalcitrant sound of that sentence describing how the flax fibres come to "the hacklers, retted, dried and scotched." It ought to be possible – take *Huckleberry Finn* as an exemplary case – to found a national literature on this scutching vernacular, just as it ought to be possible to follow popular song through the Burns stanza and the Ulster Scots employed by the rhyming weavers to build on this stanza from the ballad "Lammas Fair." The fair was originally held in Belfast:

> There sits a tinker wi' his tins
> A turner wi' his ladles
> A gleg-tongued spunkie's crying spoons
> Anither's at her fables.

The phrase "gleg-tongued" – meaning fluent of speech – might seem hampered by its sound, while the word "spunkie" – meaning an irascible person – is more vigorous and terse than its equivalent in the standard language. We admire the haggled energy of a line such as "A gleg-tongu'd spunkie's crying spoons", and, having admired it, we may feel that all the energy and vitality of our speech is the only way forward. To call the city's spoken language – its raw, tender, irascible, spunky or sparky vernacular – a cultural resource is to employ a distorting or demeaning language of consumption, but it nevertheless expresses a truth about Belfast speech, in which the wee falorie man, that rattling, roving Irishman, is forever let loose to tell us:

> I am a good ould working man
> each day I carry a wee tin can
> a large penny bap and a clipe of ham
> I am a good ould working man.

This speech is built, ironically, out of English, Irish and Ulster Scots, and it is essential to recognise that that culture which the politicians of all political parties are now engaged in extending and consolidating is one that cherishes all the languages of the province, and which looks beyond them and draws on every possible language.

As Mary Ann Mc Cracken wrote to her brother on 26th March 1791, "do not forget that the French dictionary, syntax and grammar, all of which are very necessary at present as almost everybody in Belfast are learning French". We know and celebrate the fact that there are now many other languages spoken in the Province – Punjabi and Urdu, for example.

In this context, I want to take as an example of the use of the vernacular a unique poem, "Kerr's Ass," by the revered Ulster Poet, Patrick Kavanagh:

> We borrowed the loan of Kerr's big ass
> To go to Dundalk with butter,
> Brought him home the evening before the market
> An exile that night in Mucker.

Kavanagh uses the vernacular from the opening line, and he extends it in the next stanza where, like Yeats and like "My Aunt Jane," he uses a pattern of three strong stresses and also recycles various bits and pieces:

> We heeled up the cart before the door,
> We took the harness inside —
> The straw-stuffed straddle, the broken breeching
> With bits of bull-wire tied;

> The winkers that had no choke-band,
> The collar and the reins...

Then Kavanagh shifts into another register, a more standard language beyond the vernacular:

> In Ealing Broadway, London Town
> I name their several names

> Until a world comes to life —
> Morning, the silent bog,
> And the god of imagination waking
> In a Mucker fog.

The vernacular survives and is asserted in that placename "Mucker," from the Irish for "pig", but we should note that as in Michael Longley's line "Sorry missus, I think, was what he said," the vernacular and a more standard, more classical language, work together to affirm the god of imagination waking in a Mucker fog.

It is possible to take an optimistic line and imagine the progressive enlightenment or "growing good of the world", as a Victorian novelist termed it, but in the cultural memory it is recorded battle and massacre, the damage to workers' health by the dampness and flax dust or "pouce" in the linen mills, the 1886 rioting, which produced the highest death toll of any political event in Ireland in the 19th century. We can remember the famine, the great typhus epidemic, the fact that Belfast's textile workers were among the lowest paid in the United Kingdom, and we remember the violence of 1922, as well as the outdoor relief riots of 1932, and their brief moment of working-class solidarity. We remember that the death rate from typhoid in 1906 was the highest in the UK, and we remember the Troubles of the past 30 and more years.

All this, and much much more, is remembered. But it is an expression of the sceptical, questioning, often querulous temperament of the city to carry both a doubt about the efficacy of possessing a cultural memory, and a doubt about the presentist, practical or pragmatic outlook that shrugs such a memory off. In 1791, a very early issue of that celebrated radical newspaper, *The Northern Star*, recommended "not the gloomy and precarious stillness; but that stable tranquillity which rests on the rights of human nature." Many years later, Sir James Craig reformulated that sentiment – it appeared originally in a United Irish policy document – when he described his meeting with Eamonn De Valera on May 5, 1921. De Valera, Craig said, spent almost the entire meeting "harping on the grievances of Ireland for the past 700 years, instead of coming down to practical present-day discussion". That argument between ancient grievance and present-day praxis continues, but there is another, if related, argument which expresses this city's culture, and that is the argument between a forward-looking optimism and an anti-enlightenment pessimism, which is often enshrined in the more extreme evangelical preachers and continues to attract many adherents.

This skeptical pessimism, as I'm calling it, finds one of its greatest exponents in the writings of Dostoyevski, whose tragic novel, *Crime and Punishment*, is set in St Petersburg, that "fantastic and intentional city", as he calls it, which was raised on mud like Belfast by an act of will. In his counter-Enlightenment novella, *Notes from Underground*, Dostoyevski's narrator tells us: "I am forty. I once used to work in the government service but I don't now. I was a bad civil servant. I was rude, and I enjoyed being rude. After all, I didn't take bribes, so I had to have some compensation." This is by way of explanation, but before this Dostoyevski's narrator tells us: "I am a sick man ... I am an angry man. I am an unattractive man." We may dismiss him as irrational and perverse, but the imagination that created this voice is telling us that on the one hand there is this voice from underground, and on the other there is a voice on the flat earth above it, whose favourite phrase is "of course", and which thinks every problem can be sorted out rationally. A living culture admits both voices: one which says No, Belfast ought not to become European Capital City of Culture, and then cites all those institutions and artists that it has not had. The counter-view argues that Yes, Belfast ought to become European Capital City of Culture and suggests that, as Tom Collins, chairman of the independent company set up to promote Belfast's bid, puts it: "Culture is about more than painting, music, theatre and dance. Culture is created by the things we say, make and do ... culture is about George Best, John Dunlop, Sir James Martin, who invented the ejector seat," as well as about the writers, artists and musicians it has produced.

I agree with that sentiment, and I note that Tom Collins is director of communications at Queen's University; that term "communication", employed by Milton and by Drennan, whom he influenced, is based on a belief in education. A truly vibrant and creative culture depends on a system of education which is not divided along class and sectarian lines. My understanding is that that divisive and iniquitous exam, the 11-plus, is being slowly abolished in Northern Ireland, but that there is very considerable resistance to establishing a non-sectarian education system, which will serve each and every child equally.

It is generally acknowledged that working-class loyalists have been most badly served by the education system, and it is the responsibility of politicians and civil servants to work to secure that large section of the population its rights as citizens. Culture can be the articulation in civil speech of citizenship, which is why the concept of the vernacular city has to allow for a more measured, more evenly paced discourse than any "gleg-tongued spunkie" would wish to offer.

It is possible look back in nostalgic gratitude to the education that one had in this city – I certainly do that – but I recognise that the whole system needs radical change. Teachers are the ministers and priests of culture, its practioners and its emissaries. It is from their teaching and example that a whole new culture will emerge. It is our faith in the emergence of a new, wholly peaceful culture that makes us support Belfast as the City of European Culture 2008.

This essay was first delivered at the John Hewitt Winter School, February 2002.

Tom Paulin grew up in Belfast. His most recent volume of poetry is The Invasion Handbook *(Faber, 2002).*

WEATHER REPORT: GOOD FRIDAY WEEK, 1998

Chris Agee

*Four years on, the author recalls an historic Irish
agreement at Stormont.*

Afternoon weather was the metaphor.

On the Tuesday before the talks deadline of Thursday April 9th, 1998, set by
Tony Blair early in his premiership, it had cleared suddenly to a deep and flaw-
less azure more like Provence than Ireland. Inside the talks, however, all was
gloom. The unionists were declining to accept the draft Agreement – prepared
by the British and Irish governments and presented through Senator George
Mitchell, the American chairman of the talks – as the basis for a final constitutional settlement. Predicting Thursday's outcome would, clearly, be as chancy
as prophesying the next hour's processional of cloud-laden, Turneresque
moods.

Wednesday was the archetypical Irish "dirty day": wet, bleak, grey. The
Belfast hills were topped by *tourbillons* of low mist. By late afternoon, the usual
mizzle-mist or sporadic shower had turned to a heavy downpour. But at the
talks, adjacent to the old Parliament at Stormont near Belfast, the mood was
brightening. It was just possible that a settlement ending the Thirty Years
Stalemate of the Troubles, and the most important political beginning since
Partition in 1920, was on the cards.

Ireland has what meteorologists call an "oceanic" climate, particularly in the
North. It is swept by the restless vagaries of North Atlantic isobars. Here the
trade-winds, currents and tempests from the circumnavigations of the Gulf
Stream make their far-western European landfall. The phosphorescent flares of
New England trawler-nets and the smooth brown pods of the Caribbean bean
litter the tidelines of Mayo. Year round, Irish weather is soft, clement, rain-
drenched and fickle, whereas that of its latitudinal twin, Newfoundland, with
its Arctic winter and fleeting summertime, is harsh and intemperate, a New
World Siberia. Where one might dig deep in bog in Ireland, there is tundra and
permafrost in Labrador.

Precipitation and changeability: therein lies the glory of Irish weather. Like the unique air of a culture or period, or some autochthonous ecology of light and wet, the island's weather is full of its own special blend of shimmerings and dazzles. Ireland lacks both the true wintriness that frequents Scotland and the continental warmth of the South of England at high summer. Sea-girt and sea-buffeted, it is shielded from the extremes of the great Eurasian landmass. It seldom freezes for long and is never sultry in the meridional sense. Snow is rarely more than a shallow icing. If it lacks the steady warmth and illumination of Mediterranean *claritas,* or the crisp resolutions of North American seasons, Ireland has its own its medicine-bag, its own Ariel, for meteorological enchantments.

Above all, Irish weather throbs and shines when sunlight meets the endless impressionism of ocean moisture. Cloud shadows mountain. Hailshowers in sunlight. A rainbow amid storm-darkenings over Belfast Lough. Dusk and rain-drops spangling the shimmy of a window like a bird's breast. Moon adrift in scud or rack, sunshafts fingering curtains of mist. Droplets on clover as tensile as the tremblings of quicksilver. It is an atmospheric dazzle you often glimpse in that Vermeer of sensation, Seamus Heaney: buffetings, dews, frosts, hail-stones, rinsings, lightenings, "glitter-drizzle, almost-breaths of air" and other "subtle little wets." Or even, on occasion, in Samuel Beckett, in the brighten-ing recollection of blue skies knotting the grain of his parables.

Thursday, the decisive day, dawned oceanic. Cottony dirigibles arose in the East and steamed over. It shone, darkened, gusted, showered; a stream of cycles. When my late afternoon work-out finished and I stepped from the gym in the cloud-capped shadow of Black Mountain, a splatter of hail was falling in bright sunlight. It bounced and settled on a grass verge dotted with speedwell. Endgame time. Turning the ignition I looked forward to the evening's television.

On the news the consensus was that a deal, despite impediments, was in the offing. It was the beginning of an astounding moment: modern Ireland's psychic Appomattox, though – crucially – no one was surrendering. From then on, the Irish channels – BBC Northern Ireland, Ulster Television, Radio Telefís Éireann – suspended scheduling and went more or less live. A succession of talking heads, politicians and pundits, propounded from Stormont, or studios in Belfast, London, Dublin, Brussels, America. Downstairs to make a cup of tea, I found myself thinking of that moment, on the upstairs landing, when I had shouted to my wife that the Berlin Wall had fallen. The high drama of high politics.

Only towards midnight, however, did I twig the depth of the parallel. With each new assessment of the waxing prospects, the psychic partition of the country was being breached before our eyes. The actual brick and breeze-block wall that snakes for miles through the heart of West Belfast, whose euphemism is "the peace-line", might stand for years. No jubilant crowds were gathering in the streets to deconstruct division. But just as surely, the inner Irish Wall was tottering, being chipped away by invisible, televisual legions: the spirit-troop of popular hope.

Then it happened. Perhaps there is a moment in every revolution, literal or psychological, when symbolism translates directly into the ebb or flow of power – whose momentousness lies in this very transmutation. Such was Ceausescu's speech from the balcony, Yeltsin mounted on a tank, or Mayor Daly haranguing the podium at the 1968 Democratic Convention. For it was around midnight that the panjandrum of extreme Protestantism, the Reverend Ian Paisley – high priest of bigots and homophobes, scourge of Christian charity, Jeremiah of Ulster's apocalypse – arrived at the gates of Stormont Castle to join a chanting crowd, aswirl with Union Jacks and St George's Crosses. Imagine a Cotton Mather unredeemed by humane learning; or an ignoramus instinct with charisma masquerading as Jonathan Edwards. Then imagine a party of ethnic "Protestantism" centred around such a figure. What you have, perforce, is a deformation of the Reformation.

He was let in the grounds and led his hundreds to the Soviet-style statue of Edward Carson, architect of Partition and first Prime Minister in Northern Ireland's old Parliament, prorogued in 1973 for the blatant Jim Crowism of unionist rule. It was instantly clear that despite the braggadocio of his protest against the imminence of compromise – a shot across the bows from a cunning wrecker – he was staring at a colossal miscalculation and, down the road, the political wilderness. From day one, he had boycotted the talks, a prime reason they were now succeeding against all easy expectation.

The crowd was held back, and he and a few lieutenants proceeded to the entrance of the perimeter fence surrounding the purpose-built building for the talks. Slyly, a few days earlier, the British Government had already denied him entrance, on no other grounds than astute politics, since he had long been invited and held a pass. It was a classic piece of political sharp practice within the rules of the game. He was made a gatecrasher at the moveable feast of peace. Thundering, Paisley adjourned to a Nissen hut next to the fence, there to hold forth at an ad hoc news conference: no doubt his intention all along.

Now, crying wolf for the umpteenth time, he was the true wolf at the door. The talks had overrun their midnight deadline, and though hope was escalating by the hour, it was still a close-run thing, and success might yet be tipped at the post by some unbridgeable gap. Although Paisley has always been careful not to sully his hands directly, no one person, within the structure of mindsets and forces in the North, had done more to foment years of violent unionist backlash and so pad the self-exculpatons of the IRA. His "Province" may be small as the Baltic Oblast of Kaliningrad, but his certitude is as overweening and gargantuan as Stalin's.

A truly great totalitarian (and like many others, he hails from a borderland), he has built the hot gospel of his politics and church (an offshoot of an offshoot of Presbyterianism) on one-man ground so pinched and narrow that it affords his ego a perfect fastness from which to bellow, bully, rabblerouse, threaten, instigate. (I come – two generations back – from a line of Tennessee Calvinists, and know whereof I speak). He is an adept at provoking, negatively, the inner mask of ethno-national identity that can either inflect or suppress the individual sensibility.

Nor is he simply some pre-modern dinosaur. Like so much of twentieth century religious pathology, Paisley's specious revival of "old-time religion" is a wholly modern phenomenon. It means to cherish an ignorant caricature of old faith by papering over the cracks posed either by the paradigm of science or (most dangerously) by the contemporary revision of religious sensibility. It substitutes the ardour and imagery of doctrine for a true opening to the challenge of a living and lived experience of authentic faith. Postmodernism in reverse, you might say. But by ignoring the cracks, it fails also to address them and in a sense accepts them; so it, too, is a form of unbelief, and a most invidious sort, one that will plague this century as it did the last: *religious nihilism.* That is why the patent medicine of apocalypse always has the flavour of people who despair of life, and would soon enough give it up. In truth Paisley's is not so much a theology or a politics as a perennial politico-religious psychology, no less evident in Catholicism or Judaism or Islam, that calls down ire and hellfire on the Other due to some molten angst, flaw or wound in its own spirituality. Arrogance as the obverse of deficiency. Zeal masking aggression. In this way Paisley professes Christian love even as he traduces its spirit though a tone-deaf fabulation of the letter.

Then, as I say, it happened. The hut was jammed with journalists, security officials, low-level politicos and sundry hangers-on. Outside, the night was Shakespearean — wind-tossed, lashed by bouts of rain. The cameras went live just as Paisley and his two main lieutenants seated themselves at the microphones.

"The Big Man" began to speak. It was the usual growling bellow that is slowly built up to paroxysms of high-pitched thunderings of contempt and betrayal. But no sooner had he gotten a few words out, he was being barracked by several unseen voices at the back. You could feel the whoosh of a collective televisual gasp: who *were* these noises off? In a flash it was obvious that they were *Loyalists* — the Irish descendant of a term once also used for Americans loyal to the Crown during the Revolutionary period.

Incredible moment: Paisley stood down, in the full glare of mass theatre, by his own "side". Loyalism is a strand of unionism but with a more militant, working-class, secular and (dread word) *Irish* inflection; it stands to main-stream unionism as republicanism does to moderate nationalism. Paisley, who had always presumed to lead it, instantly intuited the political danger of being hoisted on his own media petard. Although it is doubtful whether he was fully aware of it, it was the man, rather than the politician, that was being rumbled by the uncut gaze of the camera.

Paisley was flummoxed by the brickbats. One expected him to recover from the stumble and, as usual, to override the adversity, but somehow he didn't manage it. Was he getting old? A voice floated up: "Where will you take us, Ian, if we follow you out the door?" Another sang through the growing com-motion : "*The Grand Old Duke of York, he had ten thousand men . . .*"

With a sweep of the arm Paisley barked out to no one in particular: "Remove them!" He smiled inwardly, arrogantly; muttered a few words to himself, in the downward direction of the baize, with the bristling sarcasm and embattled brittleness of a fundamentalist autodidact; pursed and flattened his lips in a trademark tic of rectitude and intolerance shared by many of his Northern compatriots. He wanted a congregation, not an audience.

His tar-barrel theatricality – a hibernicized descendant of the camp revival-ism of the American Bible Belt – was malfunctioning. He who in a fog of self-righteousness had so often treated his interlocutors to extreme rudeness, was now getting a dose of his own medicine. Live coverage bore down like one of those all-seeing divine eyes, ensconced in a triangle, that adorn the Masonic regalia of Orangeism. In a few moments, with a few deft strokes, the Paul Bunyan of loyalism was outflanked, punctured like a helium float. Even many of his stalwarts must have found it difficult to suppress, as the Buddhists say, the truth of consciousness. If every dog has its day, this dog's was done, or at least ending . . . however much it might keep barking and snapping.

Weeks before the symbolism of dates had dawned on me. Happenstance symmetry, or the astuteness of those managing "the peace process" under the aegis of Anglo-Irish cooperation? The deadline for the completion of the talks was Maundy Thursday (9 April); since they were likely to run to the eleventh hour, the deal, if clinched, would be delivered to the world on Good Friday. In the first place, it seemed scheduling and political logic argued not for happen-stance but astuteness. Yet, maybe it was one of those extraordinary coincidences, like Germany's 9th of November, which has seen the end of the monarchy and the proclamation of the Republic (1918), *Kristallnacht* (1938) and the Fall of the Wall (1989)? And if a deal was indeed clinched, the Referendum would be held on 22 May; on that day two centuries before, the United Irishmen had launched, in Belfast and Dublin, their uprising for an Irish republic.

Then there was the special Irish resonance of Easter itself, evoking the republican iconography of the 1916 commemorations at Bodenstown and Milltown. It seemed extraordinary that the fracture that commenced with the Easter Rising had come full circle and begun to be annealed in a new light at the same season. On second thought, hadn't the Northern love of calendrical symbolism, and the aestheticization of violence attendant on the inevitability of such symbols – that special Ulster sense of fate, like the *wyrd* of Old English, lurking in the iconography – hadn't this love, in fact, been one of the prime sources of the glamour and ritualism of the "Troubles", so different, even in that homely label, from the true wars of the former Yugoslavia?

Of course the Easter Rising had happened not on Easter, but Easter Monday. Patrick Pearse, Gaelic scholar and aesthete that he was, would have well under-stood the symbolic distinction, whether or not it was factored into his calcula-tions or his piety. In Irish "Dé Luain" means both "on Monday" and "on the day of judgment." The Irish language poet and novelist Eoghan Ó Tuairisc titled his 1966 novel on Pearse and his leadership of the Rising just that, *Dé Luain*. When the neoclassical GPO was seized and the Republic descending from the Greeks proclaimed, it was a step into the historical dark and, for some of course, a ren-dezvous with the actual dark.

Still deeper in the background, there was the ancient pedigree of the sea-sonal meaning. The Anglo-Saxon for Easter, *Eastre,* was derived by the Venerable Bede from the name of a goddess whose feast was celebrated at the vernal equi-nox. Its ultimate root, harking back through Old Frisian and Old High German, was the Sanskrit for *morning* or *dawn*. As such it is cognate with the "aurora" of Latin and "tomorrow" of Greek.

With this image at the back of my mind, I had been hoping to take Jacob, my son, to watch the Easter dawn from the Giant's Ring at Ballyleeson, just out-side Belfast. If we rose before first light, we might get there in time, perhaps, to catch, like a harbinger, the tail of Hale-Bopp. If it was clear, we could sit on the dewiness of the immense earthen embankment and watch the molten foil spill over the mountains round Belfast, lifting shadow from the great bowl of sward and illuminating what Robinson Jeffers, who lived for a time in Belfast in the mid-twenties, called in a poem about the Ring "that great toad of a dol-men / Piled up of ponderous basalt that sheds the centuries like raindrops." (It is odd to think of the poet of the Big Sur domiciled amidst the mists and glooms of Partition, in a British backwater at the height of the Deep Freeze, a stone's throw from Yeats's "Meditations in Time of Civil War." Though, on reflection, perhaps not). In the event, two days later, when I awoke in the morning dusk of Easter, it was wet and overcast, and I scuppered the outing without wakening Jacob.

Good Friday was bright and gusty, "through-other" with sun and cloud. I woke slightly later than usual, towards ten, and straight away switched on the Tube. Atmosphere electrified the scene beamed from the carpark, where the world's media had established its carvanserai of trucks and dishes: it *had* happened, it seemed, bar the last push. A wind-buffeted microphone was swivelling between the sound-bites of pairs of politicians queuing to speak.

In my own satirical self-speak I had for some time been fond of seeing the North's lead players as either Antiques or Moderns. An Antique was a soul afflicted with the pathology of provincialism. A Modern was one who had missed or slipped it. The division transcended age, culture, creed, class, education and politics. It was more a frame of mind, or an orientation of deep formation, than a matter of the surface of self-conscious belief. Some of the worst Antiques being, in fact, intellectuals. To use a culinary metaphor, it was the difference between a cholesterol-laden "Ulster fry" (bacon, egg, sausage, black sausage, potato bread and soda bread fried in fat) and a Continental breakfast. Antique Ulster was a secret monoculture with two coloured-coded inflections that ate the same breakfast.

Over my Special K I watched the wind-jostled camera bring another pair into view: John Hume, the leader of the Social Democratic and Labour Party, the party of constitutional nationalism, and Davey Adams, one of the leaders of a small loyalist party affiliated with the Ulster Defence Association, a paramilitary organization responsible for the random killing of hundreds of Catholics. A few years earlier, months of meetings between them, let alone a meeting of minds, would have have been political pie-in-the-sky. Yet that is precisely where these two Moderns – one preeminent, one improbable – had now ended up, this very moment, stepping out of the marathon of the final all-night negotiations. Who was to be more admired, the one who had not changed, or the one who had changed?

Hume, always alert to the language of occasion, edged forward and took pole position to speak. He has always seemed to me to be cut from the same cultural cloth as his fellow Derryman Seamus Heaney. Both belong to the Redmondite tradition of constitutional nationalism, but the affinity strikes me as deeper than mere politics or even the traditional Catholicism of the upbringing of each. It is more a matter of cultural poise; of being at home in equal proportion in their *provincia,* on the island, within the wider world.

What the two make of background navigates the Scylla and Charybdis of Ulster's culture wars: the laager mentality of the unionists, and its gangrenous doppelganger, the martyrological imperative of armed republicanism. In distinct but overlapping spheres, politician and poet have fashioned a discourse of the optative Ireland where "hope and history rhyme," and where the parish is comprehended – as the great Irish essayist Hubert Butler once put it – from the vantage of the cosmopolitan: *"The interpreters will be those who can see the national life as well as live it. To acquire this detachment, they will need to have access to other forms of society, so that they can see their own lives objectively and in totality from the threshold."* And now, it seemed, was the crowning moment, when the optative had begun to transmute to the present continuous.

Visibly moved, Hume said simply, "This a Good Friday gift to the people of Ireland," before giving way to Adams, who made to speak. But all that issued was the strangled beginnings of an opening *Uh.* He was choked up, near tears. You felt the moment in yourself, the camera lulling for a second on the silent pair, before being magicked up to the anchorman in a Portacabin studio above the parking lot.

It was late afternoon when I drove home from the week's last work-out. On the hills above West Belfast the whitethorn blossom of the hedgerows put me in mind of combers foaming down through the quilted fields. It was cloudy but lightsome, and the streets, emptying early before the long weekend, were spangled with showers. A pillar-box painted green caught a sudden shaft of declining sun. By the time I reached South Belfast, the West had cleared to a deepening hue of cobalt, a last late sunshine bathing the brick of an old terrace district. The scruffy kerbstones of Primrose and Gypsy Streets were awash in a sudden preternatural glow. About this time, I would notice later on the news, the final Stormont plenary had convened for the cameras; Senator Mitchell announced "the new British-Irish Agreement"; and the eight delegations emerged successively onto the steps of Government Buildings to address the massed ranks of the global media – braving, over the next hour, and only a few miles away, a final meteorological fitfulness of gusts, drizzle, sunshowers and sleet.

Towards eight I walked out with Jacob to see what was playing at the cinema a few blocks away. A last deep glaze of jade, darkling and translucent, lay on the horizon under a streak of stratus. The Moonrise had just lifted over the silhouette of the houses beyond the thoroughfare of the Ormeau Road. Among the innumerable images for its elemental presence, would I ever quite find the one that got the beauty, the minerality, the geometry of that bright alabaster disc, its Minerva's owl's-eye, light out of the dark, magnificence reflected in the void?

Easter came chill, fresh and sunny. It blustered, and the brilliant blue of Tuesday was brindled with puffs of cumulus. Even as sun warmed the skin, there was the smoke-scent and crispness of autumn. Mid-afternoon, a low wall of grey cloud agleam, interspersed with blue, trailed a sudden manna of hail across the street-scene in my bay, rattling the panes. Within minutes, it had laid an immaculate blanket of snowy catkins on the tarmac, cars, roofs, gardens and bins. The hailstones were light, dry, peanut-sized – the largest I had ever seen – and out front the clover-and-grass seemed coated in drifts of Styrofoam. Suddenly the air had the high-altitude freshness of a timberline.

Just as quickly, the downfall was changing to a slush the colour of mothballs. The sun shone on the steaming street's meltwater, and the last white on the facing roof was like fallen blossom. Soon nothing was left of the day's visitation of hail but a few white shadows in the green shade of hedges. An hour later, all was rinsed, the light crystalline. The large camellia five doors down, its fall of magenta daubing the footpath, reminded me of Chagall. Incontrovertibly, something new was in the air.

Chris Agee is the Editor of this journal. His third volume of poems, First Light *(The Dedalus Press), will appear in 2003.*

THOUGHTS IN THE PRESENCE OF FEAR

—

Wendell Berry

—

The Eleventh of September.

I

The time will soon come when we will not be able to remember the horrors of September 11 without remembering also the unquestioning technological and economic optimism that ended on that day.

II

This optimism rested on the proposition that we were living in a "new world order" and a "new economy" that would "grow" on and on, bringing a prosperity of which every new increment would be "unprecedented."

III

The dominant politicians, corporate officers, and investors who believed this proposition did not acknowledge that the prosperity was limited to a tiny percentage of the world's people, and to an ever smaller number of people even in the United States; that it was founded upon the oppressive labor of poor people all over the world; and that its ecological costs increasingly threatened all life, including the lives of the supposedly prosperous.

IV

The "developed" nations had given to the "free market" the status of a god, and were sacrificing to it their farmers, farmlands, and rural communities, their forest, wetlands, and prairies, their ecosystems and watersheds. They had accepted universal pollution and global warming as normal costs of doing business.

V

There was, as a consequence, a growing worldwide effort on behalf of economic decentralization, economic justice, and ecological responsibility. We must recognize that the events of September 11 make this effort more necessary than ever. We citizens of the industrial countries must continue the labor of self-criticism and self-correction. We must recognize our mistakes.

VI

The paramount doctrine of the economic and technological euphoria of recent decades has been that everything depends on innovation. It was understood as desirable, and even necessary, that we should go on and on from one technological innovation to the next, which would cause the economy to "grow" and make everything better and better. This of course implied at every point a hatred of the past, all things inherited and free. All things superceded in our progress of innovations, whatever their value might have been, were discounted as of no value at all.

VII

We did not anticipate anything like what has now happened. We did not foresee that all our sequence of innovations might be at once overridden by a greater one: the invention of a new kind of war that would turn our previous innovations against us, discovering and exploiting the debits and the dangers that we had ignored. We never considered the possibility that we might be trapped in the webwork of communication and transport that was supposed to make us free.

VIII

Nor did we foresee that the weaponry and the war science that we marketed and taught to the world would become available, not just to recognized national governments, which possess so uncannily the power to legitimate large-scale violence, but also to "rogue nations," dissident or fanatical groups and individuals – whose violence, though never worse than that of nations, is judged by the nations to be illegitimate.

IX

We had accepted uncritically the belief that technology is only good; that it cannot serve evil as well as good; that it cannot serve our enemies as well as ourselves; that it cannot be used to destroy what is good, including our homelands and our lives.

X

We had accepted too the corollary belief that an economy (either as a money economy or as a life support system) that is global in extent, technologically complex, and centralized is invulnerable to terrorism, sabotage, or war, and that it is protectable by "national defense."

XI

We now have a clear, inescapable choice that we must make. We can continue to promote a global economic system of unlimited "free trade" among corporations, held together by long and highly vulnerable lines of communication and supply, but *now* recognizing that such a system will have to be protected by a hugely expensive police force that will be worldwide, whether maintained by one nation or several or all, and that such a police force will be effective precisely to the extent that it oversways the freedom and privacy of the citizens of every nation.

XII

Or we can promote a decentralized world economy which would have the aim of assuring to every nation and region a local self-sufficiency in life supporting goods. This would not eliminate international trade, but it would tend toward a trade in surpluses after local needs had been met.

XIII

One of the gravest dangers to us now, second only to further terrorist attacks against our people, is that we will attempt to go on as before with the corporate program of global "free trade", whatever the cost in freedom and civil rights, without self-questioning or self-criticism or public debate.

XIV

This is why the substitution of rhetoric for thought, always a temptation in a national crisis, must be resisted by officials and citizens alike. It is hard for ordinary citizens to know what is actually happening in Washington in time of such great trouble; for we all know, serious and difficult thought may be taking place there. But the talk that we are hearing from politicians, bureaucrats, and commentators has so far tended to reduce the complex problems now facing us to issues of unity, security, normality, and retaliation.

XV

National self-righteousness, like personal self-righteousness, is a mistake. It is misleading. It is a sign of weakness. Any war that we may make now against terrorism will come as a new installment in a history of war in which we have fully participated. We are not innocent of making war against civilian populations. The modern doctrine of such welfare was set forth and enacted by General William Tecumseh Sherman, who held that a civilian population could be declared guilty and rightly subjected to military punishment. We have never repudiated that doctrine.

XVI

It is a mistake also – as events since September 11 have shown – to suppose that a government can promote and participate in a global economy and at the same time act exclusively in its own interest by abrogating its international treaties and standing apart from international cooperation on moral issues.

XVII

And surely, in our country, under our Constitution, its a fundamental error to suppose that any crisis or emergency can justify any form of political oppression. Since September 11, far too many public voices have presumed to "speak for us" in saying that Americans will gladly accept a reduction of freedom in exchange for greater "security". Some would, maybe. But some others would accept a reduction in security (and in global trade) far more willingly than they would accept any abridgement of our Constitutional rights.

XVIII

In a time such as this, when we have been seriously and most cruelly hurt by those who hate us, and when we must consider ourselves to be gravely threatened by those same people, it is hard to speak of the ways of peace and to remember that Christ enjoined us to love our enemies, but this is no less necessary for being difficult.

XIX

Even now we dare not forget that since the attack of Pearl Harbor – to which the present attack has been often and not usefully compared – we humans have suffered an almost uninterrupted sequence of wars, none of which has brought peace or made us more peaceable.

XX

The aim and result of war necessarily is not peace but victory, and any victory won by violence necessarily justifies the violence that won it and leads to further violence. If we are serious about innovation, must we not conclude that we need something new to replace our perpetual "war to end war"?

XXI

What leads to peace is not violence but peaceableness, which is not passivity, but an alert, informed, practiced, an active state of being. We should recognize that while we have extravagantly subsidized the means of war, we have almost totally neglected the ways of peaceableness. We have, for example, several national military academies, but not one peace academy. We have ignored the teachings and the examples of Christ, Gandhi, Martin Luther King, and other peaceable leaders. And here we have an inescapable duty to notice also that war is profitable, whereas the means of peaceableness, being cheap or free, make no money.

XXII

The key to peaceableness is continuous practice. It is wrong to suppose that we can exploit and impoverish the poorer countries, while arming them and instructing them in the newest means of war, and then reasonably expect them to be peaceable.

XXIII

We must not again allow public emotion or the public media to caricature our enemies. If our enemies are now to be some nations of Islam, then we should undertake to know those enemies. Our schools should begin to teach the histories, cultures, arts, and languages of the Islamic nations. And our leaders should have the humility and the wisdom to ask the reasons some of those people have for hating us.

XXIV

Starting with the economics of food and farming, we should promote at home, and encourage abroad, the ideal of local self-sufficiency. We should recognize that this is the surest, the safest, and the cheapest way for the world to live. We should not countenance the loss or destruction of any local capacity to produce necessary goods.

XXV

We should reconsider and renew and extend our efforts to protect the natural foundations of the human economy: soil, water, and air. We should protect every intact ecosystem and watershed that we have left, and begin restoration of those that have been damaged.

XXVI

The complexity of our present trouble suggests as never before that we need to change our present concept of education. Education is not properly an industry, and its proper use is not to serve industries, neither by job-training nor by industry-subsidized research. It proper use is to enable citizens to live lives that are economically, politically, socially, and culturally responsible. This cannot be done by gathering or "accessing" what we now call "information" – which is to say facts without context and therefore without priority. A proper education enables young people to put their lives in order, which means knowing what things are more important than other things; it means putting first things first.

XXVII

The first thing we must begin to teach our children (and learn ourselves) is that we cannot spend and consume endlessly. We have got to learn to save and conserve. We do need a "new economy", but one that is founded on thrift and care, on saving and conserving, not on excess and waste. An economy based on waste is inherently and hopelessly violent, and war is its inevitable by product. We need a peaceable economy.

Wendell Berry, a poet and essayist, lives in Kentucky. His most recent volumes are Life is a Miracle *and* Jayber Crow *(both Counterpoint Press, 2000). This essay is published courtesy of* The Orion Society.

MÓRTAS NA MNÁ PALAISTÍNÍ

Cathal Ó Searcaigh

Tá sé doiligh dánta polaitiúla a scríobh gan dul i mbaol agus i mbannaí na bolscaireachta. Sin *dilemma* an dáin go minic. Conas d'aghaidh a thabhairt ar mhairgí móra an tsaoil i bhfilíocht? Caidé mar is feidir é seo a dhéanamh go fírinneach nuair nach bhfuil á chaitheamh agat féin ach saol beag suarach, sábháilte, saor ó bhroid agus ó bhuaireamh? Níl de fhreagra agam air sin ach gur dóigh liom go mbíonn filíocht mhaith ar thaobh an tsolais agus ar thaobh na beatha i gcónaí. Tá claíomh solais na Saoirse ag soilsiú, ag glinniúint i gcroí an fhile. Tá a thír dhúchais i gcroí an ndaoine atá faoi dhaorsmacht.

Is é ata sa dán seo ná bean Phalaistíneach agus í ag cur síos go neamhbhalbh ar an éagóir atáthar a dhéanamh ar a daoine. Le déanaí bhí mé ag léamh dornán dánta le Tawfiq Zayyad, file óg Palaistíneach, a chuaigh i bhfeidhm go mór orm. Bhain said siar asam le binb agus boirbe a ngutha. Shamhlófá go raibh nathair nimhe ag siosarnaigh agus ag slabhrú istigh i ngach ceann acu. Bhí ort a bheith ar d'fhaichill nó bheadh daor ort.

As an teagmháil sin le dánta Twfiq Zayyad a tháinig an dán seo. Is é ár ndán a bheith rannpháirteach i gcinniúint a chéile. Caithfidh muid comharsanacht mhaith a dhéanamh lenár gcomhdhaoine, cé acu i nGaza atá cónaí orthu nó i nGleann an Átha.

MÓRTAS NA MNÁ PALAISTÍNÍ
(i gcead do Tawfiq Zayyad)

Anseo i Lidda, i Ramla, i nGailílí,
fanóidh muid ag buanú ár gcineáil is ár ndlí.
Cha ruaigeann tú muid as do shlí.

Le súil nimhe an naimhdis
dhéanfaidh muid tú a chiapadh.
Le horthaí ársa an díoltais
dhéanfaidh muid tú a shárú.
Le gaineamh síobtha an tseachráin
cuirfidh muid tú amú.

Fanóidh muid go buan
ag sclábhaíocht, más gá, ó Luan go Luan;
ag scuabadh agus ag sciúradh
go béasach in bhur dtithe bodaigh;
ag freastal agus ag friotháladh
go dúthrachtach in bhur dtábhairní;

Inár scarbhóntaí agus inár seirbhisigh,
géilliúil agus cuideachtúil,
sa chruth go dtig linn, mall agus luath,
greim bídh a ghoid go trathúil,
deaslámhach, d'ár gcuid páistí gortacha
ó chrúba craosacha bhur bhfuath.

Fanóidh muid anseo go dochlóite
ag déanamh angaidh mar dhealga an chactais
i gcroí bhur gCinnteachta, i gcnámh droma bhur gCumais;
ag canadh amhráin ár gcráiteachta;
ag leirsiú ar shráideacha na hagóide;
ag líonadh na bpríosún le dínit na tragóide.

Cosnóidh muid an crann fige
agus an crann olóige;
cothóidh muid réablóid
i groí na hóige
mar an giosta seo atá ag éirí
i dtaos aráin ar an tinidh.

Anseo i Lidda, i Ramla, i nGaililí
gur beo a bheas muid, Palaistínigh
i mbuanseilbh ár mbuanchónaí.

———

It is difficult to write political poems without the risk of straying into the realms of propaganda. That is often the dilemma of a poem. How does one address the great woes of the world in poetry? How can one do this with integrity when one is living a cosy and safe little life free from distress and sorrow? My only answer is that I believe good poetry always takes the side of light and life. The luminous sword of freedom shines and beams in the heart of the poet. His native land is in the heart of the oppressed.

The following poem concerns a Palestinian woman defiantly telling of the injustice being carried out on her people. I recently read and was greatly impressed by a selection of poems by the young Palestinian poet Tawfiq Zayyad. I was taken aback by the venom and fierceness of their tones. One could also imagine that a serpent writhed and hissed in each one of them. One had to exercise a sense of caution or risk being dragged in.

The current poem is a direct result of that encounter with the poetry of Tawfiq Zayyad. Our separate destiny is to participate in our collective fate. We must strive to be on neighbourly terms with our fellows, should they live in Gaza or Gleann an Átha.

A PALESTINIAN LADY'S PRIDE
with deference to Tawfiq Zayyad

Here in Lidda, Ramala and Gallilee
we shall remain and perpetuate our people and our laws
you shall not clear us from your path.

With the evil eye of enmity
we shall torment you.
With ancient incantations of revenge
we shall overpower you.
With the shifting sands that waylay
we shall confound you.

We shall remain for ever
slaving, if needs be, week in week out
politely brushing and bleaching
in the houses of your grandeur
diligently waiting, hand and foot,
in your public houses,

as servants and bondswomen
we are submissive and sociable
from dawn to dusk that we might

seize the chance to pilfer with nimble hand
crusts from the greedy claws of your loathing
to feed our starving children.

We shall remain here unbowed
festering like the cactus thorns
in the heart of your Certainty, the spine of your Power;
singing the songs of woes
demonstrating in public protest,
filling the prisons with the dignity of the tragedy.

We shall protect the fig tree
and the olive branch;
we shall nourish revolt
in the heart of our young
like the yeast rising
in the bread baking on our hearths.

Here in Lidda, Ramala and Gallilee
we, Palestinians, shall prevail
dwelling for evermore in our eternal homeland.

Translated by Art Hughes

Cathal Ó Searcaigh is the Irish Language Editor of this journal. His most recent volume of poetry is Ag Tnúth Leis an tSolas *(Clo Iar-Chonnachta).*

IN OTHER WORDS: FROM THE ARABIC

Zakaria Mohammed

A suite of poems from the West Bank.

THE BIT

The boy watched
the black horse
with a white star
set in its forehead

The black horse watched
nothing
He lifted one hoof
from the ground

The meadow was lush
under the scorching sun
The horse's star blazed
under his forelock

The horse
wore no bridle
He had no bit
in his mouth

But still he champed
and champed
rearing his head
while hot blood spilled
from his lips

The boy was amazed
What is the black horse chewing?
he asked,
What does it chew?

The black horse
is chewing
a bit
of memory

forged from cold steel
to be champed on
and champed on
till death

COMING HOME

I left and came back

What was green had ripened

Fodder for caterpillars
Flesh to be chewed on like *qat*

THE DEAD

Father, what are these trees
that stretch to the horizon
in an unbroken row?

The dead, my son,
who left for the war
and couldn't return

Watch them line up
like peasants at checkpoints
longing to enter the city

But the huge gates are barred
and the watchtowers are manned
with fire and with arrows all night

STRANGERS

Fearful of light
they cower in the shadows

slinking through the trees
from trunk to trunk

cautiously
scanning the horizon

But I know their sort
Like rabbits in car headlights

the lunge of my torch
knocks them to their knees

hands raised for the handcuffs
instant caged birds

WAR

Kidnap the young goat
while its mother's not looking

Take it away
then stitch up her udder

Let the kid bleat
till even the rocks can hear it

Let the kid bleat
till even God will listen

Let the milk fatten
hyenas and wolves

So that war is enflamed
between the mouth and the udder

between a child and its mother
between God and the believer

PUPPET SHOW

The rose and death and I are centre stage
For fun we swap masks

Sometimes I am death
blasting everything
with my fearsome hand

Or death blossoms
as a rose on the fence

Or the rose turns into
a deadly shrapnel of glass

The three of us are on the stage
One hand pulls the strings

Who's hand is it?
Who's hand makes passes above our heads?

God's hand, said the rose
The devil's, said death

I don't breathe a word

Death covered my lips with its finger
before I could say my piece

DEATH

He has fallen asleep
He dreams of a meadow

A herd of sheep graze in the meadow
sheep-bells clang on their necks

As the bells clang
he falls deeply asleep

No one comes to wake him
No ram prods him awake with its horns

The night comes down
The sheep clatter off

He follows their sheep-bells
all through the night

as all through the night
the rams lead the sheep on

drawing down the night
with the tips of their horns

cloaking the meadow
with infinite night

(UNTITLED)

One rock beached on my beach
bears all the guilt of the rubble

THE SECOND BROTHER

I followed in your footsteps
I trod in your shadow

till you fell
in the pit of the dead

They made me first
the ram with no horns

But I will be second forever
forever printing my footprints

over those invisible footprints
that stretch out into pitch dark

BIRTH MARK

A birth mark like a vine leaf
is branded under my breast

How I hate my prefigured death –
crushed in the winepress one August

How I wish that my mother
hadn't craved grapes

I long for a birthmark
shaped like a lemon

If she'd craved lemons
I'd live until autumn

One afternoon I'd fall asleep
under our old lemon tree

mesmerised by its thorns
by its fat fruit like teardrops

The sad weeping lemons
mourning my passing

THE WOMAN'S DREAM

A small grey bird crashed into the fence
my fence
its cries like steel scissors slicing the air

My heart sank
my very worst nightmare
rose in my gullet —

those scissors
spinning about me
shearing my dress

those excitable scissors
stripping me naked
with their sharpened, stiff blades

THE JUG

Smash it with your stick,
my love

this fragile jug,
my heart

Splash its liquid
in the dust

or hold it high
above your head

to let it spill
into your mouth

But don't touch your lips
with its ochre clay:

Death is fired
on the lip of the jug

death is fired
in its clay

THE LIZARD

Toughened hide of rough bark
the lizard climbs the rock at noon

salaaming to a martinet
a cryptic autocrat

a hanging judge
whose mercy is the jackboot and the fist

Toughened hide of rough bark
the lizard climbs the rock at noon

salaaming, bowing
flummoxed by the arcane rules

at the wrong end of the stick
He ducks his head

hammered by the naked sun
He bows his head

certain that a breeze must come

NIGHT

Night is unfurling its blackhearted flower
for those who stumble
down steps and stairs

Night is unfolding its dark little buds
for those who slink out
of backrooms and basements

Night is opening its pitchblack bloom
as dread tumbles down
like a melon

GHOSTS

Their souls are like swifts
flicking their wings
at the corner of your eye

Their souls flit
from room to room
snuffing the candle
slamming the door

Garlic and mothballs
are pointless
You've got to burn down the house
to fumigate ghosts

All night the ghosts
swing from the coathangers
upsidedown like bats

THE LAST ONE

Spare me
the last bullet in the revolver
so death can wait at the doorway

Spare me
the last gasp in the lungs
so breath can expire with hard labour

Spare me
the last copy of the key
so only the ghosts can get in

Translated by Sarah Maguire

A NOTE ON THE POET

Zakaria Mohammed is one of the leading poets of his generation. Born in 1951, he was brought up in a small village outside Nablus. He left Palestine to study Arabic Literature in Baghdad, and then began a long and distinguished career as a political and literary journalist, living in exile in Beirut, Tunis and Amman, until his return to Palestine in 1996. Since then he has lived with his family in Ramallah, where he was the senior editor of *Al-Karmel*, the prestigious literary quarterly published by Mahmoud Darwish. His highly acclaimed columns in *Al-Ayyam* newspaper have attracted serious criticism from conservative and Islamic elements in Palestinian society. Also a sculptor, novelist and playwright, Zakaria Mohammed is best known for his ground-breaking collections of poetry, including *Last Poems* (Beirut, 1981), *Hand Crafts* (London, 1990) and *The Horse Passes Askidar* (London, 1994). His poems have been described as being "one of the great examples of modernist Arabic poetry... in which language echoes the real pulse and rhythms of contemporary Arab life".

AFTER NATURE
(Section 6, Part III)

W. G. Sebald

(1944- 2001)

When morning sets in,
the coolness of night
moves out into the plumage
of fishes, when once more
the air's circumference
grows visible, then at times
I trust the quiet, resolve
to make a new start, an excursion
perhaps to a reserve of
camouflaged ornithologists.
Come, my daughter, come on,
give me your hand, we're leaving
the town, I'll show you the mill
set twice each day in motion
by the sea's current,
a groaning miraculous construct
of wheels and belts
that carries water power
right into stone, right
into the trickling dust and
into the bodies of spiders.
The miller is friendly,
has clean white paws,
tells us all kinds of lore
to do with the story of flour.
A century ago Edward Fitzgerald,
the translator of Omar Khayyam,
vanished out there. At an advanced age
one day he boarded his boat,
sailed off, with his top hat

tied on, into the German Ocean
and was never seen again.
A great enigma, my child,
look, here are eleven barrows
for the dead and in the sixth
the impress of a ship with forty oars
long since gone, the grave of
Raedwald of Sutton Hoo.
Merovingian coins, Swedish
armour, Byzantine silver
the king took on his voyage,
and his warriors even now
on this sandy strip keep their weapons
hidden in grassy bunkers
behind earthworks, barded wire
and pine plantations, one great
arsenal as far as the eye can see,
and nothing else but this sky,
the gorse scrub and, now and then,
an old people's home,
a prison or an asylum,
an institution for juvenile delinquents.
In orange jackets you see
the inmates labour
lined up across the moor.
Behind that the end
of the world, the five
cold houses of Shingle Street.
Inconsolable, a woman
stands at the window,
a children's swing
rusts in the wind, a lonely
spy sits in his Dormobile
in the dunes, his headphones
pulled over his ears.
No, here we can write
no postcards, can't even
get out of the car. Tell me, child,
is your heart as heavy as

mine is, year after year
a pebble bank raised
by the waves of the sea
all the way to the North,
every stone a dead soul
and this sky so grey?
So unremittingly grey
and low, as no sky
I have seen before.
Along the horizon
freighters cross over
into another age
measured by the ticking
of Geigers in the power station
at Sizewell, where slowly
the core of the metal
is destroyed. Whispering
madness on the heathland
of Suffolk. Is this
the promis'd end? Oh,
you are men of stones.
What's dead is gone
forever. What did'st
thou say? What,
how, where, when?
Is this love
nothing now
or all?
Water? Fire? Good?
Evil? Life? Death?

Translated, from the German, by Michael Hamburger.

This extract appears courtesy of the the translator. After Nature *will be published by Penguin later this year. W. G. Sebald died in a traffic accident in East Anglia in December 2001.*

TRANSLATOR'S NOTE ON *AFTER NATURE*

The lines here translated here constitute Section 6, Part III of W.G. Sebald's book-length poem *Nach der Natur*, published in 1988 before the unclassifiable prose books that won him his international readership and acclaim. A straight translation of the title, *After Nature*, renders the terrible ambiguity which Sebald must have intended. "Post-nature", like "post-Modernist", is likely to become part of the stock of political-cum-cultural correctness, as indicated in a recent prominent anthology of twentieth-century verse.

Readers of the prose books will recognize the questing and questioning mobility that distinguishes Sebald's writing, the connections he make between seemingly disparate phenomena and orders of experience, his peculiar leaps from the immediately observed to historical enquiry and an imaginative free-dom usually expected only of fiction. If they are struck by the gloom of Sebald's respond to East Anglian impressions here, the ambiguity of the title is one clue to it. Another is that he was born in an alpine region of Germany, shortly before the end of the war, and a region so remote from post-natural develop-ments that it was spared the destruction by aerial bombardment that is the theme of Sebald's most recent prose book, not yet available in English. A third, perhaps, that, unlike more spectacular regions, East Anglian landscapes and seascapes grow on one, as I can testify as a fellow immigrant to the region. Although Sebald's vision – in *The Rings of Saturn* also – is marked by a melan-cholia induced less by his voluntary displacement than by a deep concern with the horrors and upheavals of the century now ended, the East Anglia of the prose book is more differentiated than that of the poem – not least because it draws on longer and wider familiarity, not the single excursion that assumes its full significance only in the context of the other landscapes, including an American one, evoked in the whole long poem.

One thing that drew me to this extract was that my first visit to East Anglia was an even stranger one: on a military exercise in wartime – probably 1944, the year of Sebald's birth – so secret that I discovered only later that it took place in West Suffolk. On this exercise, because of my knowledge of German, my part was to impersonate a German soldier to be taken prison and interro-gated by Polish troops involved in it. This surreal experience left impressions even more sinister and absurd than any of Sebald's. No wonder that for holi-days in later years I chose the Cornish and Welsh coasts, with their defiantly rocky cliffs and the rock-pools teeming with marine life I had explored ever since my childhood – until we moved to East Suffolk, slowly learning to love a bleaker sea, not always as grey as that of Sebald's poem, and be content with the undulations of land that had seemed flat at first. This became one of many links to Max Selbald, his person and his work. In our rare meetings and correspondence, just as in his texts, everything comes to hang together.

(1999)

ON THE DEATH OF W.G. SEBALD

Still stunned by his sudden death, I can't write anything as public as an obituary for W.G. Sebald the author or Max, my friend. Nor would he have wished me to, knowing that I've dropped out of literary criticism and never wrote about his books in his lifetime, beyond a little note attached to an extract from my translation of his long poem *After Nature*. That he was a writer unlike any other, therefore irreplaceable, was generally and internationally recognized ever since the publication of his unclassifiable prose works, if not that of the earlier "elemental poem", as he called it, just as unclassifiable, in 1988. A proof of the English version of that poem with the virtues of his prose was in the post to him and me for a last revision at the moment of his death; and on top of a pile of unopened mail on a table in his house I saw the letter I'd written to make arrangements for this joint finalization of the text.

That was after his funeral service in a little Norman church within walking distance of his house. The service was Anglican, as brief and unceremonious as he had wished it to be, and as private, confined to his family and a few invited friends. There, too, nothing was said about his eminence as a writer or teacher. No hymns were sung – only two Schubert songs, unaccompanied, by his brother-in-law, a secular song and the 'Ave Maria'. After the service and burial, at his house an artist friend from Alsace read out some of his last brief poems, those about death by allusion, ellipsis and sardonic understatement – the humour that made this collector of existential extremities accessible to more British readers than he is likely to have had without it – or without the sharp, loving eye for seemingly trivial minutiae so rarely combined with a panoptic, visionary momentum, as in him.

In all his works, not excluding the studies, not yet translated, of writers mainly Austrian or Alemannic, Max wrote as a voluntary immigrant, as much at home in his adopted country – or anywhere – as in his peripherally German native region, to which he remained attached by biographical and family – not national – ties. The little Norman church, of course, had been Roman Catholic before it was Anglican. The house he had made his home was a former rectory. His last resting place, therefore, accords as well as any other that could have been chosen with Max's peripatetic writings and the magnanimous imagination, sympathies, affinities and curiosities from which they sprang. So did the unceremoniousness and privacy of his exit.

What no one present at his funeral will yet be able to accept or understand is its suddenness, the abrupt termination of a life and work so intricately rich that it seemed to call for a long continuation. Max may have known better, as his minimal last poems suggest. There was so much he knew at which he only hinted, so much that can never now be told.

Michael Hamburger

See page 228 for a further discussion on W.G. Sebald.

THREE POEMS

—

Michael Hamburger

—

INTERSECTION, DECEMBER

Easter music at Advent, Victoria's,
And the songbirds all silenced.
Moon snowlight briefly before the sun
Gilds one crack willow's limbs,
More black than green beside slanted rays
Conifers bulk till, a mist rising,
Even the black shapes skulk in air
Lentenly mild, and a heron, ghostly,
Stalked to the pond, stabbed
The fishes no slab of ice now
Nor stillness hid from his raptor's eye
So sharp that the smallest fed
The microscope fixed to that hunger.

But the heron survives, you were glad
Of such bitter grace, condescension
Of heavy wild wings to our patch,
Of their slow passage then
From birth and death commingled
Into whatever light,
The season's, the day's, the minute's,
Glimmers inhuman, beyond us yet.

FOR TED HUGHES

(October 29th, 1998)

After gale and flood, on the brink of winter I see
A faint half-moon haloed in haze half-earthly,
The huntress's light, Artemis, delicate as a cat
In her art of killing, self-contained as a cat,
Adored for that, seducer to sacrifice.

But morning's, Apollo's and Aphrodite's
Cruelly too shines on the planters, the breeders
Of perishing cattle, crops.
Then it is love that hurts, not coldness.

Both he must serve who was born in high summer,
Compelled to mother the children half-orphaned,
Magnanimous helper, friend.

Uneaten this day of death
In either light the dark Devonshire apples lie
That from seed I raised on a harsher coast
In remembrance of him and his garden.
Difference filled out the trees,
Hardened, mellowed the fruit to outlast our days.

SPINDLEBERRY SONG

Winter: endure and wait
While frost cleanses the air,
The sky widens with light
Harder, more pure, more clear.

Half-awake your eyes will see
Those only a dream allowed,
Golden-winged swallows fly
Back to the home of the dead.

Fallen leaves, let them stay
Where they stopped, weighed down with rain.
From the season for lying low
Get up again if you can.

But time's the mere measurement
Of motion, mutation in space.
Unbleeding though bare from this plant
Hangs the heart-shaped seed-carapace.

Michael Hamburger, a poet and translator, lives in East Anglia. His latest collection of poems is Intersections *(Anvil, 1999).*

THE STRUGA ADDRESS

&

TWO POEMS

—

Seamus Heaney

—

The Struga Poetry Festival is one of Eastern Europe's most prestigious literary gatherings. Struga is a small resort town on the shores of Lake Ochrid, in the southwestern corner of Macedonia. Each year, the Festival chooses an "honouree" and presents him or her with the Golden Wreath in recognition of preeminent poetic achievement. Past recipients include W.H. Auden, Pablo Neruda, Eugenio Montale, Hans Magnus Enzensberger, Allen Ginsberg, Adonis, Yves Bonnefoy, Ted Hughes and Joseph Brodsky. The festival also includes several dozen other poets reading their work over the course of a week. Heaney's first visit to the Struga Festival in 1978 is recounted in "Known World," a poem included his last collection, Electric Light.*

As Heaney rose to speak to a large audience in the Kalishta Monastery on the shores of Lake Ochrid last August, Macedonia teetered on the verge of a full-scale civil war between its Slav and Albanian populations. It was the gravest crisis since the country's independence from Yugoslavia in 1992. Troops had mobilised throughout the country, setting up checkpoints, posting guards, and moving through the streets in a manner reminiscent of Belfast.*

The Editor

—

Prime Minister, Mayor, Your Excellency, members of the Struga Poetry Evenings: I want to begin by quoting a line from an old Irish legend. In the legend, the hero is asked a question. His comrades want to know what is the best music in the world. And the hero answers, "The best music in the world is the music of what happens". This statement may not always be true, but it was true in Struga this week. We heard the music of poetry in many languages; we heard the music of welcome in Macedonian; and I heard with great delight my own poems in translation. I want to thank the actors for their wonderful performance, and I want to thank especially the translators. A poet can have no more valuable gift than the full attention of another poet, and I have been doubly lucky, because I have been attended by two of the best in Macedonia. I go back to Ireland proud and happy – bearing the Golden Wreath of Struga; but even prouder and happier, this evening, because of the praise – the grave and generous praise – of Bogomil Gjuzel.

I began with an old Irish hero and I want to end with a hero from ancient Greece – with Orpheus, the archetypal poet. Orpheus could make the stones dance and the animals listen by the power of his art. But what we remember most about him is his backward look, his need to make sure his beloved Eurydice was following him up the dark slope. His human fear and his human love made him disobey the order of the gods. So he turned his head – and in that instant lost Eurydice forever. And it is that moment of human weakness and human loss that has stayed in our consciousness for more than two millennia.

But, at this moment in Struga, at this moment in Macedonia, what I want to recall is Orpheus' moment of human strength and his moment of unparalleled triumph. Because Orpheus, let us not forget, had persuaded the King of the Dead to change the laws of the land of the dead, and to allow Eurydice to go back to the land of the living. And Orpheus had achieved this by the practice of his art. He played his lyre and sang; and as he sang, the whole of the underworld listened. Axion's wheel stood still; Sisyphus stopped pushing his boulder; and the Fates stopped spinning their thread. And Hades, the Lord of the Underworld, relented, called Eurydice forth from among the shades, and let her go up the slope towards a new life. Orpheus, holding his lyre like a shield against the dark, leading his beloved up the dark slope towards the light – these are images of poetry and the poet's work that I want to invoke at this moment in Struga. Macedonia has suffered unfairly, the Fates have dealt the nation a hard blow; but from what I know of the Macedonian spirit, I know there is a Macedonian ability to keep facing the light. And from what I know of Macedonian poets, I am confident that they are ready to lift their lyre and raise their voice and sing the song of the future. They will do what poets always do: they will listen to the music of what is actually happening, but they will answer it by playing the music of what might happen. And in this vital work, we wish them all good luck.

A KEEN FOR THE COINS

O henny penny! O horsed half-crown!
O florin salmon! O sixpence hound!
O woodcock! Piglets! Hare and bull!
O mint of field and flood, farewell!
Be Ireland's lost ark, gone to ground,
And where the rainbow ends, be found.

SANTIAGO DE COMPOSTELA

What stays with me from my time in Santiago
Is midnight rain scourging the big square,
Lashings of water off the fountain lips,
Spouts and gutters plenished and replenished.

        Also stone purgatorial flames –
Unfannable, no matter what wind blew –
Surmounted by stone faces on the carved
Pediment of *Las Animas.*

           And beneath the steps
Of the Hotel of the Catholic Kings, the tongue
Of a panting mongrel, for all the world
As desperate as Dives ever was
For a touch of Lazarus' wetted fingertip.

Seamus Heaney was awarded the Nobel Prize for Literature in 1995. His latest collection of poems is Electric Light *(Faber, 2001).*

A KEEN FOR THE COINS

—

Carolyn Mulholland

—

Carolyn Mulholland grew up in Lurgan and now lives in Dublin. Renowned for her work in bronze, she has worked as a self-employed sculptor since 1966. The bronze collaboration with Seamus Heaney (see above photographs and the facing poem, "A Keen for the Coins") marks the demise of Irish coinage, whose design was overseen, after independence, by W.B. Yeats in his capacity as a Senator in the Dáil.

DÁNTA

Nuala Ní Dhomhnaill

AN T-OTHAR

Tá smaoineamh éigin fós ina ceann
Cé nach féidir léi é a chur i bhfoclaibh
"An leaid óg sin arís, – tá sé, –"
(sos beag us creathán ina láimh)
"tá sé, – tá sé –
tá sé in áit dhorcha."

Cé tá i gceist aici? –mo mhac?
M'fhear chéile, nó duine éigin eile den gclann?
Nó an bhfuil sí, ar leibhéal éigin
Ag trácht uirthi féin?

Bhí sí riamh domhain,
Ach anois tá sí ag labhairt aníos chughainn
As tobar gan tóin.

FÉILIRE

Gaoth láidir anoir aduaidh
ag séideadh feadh na h-óiche go teann.
Níl aon bhád farantóireachta amuigh.
Tá capaillíní Mhanannáin ar Mhuir Mheann.

Níor chodlaíos luid le heagla gaoithe.
"Dúchas is ea é sin", adeir m'aintín, "ón Seana Ghleann.
Nach raibh oíche ansan thuas sa Droch-Shaol
gur buaileadh an díon go léir anuas don dtigh,
ceann, cearachaillí agus uile
is gur leaindeáladh amach ar an mbuaile iad!

Ní raigh aon oíche riamh ina dhiaidh sin
gur ardaigh puth beag gaoithe
ná gur thóg do shin-shean-uncail, Seán Deartháir,
é féin is a ghiobal beag súsa leis síos an gheaird
is dhein leaba do féin istigh faoin gcairt sa stábla
mar dhea is dá séidfi an ceann anuas air
go sábhálfadh an chairt é."

Tá cuid eile de mo mhuintir is níl aon trua acu dom.
"Táimid bog ort", adeir siad.
"Nách ort atá an rath a leitheid seo d'oíche
ná fuileann tú i do mhairnéalach ar bord loinge
i lár na mara móire."
Is fíor dóibh. Is fíor san.

Gan trácht ar
Gan na Lochlannaigh a bheith ag foghail a thuilleadh
Ar Mhuir Mheann.

Nuala Ní Dhomhnaill lives in Dublin. Her most recent collection of poems is Cead Aighnis (2001).

ANCIENT SALT, AMERICAN GRAINS

—

Daniel Tobin

—

On the poet as scavenger.

Since Ralph Waldo Emerson in "The Poet" declared that America needed to begin mining its own poetic resources instead of deriving the raw materials and methods of its art from England, and Walt Whitman heeded Emerson's call and largely re-invented American poetry in his own expansive image, poetry in America has succeeded in building an indigenous tradition on the foundation of Emerson's and Whitman's essentially futurist vision of the poetic imagination. America is an "open road," and the democratic and geographical vistas it surveys require an equally open art. In contrast, it is tempting to invoke Emily Dickinson as the avatar of a contrary poetic, one that while being distinctly American nonetheless preserves its formal and, in particular, its metrical ties to the past. That, at least, is New Formalist Timothy Steele's claim in *Missing Measures*. In his scenario, Whitman, Eliot, Pound, Williams, Olson and their contemporary inheritors compose a dominant experimental lineage alongside that of Dickinson, Robinson, Frost, Bogan, Wilbur, Hecht, and the newer practitioners of the earlier dispensation of meter and form.

If American poetry's double inheritance seems overly pat and polarized in this particular narrative, one need only turn to the recent Special American Issue of the Irish journal, *Metre* (Spring/Summer 2000) for confirmation of the rift from both sides of the chasm. "American poetry, as such, began with two geniuses" who cut "the Anglo-nostalgic umbilical tube with impertinence, impenitence," so Calvin Bedient writes. In his sweeping condemnation "alot of current American poetry is ... not American, but still English". Michael Donaghy, an expatriate American poet living in London, counters Bedient's claim by denouncing the "two-party system" of American poetry. Far from muzzling Dickinson's explosive silences under Whitman's impertinent yawp, Donaghy places her work centrally within a metaphysical tradition going back to Herbert and Donne. Another salvo finds Robert Mezey answering what he calls Diane Wakoski's "foolish rant" that she heard the devil in the poetry of John Hollander, as well as her endorsement of the simplistic notions that rhyme and meter underwrite political conservatism and that Robert Frost is "a bad European influence". For Mezey, Diane Wakoski doesn't have "the faintest idea what she is talking about," and as such she represents the Zeitgeist "in one of its cruder and more mindless aspects". Though I agree with Mezey in his condemnation of Wakoski's glib remarks, in such exchanges legitimate questions of technique, aesthetic orientation, tradition, and period style devolve into the memorable skittishness of a Saturday Night Live routine: *"Robert, you impotent prig." "Diane, you ignorant slut."* Yet, it seems to me a poet inevitably writes at least in part out of the faith that genuinely good poetry – and certainly great poetry – transcends even the limits of its maker's stylistic assumptions as one of the necessary conditions for its being able to last beyond its own narrow historical moment. Out of the quarrel with others one makes rhetoric, so Yeats claimed, and out of the quarrel with self poetry. To what extent can American poets shift the locus of the conflict between the "closed" forms of traditional poetics and the "open" forms of a long-established *avant guard* from the contentious realm of rhetoric to the combustible arena of the individual imagination?

As if implicitly to answer this question, Robert Hass in his essay "Listening and Making" shifts the conflict between closed and open form to a productive though similar binary opposition. In poetry, Hass observes, "repetition makes us feel secure and variation makes us feel free". In this formula, the metron or "measure" with its natural insistence on the closed system of reiterated feet becomes a vehicle for speech when it is freed, so to speak, by variation. Though one might argue that mere variation at best creates a limited opening for speech within the strict framework of meter, it might also be answered that non-metrical poetry depends on the metrical system as a ghost in the poetic machine. Free verse is variation writ large, hardly playing tennis without the net (to recall Frost's pithy condemnation), since the net is skirting the iamb. As Hass observes, "freedom from pattern offers us at first an openness, a field of identity, room to move". At the same time, however, "it contains the threat of chaos, rudderlessness, vacuity." Or, one may add, the mere flatness of much contemporary poetry. In contrast, for Hass, the "reverse face" or shadow side of repetition is claustrophobia, a kind of neurotic nostalgia for the safety of the metrical system. One can hear such nostalgia when Timothy Steele claims, excessively it seems to me, that the free verse poems of Pound and Eliot in both their more experimental and less strident manifestations, "undermine the norm [of measure] itself". Steele's stance here is nostalgic because the perfect iamb is an abstraction, and as such the norm is not the grid or temporal lattice of measure but the poet's living speech – heightened, dramatized – by its transfiguration into the poem. The norm in the sense I intend is Shakespeare:

"When in disgrace with fortune and men's eyes." The last two feet of the opening line of this famous sonnet are pushed toward iambic by the metrical expectation, though "men's eyes" by any account of the line's spoken quality is a spondaic foot. In short, the iambic regularity of the line is brought under the rule of the voice through syntax, which – thankfully – avoids making the iamb a metronome. Of course, it would be wrong to discount Steele's more incisive claim that at its best "conventional versification accommodates personally distinctive rhythm", and indeed Shakespeare's line exemplifies Steele's claim perfectly.

In modern poetry surely the paradigmatic example of this indisputable truth is the poetry of William Butler Yeats. Yeats, it goes without saying, is a poet for whom the closure of meter and form is emphatically necessary, and his antipathy to more open modes (not to mention his politics) would be strident enough in our day to incite Diane Wakoski's anti-conservative tirades. Here is his classic statement on the matter:

> All that is personal soon rots ... If I wrote of personal love or sorrow in free verse, or any rhythm that left it unchanged, I would be full of self-contempt because of my egotism and indiscretion, and foresee the boredom of the reader. I must choose a traditional stanza, even what I alter must seem traditional... Talk to me of originality and I will turn on you with rage. I am a crowd. I am a lonely man. I am nothing. Ancient salt is the best packing.

Isolated in this way, I imagine that to most contemporary American practitioners of the poet's art for whom the norm is free verse and not meter (inheritors of a confessional aesthetic and inhabitants of a climate that often praises and rewards a poet's message and affiliation – what Yeats called "the literature of the point of view" – over the mastery of their medium) Yeats's observations on craft could hardly seem more antiquated and curmudgeonly. "American poets learn your trade," he might say. Indeed, Yeats's way of working flies in the face of the American poetic ideal as framed by the Whitman tradition of openness and the worship of originality. His own rage for order, "to hammer his thoughts into unity," more often required him to fashion his traditional stanzas out of loose paragraphs and fragments – the very stuff of some modern and postmodern poetry: heaps of broken images, fragments shored against ruins. From the vantage of a century of experimentation, and the triumph of free verse as a mode seemingly consubstantial with the American idiom, it would seem that Yeats's need to pack the personal in the "ancient salt" of traditional form bears little if any relevance to writing, as Williams suggested, in "the American grain." Or, if it does, it would seem to place itself within the context of a polemical aside nostalgic in its understanding of the art and contrary to the real force and scope of the American experience.

Yeats's appeal to the ancient salt of tradition represents the technical application of his Platonic ideal. Though, as he remarks, "a poet writes always of his personal life" at the same time "he is never the bundle of accident and incoherence that sits down to breakfast; he has been reborn as an idea, something intended, complete". The closure Yeats seeks is not only technical and historical but, as implied here, metaphysical. The formal qualities of compression and closure that Yeats requires of his art are the artistic manifestations of ethical and ultimately spiritual needs. But Yeats by his own lights also cries "in Plato's teeth." The desire to be reborn into a Platonic idea complete and intended, and therefore secure in the safe but claustrophobic neatness of the poem, is countered in the work by the answering gravity of the heart's "foul rag and bone shop" – the very accidence he seeks to escape. Plato's launch into formal idealism is rebutted by Aristotle's plunge into accident, into the disruptive but freeing processes of life. For Yeats, vivid speech is the embodiment of this counterforce within the poem:

> It was a long time before I had made a music to my liking; I began to make it when I discovered some twenty years ago that I must seek, not as Wordsworth thought, words in common use, but a powerful and passionate syntax for passionate subject matter.

Though Yeats further states that he compels himself "to accept these traditional metres that have developed in the language," the measure of his lines never reify into the mere mechanics of verse as though they were the imitation of some ideal form; rather, measure in Yeats's poetry realizes a personal though distinctive rhythm through the way passionate syntax fuses with the metron, creating rhythm, combining itself with other textures of sound:

> That is no country for old men. The young
> In one another's arms, birds in the trees
> —Those dying generations – at their song,
> The salmon-falls, the mackerel-crowded seas,
> Fish, flesh, or fowl, commend all summer long
> Whatever is begotten, born and dies.
> Caught in that sensual music all neglect
> Monuments of unaging intellect.

Thematically these famous opening lines from "Sailing to Byzantium" embody the fundamental tension in Yeats's work, the conflict between flesh and spirit, the Platonic idea and the Aristotlean attention to process. Thematically Plato has the upper hand, for Yeats clearly favors the monumental endurance of art over the passing pleasures of the dying generations. By the end of the poem he transmutes himself into a golden bird, abstracted from life but nonetheless able to bear witness to it. He has become the ideal transfigured from mere accidence. However, if we look even momentarily at the dynamic rhythm of Yeats lines – rhythm created by the pressure of his syntax – we realize that in fact the sensual music of the poet's own impossible longing passionately shapes his declamation of the ideal. To my ear only three of these eight lines – 3, 4, and 6 – can be read as purely iambic, and all of them evoke some attribute of the passing fleshly world rather than the ideal realm of art. The second line is also iambic with a trochaic substitution in the fourth position, and likewise evokes the passing world with its doomed lovers. In lines 1, 5, 7, and 8, however, Yeats's syntax alters the percusive iamb according to the designs of the speaker's passion, his disgust with age, his muted jealousy of the young, his anger at impending death, his raging need for an eternity intuited paradoxically by the intellect alone. The greatest departure from the iambic back beat occurs in the fifth line where the rhythm becomes positively sprung, the added stresses – "Fish, Flesh, or fowl, commend all summer long" – combined with the textures of the three initial fricatives modulating into the quieter, liquid double "m"s and "l"s – communicate the poet's almost speechless combination of fury and longing. The result of this yoking of meter and syntax here is energy, tension, intensity, while the last three feet of the stanza's final line return the poem to an iambic equilibrium. Scoring into the poem Yeats's unrelieved quarrel between flesh and spirit, this interplay between traditional meter and passionate syntax continues throughout the poem with tonal variations until it reaches its final equilibrium in the last line with the straight iambic pentameter of "of what is past, or passing, or to come."

One could have continued the analysis, enjoining Yeats's management of enjambment, caesura, and octava rima, but the essential point is that in a great poet like Yeats the seemingly closed system of meter and form becomes a vehicle in which passion is freed into the poem. "How can we know the dancer from the dance?" Yeats asks at the end of "Among School Children," knowing well that even improvisational dance requires a sense of form in order to liberate emotion. Nevertheless, given the American tradition of formal experimentation, do poets working in traditional meter and form comprise only a minor company within the American mainstream? Is the ancient salt really anathema to the American grain? The aesthetic claims that prompt such questions seem strained, and are finally a matter of polemics instead of practice. Neither Robinson, nor Frost, nor Wilbur, nor Nemerov, nor Hecht – regardless of what one might think of their poetry – are "English" poets because they write in traditional meter and form, no more than are David Jones and Basil Bunting "American" poets because they followed the example of Pound in a British context that has remained closer to the grain of an indigenous tradition in which meter and form figure largely. Richard Wilbur's formalism, in turn, suggests nothing new except that it is a squarely American incarnation of historically longstanding traditions. Not unlike Yeats, at his best he appeals to ceremony without devolving into the ceremonious. And, of course, the formalism in English language poetry is in fact multinational. Sonnets traveled from Italy to England during the Renaissance. Sestinas and villanelles came into the language from the French. Pantoums are a Malaysian form. Ghazals, a burgeoning form in contemporary American poetry through the work of Agha Shahid Ali, find their origin in Persian culture. It is simply absurd to say that non-metrical poetry is the only legitimate mode for American poets, and that to work otherwise is to engage in a marginal art, or at worst an un-American activity. Pound, the most vigorous advocate of the free verse revolution ("Compose in sequence of the musical phrase, not in sequence of metronome") was a Fascist. There is no inherent correlation between politics and style, and indeed the most liberal art can become dogmatic under the pressure of polemics.

Putting aside such prejudices, it is possible to explore for example how Yeats's ideas about passionate syntax might reverberate in an American context with Frost's theory of sentence sounds. "A dramatic necessity," Frost observed, "goes deep into the nature of the sentence. Sentences are not different enough to hold the attention unless they are dramatic ... All that can save them is the speaking tone of voice somehow entangled in the words and fastened to the page for the ear of the imagination". In essence, this is Frost's theory of the sound of sense, or sentence sounds. His claims for speech and the dramatic organization of the sentence reiterate in an American context Yeats's enthusiasm for passionate syntax. Even the blank verse of an essentially meditative poem like "Directive" manifests dramatic energy through its sentence sounds:

> Back out of all this now too much for us,
> Back in a time made simple by the loss
> Of detail, burned, dissolved, and broken off
> Like graveyard marble sculpture in the weather,
> There is a house that is no more a house
> Upon a farm that is no more a farm

And in a town that is no more a town.

Far from organizing itself according to some iambic drum machine, the first line is both syntactically and metrically disruptive. Though still within the contours of an indigenous speech, the line is speech that "makes strange" in a manner that – even more strangely – anticipates the contortions of Charles Olson's work. The second line intensifies the poem's energy through anaphora, the repetition of "back" placing the reader like the speaker in a kind of time warp. This is real retrospective movement and not nostalgia, a backward thrust and not merely a backward look. Were we to closely analyze Frost's metrical pyrotechnics here, we would find very few regular feet through the poem's first four lines, while the last three lines that comprise this opening sentence resolve into regular iambics – a sentence sound that shifts dramatically from a jarringly propulsive beginning to its soft landing, as it were, in the past. Though constructed word by word, the sound experienced in these lines is the entire sentence woven through the temporal grid of Frost's blank verse, and so to place the burden of Frost's music entirely on measure as though each note were greater than the symphony, is to miss Frost's fundamental insight about the nature of working in traditional meter. The net is important, but the play is more important. As is so often the case in Frost's greatest work, the sound of sense is both serious and ironic at the same time. There is no safety in the past, though there may be the illusion of safety – or a momentary stay against confusion – that the poet at once requires and keeps from hardening into finality. "Here are your waters and your watering place. / Drink and be whole again beyond confusion" epitomizes the paradox of closure with an opening, since the poem gives us no real faith that finding even a toy Holy Grail is at all within our power, though our better angels would believe that finding it must be possible.

One might say that for Frost the form of a poem emerges from the evolving shape of its sentence sounds, with the provision that Frost saw meter as the necessary skeletal frame that had already established itself in the greater body of the art. Something similar might be said of Yeats. Finding his paradigm in organic theories of form extending back at least as far as the Romantics, Robert Hass in "One Body: Some Notes on Form" locates the formal sense literally and not just metaphorically in a human biological necessity. "Maybe our first experience of form is the experience of our own formation," Hass remarks. Not surprisingly, for Hass this intuition of the organic sources of form extend to poetry generally, and not just free verse:

> We speak of the sonnet as a form when no two sonnets, however similar their structures, have the same form ... The form of a poem exists

in the relation between its music and its seeing; form is not the number or kind of restrictions, many or few, with which a piece of writing begins. A sonnet imposes one set of restrictions and a poem by Robert Creeley with relatively short lines and three- or four-line stanzas another. There are always restrictions because, as Creeley says, quoting Pound, "Verse consists of a constant and a variant."

It is easy to misconstrue organicism in poetry as advocating a kind of free-flowing, intuitive profusion as if nature gave no restrictions to its apparently limitless productions. But variation is not formlessness. Coleridge, following Schelling, envisioned a poetry coincident with the *naturans* – the "organic form" shaping itself "as it develops from within" –rather than the *naturata*, nature's particular manifestations. Yet Coleridge wrote in meter and form, and disputed Wordsworth's claim in his "Preface to the Lyrical Ballads" that poetry should be written in the common speech of ordinary people. On the contrary, like Yeats after him he believed it should be dramatized, heightened from life, but not antiquated or artificial. For Coleridge there was no inherent contradiction between organic form and the inherited conventions of poetry. In our own time, Hass's biological understanding of poetic form grows out of Coleridge's organic conception, and yet Hass himself remarks "now, I think, free verse has lost its edge, become neutral, the given instrument". How extraordinary to find so eloquent an advocate of organic form in agreement with one of the basic tenets of the New Formalism, that the "official art of free verse" has become ineffectual, even decadent (Steele). Conversely, when Timothy Steele laments the Victorian tendency to read "poems in a sing-song way to bring out their metrical identity" as an unfortunate practice that obliterated "natural degrees of relative speech stress within lines", he essentially brings meter under the governance of speech. As such, he is in essential agreement with Hass's claim that "the pure iamb can't be rendered; it only exists as a felt principle of order, beneath all possible embodiments, in the mind of the listener. It exists in silence, is invisible, unspeakable. An imagination of order. A music of the spheres". If scansion is not meter, then meter comes to life only in speech. The remote godhead of the metron cannot exist without the body of the living word.

The idea of meter as some outmoded deity relevant to only a few remnant disciples is an exaggeration, of course, but from the standpoint of some of the twentieth century's more radical declarations of poetic independence the likening of traditional meter and form to an antiquated and soon-to-be extinct faith is not entirely inaccurate. In his essay "The Poem as a Field of Action,"

William Carlos Williams proposes "sweeping changes from top to bottom on the poetic structure ... I say we are through with the iambic pentameter as presently conceived, at least for dramatic verse; through with the measured quatrain, the staid concatenations of sound in the usual stanza, the sonnet". If Pound for all his revolutionary fervor saw rhythm as a "form cut in time," then Williams in announcing poetry through with the measured quatrain and usual stanza shifts the locus of form from time to space. The poem is a field of action or energy, and if the temporal unfolding of passionate speech or sentence sounds exists, it is registered more in the spatial display of the page rather than in the temporal interplay of meter and line. The ramifications of this shift, so significant for some postmodern poetry, are even more emphatically articulated in Charles Olson's polemical treatise, "Projective Verse." In Olson's diatribe against traditional poetics, the tension within the "closed" and "open" attributes of poetry becomes a gulf between seemingly mutually exclusive approaches to the art.

The primary source of Olson's complaint against "closed" or "non-projective" verse is that, he claims, poetry since Shakespeare has gradually lost its grounding in the voice and has become "print bred". It therefore has ceased to be a "reproducer of the voice" since rhyme and measure have outlived their necessity as aids to memory. In contrast, "projective" or "open" verse eschews the inherited line, stanza, and overall form in favor of "composition by field" in order to restore "a point by point vividness" to the speech of poetry. For Olson, the locus of vivid speech lies initially in the syllable and then in the line understood as a kind of inscription of the poet's breath. "The line comes... from the breath," Olson writes, "from the breath of the man who writes," though everything "starts from the syllable". From this core idea Olson elaborates his program for revolutionizing modern poetry:

> It is by their syllables that words juxtapose in beauty, by partaking of sound, the minimum source of speech ... It would do no harm, as an correction to both prose and verse as now written, if both rime and meter, and, in the quantity of words, both sense and sound, were less in the forefront of the mind than the syllable, if the syllable, that fine creature, were more allowed to lead the harmony on.

The field of Olson's projective verse is essentially a field of the voice, but it is voice operating at a register of sound before sense rather than the sentence sound, as in Frost's poetry. Here is an excerpt from "I, Maximus of Glouchester, to You":

in! in! the bow-spirit, bird, the beak
in, the bend is, in, goes in, the form
that which you make, what holds, which is
the law of object, strut after strut, what you are, what you must be, what
the force can throw up, can, right now hereinafter erect,
the mast, the mast, the tender
mast!

As should be clear from these lines, the speech of Olson's poem intends to affect "the listener" in a manner that, initially at least, short-circuits any rush to comprehension. The syntax of this speech likewise intends to be passionate, but in a manner that elides the personal voice entirely, as we find it in Yeats's poetry. What we hear instead is the voice-as-medium in which, to use Olson's words, syntax is "kicked around" for the purpose of generating a different kind of kinesis. The lines read either like the words of a person gradually losing consciousness, or those of a person overtaken by an oracle whose meaning cannot be fully expressed in completed thoughts. The emphasis finally is on process rather than closure, since in Olson's understanding of poetry every line-break constitutes a new turn of breath that carries with it a possibility for furthering the voice's projection, and therefore the poet's need to pursue every worthy impulse. As they stand, the lines compress the action and thus the metaphor of the boat's bow-spirit plunging into the waves like the beak of a bird, and then pressing beyond that first sense to the matter of the poetic process itself, the boat as sea-going craft transforming itself into the craft of making: "the form / that which you make, what holds..." Though the point is that the craft of poetry should refuse holding, refuse closure for the sake of what the force of breath itself "can throw up" in the process of discovery, instead of being content to remain harbored (to push the metaphor perhaps too far) within vessels of received form.

In addition to exemplifying his own practice, Charles Olson's program of projective verse is particularly significant because it both gathers into itself many of the innovations advocated earlier in the century by Pound, Eliot, Williams, and others, and sets the table for the more radical postmodern poetries that have followed us into the new century. For example, it is possible to foresee Susan Howe's linguistic montages in Charles Olson's claim that the new technology of the typewriter can indicate "exactly the breath, the pauses, the suspensions even of syllables, the juxtaposition of even parts of phrases" and so for the first time "without the convention of rime and meter, record the listening [the poet] has done" and so further "indicate how he would want any reader ... to voice his work" . How much more would Olson see the computer developing this potential even further? Notice, however, that Olson's concern is with the breath, with speech, and that the page – the typewriter's field of action – suggests a spatial orientation exclusive of those oral traditions that have shaped traditional meter and form. Of course, stanzas by definition are "little rooms," but the spatial metaphor in the word's etymology does nothing to diminish the oral and therefore temporal dimension of poetry. People on the street do not speak in octava rima or blank verse, but Yeats's and Frost's uses of these conventions on the page have less of a visual appeal than the deconstruction of traditional form into atomized, "non-traditional" parts on the page, whether by pauses, syllables, or juxtapositions of phrase. The phrase "composition by field" clearly suggests as much, and visual poems like George Herbert's "Easter Wings" and "The Altar," and John Hollander's "Swan and Shadow" are exceptions that prove the rule. So by a strange reversal of original intent, Olson's program might be said to more deeply entrench the poet in the print-bred culture from which he sought to liberate it, as well as the burgeoning digital culture, precisely because the freedom brought by scraping traditional meter and form makes positioning on the page even more integral to indicating how the reader ought to listen to the moves the poem makes.

A second problem, suggested earlier, concerns the issue of what Charles Olson's friend Robert Creeley called restriction. Because projective verse (and potentially all free verse) calls for a radical adherence to openness, to a furtherance of the poet's impulse to discover, there is nothing to stop the poem from not stopping. The obvious result is shapelessness, which is one of the reasons why Hass fears that free verse has run its course. Pound's *Cantos*, Williams's *Paterson*, Olson's own *Maximus Poems*, all lose in formal integrity because, in the final analysis, they have no closure. In contrast, a long sequence like Berryman's Dream Songs, though clearly open in its articulation of Henry's angst-ridden musings, nevertheless obtains an accrued sense of closure through Berryman's elongation and re-formalization of the sonnet. Likewise, though multifarious in the formal expression of its parts, Irish poet John Montague's *The Rough Field* obtains closure through the leitmotif of the journey and the sequence's overall circular structure. It almost goes without saying that if the great pitfall of traditional verse is a staid satisfaction in filling out the form to the letter of its convention, the great pitfall of non-traditional verse is to make convention out of originality. The result is verse that reads like the proverbial chopped prose, or as seems more and more the case, verse that runs like words in spate in lines that confuse excess with passion. At the far side of the gulf between open and closed poetries, lies mannerism: on the one hand an idolatry of tradition and form that mistakes security for achievement; on the other a pretentious radicality that mistakes faddishness for sophistication.

Whether Olson's is a program for a more sophisticated poetry or not, if literary historian David Perkins is right in observing that he "writes in a language that was never spoken anywhere", then the irony of "Projective Verse" is that it reminds us that poetry ought to have the strength and vigor of speech that the best poetry has never lost, and it does so with practical acknowledgement that speech is not merely a recording of what might be heard in conversation but is speech shaped by the ear of the poet. To re-double the irony, despite his desire to escape the metrical strait-jacket, the last run-over line from "Maximus" quoted above is pure iambic tetrameter ("the mast, the mast, the tender / mast"); which perhaps only suggests that measure does exist in the rhythms of speech, however "kicked around" that speech might become, and it is one of the poet's essential jobs to listen for it. Despite Olson's objection to traditional meter and form, some of the ancient salt gets into the American grain. Moreover, in instances where attentive listening shapes the process of composition, I would argue that the gulf between closed and open modes collapses, and does so regardless of the individual poet's particular aesthetic or polemical program.

A.R. Ammons's "Corson's Inlet" is undoubtedly a poem shaped by the poet's embrace of open poetics and his refusal to be limited by what he called in the long poem *Garbage* "the tidy boxes" of conventional stanzaic structure. I know of no other poem that locates itself and its poet more steadfastly within the tradition of organic verse. Indeed, "the field of action" envisioned in "Corson's Inlet" translates the biological metaphor underlying organicism into an overall poetic structure derived from contemporary physics. Like any shoreline, the size of Corson's Inlet depends on the scale of measurement. On the scale of maps a given shoreline might be ten miles long, but even if one were to measure the inlet with a straightedge the minute curves and juttings of the shoreline would be missed. To obtain the "actual" length of the shoreline you would need a still more subtle device, though the smaller and presumably more intimate the scale of measurement the more intricately formed the shoreline reveals itself to be. Corson's Inlet is a fractal shore, and as fractal geometry demonstrates, its ever finer edges can be measured infinitely. Ammons's walk is an encounter with infinity, with the ultimate openness of form that finally composes all of nature, indeed all of physical reality, and the poem is not only shaped by the poet's recognition of that openness but becomes a self-reflexive model for it:

> I allow myself eddies of meaning:
> yield to a direction of significance
> running
> like a stream through the geography of my work:
> you can find
> in my sayings
> swerves of action
> like the inlet's cutting edge:
> there are dunes of motion,
> organizations of grass, white sandy paths of remembrance
> in the overall wandering of mirroring mind...

As these lines suggest, Ammons's poem intends to be an *ars poetica* mimetic of the inlet's own structure and organization, and not merely an objective meditation on the scene. As such, the ultimately open form of physical reality guides the poet's reflections. "I have reached no conclusions," he continues, "I have erected no boundaries / shutting out and shutting in, separating inside / from outside: I have drawn no lines ..." The poet's whole effort is to follow the motion forward, continually breaking beyond the boundaries of line and stanza into wider more rarified "fields of order." The poem is therefore a model of projective verse, its ideal "an order held / in constant change" without "finality of vision." In keeping with this open ideal, "Corson's Inlet" is a single sentence held together by thresholds of colons. As such, the poem's self-reflexive liminality extends to grammar and syntax. What would Frost make of this sentence sound? Is Ammons just playing tennis without the net? And if, to borrow Yeats's phrase, any poem looks "out of shape from toe to top" it seems to be this one.

Yet, as in any successful poem whether open or closed, "Corson's Inlet" exhibits a perfect coincidence between content and form. At the same time, it could be easy to justify the arbitrary management of lines in a poem simply by appealing to the ephemeral nature of the world: "I make / no form / of formlessness." In this scenario, a single line might read "as" as it does in Ammons's poem, a line arguably as far from any rhythmic vitality as from any metrical validity as one could possibly write. Arguably, however, the success of Ammons's poem even in the matter of this single word line springs from the poem's orchestration of texture and structure in achieving its overall form. In her essay "The Flexible Lyric," Ellen Bryant Voigt describes the relationship between these three elements of a poem—texture, structure, and form—in the following way:

To say a building has a sound structure means that the foundation and frame are adequate for the shape and weight ... By extension, structure in poems seems neither "paraphrasable" content... nor "achieved harmony"... but rather the support for both content and its embodiment in the words chosen and arranged in harmony or tension. That is, structure is the way all the poem's materials are organized, whether they are abstract or concrete, precise or suggestive, denoted or connoted, sensory or referential, singular or recurring. Since almost all poems in English are linear – read left to right down the page – structure is also the purposeful order in which materials are released to the reader, whereas form creates pattern in these materials, to establish pleasing proportion, balance, unity –"a single effect"– in an otherwise overwhelmingly various texture.

Given Voigt's luminous discrimination, the question to ask of a free verse poem like "Corson's Inlet" is whether and where "texture has been used in the service of structure" and where it has been used to achieve "a formal arrangement". While one could trace how the poem successively and successfully builds structure and formal integrity from the textural sub-structures of Ammons's swerving lines, the poem's most achieved scale of measurement is precisely what Ammons's says eludes him in the poem: the Overall. Though "Corson's Inlet" portrays a manifold and elusive order, the poem's formal achievement – the "shape of its understanding" – rests in its ability to attain a suitable and pleasing closure despite textures that easily could have dispersed into overwhelming variety: "not chaos." The overall pattern or form of the poem is circular: "I went for a walk over the dunes again this morning... tomorrow a new walk is a new walk." Across the span of its one sentence the circular movement of the poem is dynamic because it speaks to the deep reality of recurrence, and not just the poet's personal habit of taking walks. "Corson's Inlet," to borrow the subtitle of Ammons's book-length poem *Sphere*, has "the form of a motion." Recurrence is an open circle. It is the poem's overall formal organization, realized through its textures and structural "fields of action," that finally lends even a one word line like "as" credibility, since the line finds its true measure on a different order of scale – not the syllable, not the metron, nor the line, but the overall. And "as" as a line also makes paraphrasable sense, since the word embodies in microcosm the ambitious mimetic intentions of the poem, the co-terminus spaces of the poet's mirroring mind and the equally mind-mirroring reality of the world.

Underlying Ammons's use of open poetics in "Corson's Inlet" is an idea of order that presumes a deep formal correspondence between the poem and reality. Unlike the seashore encountered by the singer of Wallace Stevens's "The Idea of Order at Key West," the inlet on which Ammons's walker meditates offers a version of the sublime that need not be "mastered" or "portioned out" because the poem and the world on which the poem reflects are finally all a part of one flow. The "blessed rage for order" has resolved into a blessed acceptance of organic and even sub-atomic form. The conflict between one poet's desire to impose order on reality by means of what Olson called "closed verse," and another poet's desire to discern in reality a more rarified and open conception of form originates in the apparent gap between two seemingly contrary ontologies. Do poems master or receive the world? But the opposition is false, since the world is rife with formal symmetries and mathematical structures, rhythms, recurrent measures, all manifesting themselves both within and as the natural expression of the flow. Perhaps, given the mainstream tradition of American poetry and the fragmented nature of our postmodern world, the traditional formal poem seems for many too tame, too tended within the present historical and cultural context, while for those across the divide open verse appears a culpable indulgence in formlessness.

Steering her own craft beyond the contentious seas between these clashing rocks, Elizabeth Bishop offers a model art gratefully above polemics in which fixed ideas of order give way to the patient practice of the repertoire. Equally masterful at couplets, quatrains, ballads, sestinas, the villanelle – "The Prodigal" is formally a double sonnet! – and free verse, Bishop's work has risen to such universally high regard precisely because her poems manifest an openness to the world's variety and the poet's own contrary impulses without losing artistic control, intelligence, and their unique brand of restrained but unmistakable passion. Written in free verse, "At the Fishhouses" manifests Bishop's genius for showing us a world, for pacing us through that world with measured attention to the right detail given at just the right time until, by the poem's end, textures that might have seemed random have fallen together with explosive continuity:

> Although it is a cold evening,
> down by one of the fishhouses
> an old man sits netting,
> his net, in the gloaming almost invisible,
> a dark purple brown,
> and his shuttle worn and polished.

As the opening of her poem demonstrates, the acuity of Bishop's visual attention is fine almost beyond comparison, but what gives the scene its subtle intensity is the audible pacing of the lines. Each is a complete phrase that gradually releases and concentrates the poem's dramatic focus. Moreover, it contains the most delicate of alterations – the comma after netting and the subsequent line break that place's the old man's net in clear juxtaposition to the gloaming which renders it nearly invisible. This blending of the human landscape with the surrounding non-human atmosphere will become crucial to the poem, and the net as a tool that permits access to the sea's otherworld resonates with the apparently frail but secure device of the poem itself as it lowers the reader ever more deeply into the liminal world of the fishhouses. Of course, the consonance and assonance of the lines does its work as well – "although," "cold," "old," "gloaming," "almost," "invisible," "purple," "shuttle," "polished." The poem's sonic textures, filled with liquids, announce the sea's "heavy surface" as well as its unbearable depths before it even appears on the poem's thirteenth line, its opacity a muted contrast to the silver translucence of the dock area with its gangplanks, gables, wheelbarrows and fish tubs. But for the emerald moss of the shoreward houses and the rust on the old capstan like "dried blood" the world of the poem is nearly monochromatic.

Beyond Bishop's vivid description, the significance of these details derives from the pacing. After the opening five lines, Bishop departs from her focus on the old man and spends the next twenty-five describing the indigenous surroundings. In short, she slows the pace even further in order to widen the aperture of the poem's focus. The details and textures throughout these lines compose a living map and not merely a random survey of the scene. She is defining the space of the poem in a way that inevitably returns us to the old man who now ceases to be part of a painterly setting and is revealed as a friend of the poet's grandfather. How many lesser poets would have cut the preceding twenty-five lines, or condensed them and re-structured the poem around this personal detail, thereby having marred the vivid surfaces – "the principal beauty" – that the poem regards so patiently, so lovingly? But neither is this personal detail superfluous, for it introduces the past and therefore time into the poem, a crucial move at this juncture, for it is between time and timelessness that the poem's spaces hover. This becomes apparent in the short strophe that follows with its interplay of verticals, "down" and "up" balancing each other on the water's edge until the brief scene comes to rest on the horizontal tree trunks – again silver, and a threshold between the historical human world and the timeless world of the sea. Here, as it were, is the poem's spirit level, its balance point between alternate universes:

Cold dark deep and absolutely clear,
element bearable to no mortal,
to fish and to seals ...

Rhetorically these lines constitute a dramatic shift in tone in which the world's fleeting principal beauties, unlike the iridescent scales of fishes taken up from this otherworld, encounter an impenetrable limit. The arrival of the seal in the poem, to which the poet with marvelous good humor sings Baptist hymns, suggests the possibility of mediating these worlds, the absolute world of the sea and the ephemeral human world. One might hear, even in a good workshop, someone suggest that this detail is distracting, an unnecessary re-direction in a poem that directs us all too often, before us and behind us, up and down. But the seal is a mediator, like the hymns to which it appears to listen and shrug off, a mediator between worlds. Likewise, the second re-direction to the tall firs, a million Christmas trees, underscores the restrained religious sense that has entered the poem. The poet, like the seal, is a believer in "total immersion," though so extreme a baptism in this context represents a loss of identity rather than a fulfillment of religious promise. Bishop, as always, moves by margins and reversals to the center, though none of those margins, reversals, or re-directions are extraneous to the shape of the poem's understanding. The icy freedom of the water above the stones and then "above the world" is a perceptual trick, an illusion that reveals the truth of the sea as a kind of radioactive sub-space, a metaphor not for the Ground of Being but for an ontological flow that finally permeates Bishop's shore as well, and that resists full translation into human terms:

If you should dip your hand in,
your wrist would ache immediately,
your bones would begin to ache and your hand would burn
as if the water were a transmutation of fire
that feeds on stones and burns with a dark gray flame.

The water is a transmutation of fire, like all things a metamorphosis from primal energy. At this point Bishop's lines lengthen to accommodate the increase in the poem's intellectual and emotional resonance. One would think the ontological nature of the world would be enough for one poem to tackle, and to do so in utterly concrete terms that allow for remnant old men as well as comical seals, but as its final move "At the Fishhouses" re-directs us again, from ontology now to epistemology, and so to the historically conditioned nature of all knowledge, and therefore all talk about that Beyond the sea represents. As in "Corson's Inlet," Overall transcends the poem's widening scope, but whereas Ammons's poem confidently models the poet's work on a subliminal, primal, and recurrent flow Bishop's poem offers a more circumspect vantage. In "At the Fishhouses," to drink from the sea is not the same as drinking from Frost's imaginary grail to become "whole again beyond confusion," or lifted like Yeats's bird out of the sensual music. The world resists us, and knowledge of it is often bitter and briny, and certainly fleeting. With this final realization, Bishop's resolutely paced and tightly controlled free verse in "At the Fishhouses" offers a closure more free than the circular path of "Corson's Inlet" for at the poem's end she launches us expressly into the open. Tomorrow, a new walk might be a new walk by the fishhouses, but though flowing eventually our knowledge of the world will be "flown." From the perspective of Bishop's poem, Ammons's faith in scientific knowledge as a model for poetic form is merely one more conditioned way of envisioning the world and the poems that seek to derive order from it. Despite his preference for open form, I doubt whether Ammons would deny Bishop's insight. In the final analysis the two poems offer overlapping rather than contrary visions of the world, and the formal approaches poems might employ to respond to the world.

"Everything only connected by 'and' and by 'and'," so Elizabeth Bishop observes in "Over 2000 Illustrations and a Complete Concordance," a phrase that could have been incorporated by Charles Olson in "Projective Verse." And yet within her poems a world defined by contiguity and resistant to metaphor progressively gains in metaphorical intensity and revelatory power. In turn, the world of her poems resists neat closure while still embodying formal necessity, and retains its openness to new impulses while securing its textures within the larger order of the whole. Whether she is writing a villanelle or a free verse meditation her forms are always actively engaged with the world she encounters and imagines, never slack or intransigent or merely imposed on the elusive conditions of life, which finally is characteristic of all good poems whether packed in the ancient salt or orchestrated in the American grain. Regardless of school, program, or ideology, good poets are scavengers who somehow manage to find what they need, and good poems of any formal orientation embody the desire to clarify life out of the welter of experience. In such poems the walker becomes a dancer whose mastery we know by the choreography of the dance, the world another dance we are called to join again and again in its passing, and in our passing to know with ever greater intimacy and integrity.

Daniel Tobin is Chair of the creative writing programme at Emerson College in Boston. His second book of poems, Double Life *(Louisana State University Press), will appear in 2003.*

TWO POEMS

Samuel Menashe

GHOST AT THE WAKE

For all I know
Of love and woe
My all and all
Forgoes no feast
Or show of grief
For me, his ghost
At this banquet –
He eats the most
And yet he weeps
For now he knows
I'm his, for keeps.

MARCH

February's iron
Has lost its starch
And now becomes
The mud of March

Puddles mire
Shoe and tire
But do not speck
What they reflect

The sky looms higher

Samuel Menashe's most recent book of poems is The Niche Narrows: New and Selected Poems *(Talisman House, 2000). He lives in New York City.*

PORTFOLIO:PORTRAITS OF WRITERS

John Minihan

William Trevor, Devon, England 1988

John Minihan is one of Ireland's foremost photographers. He has published three major books of photographs in recent years: Photographs of Samuel Beckett *(Secker, 1995),* Shadows from the Pale *(Secker, 1996), and* An Unweaving of Rainbows: Portraits of Irish Writers *(Souvenir Press, 1998). A retrospective of his work was shown in the National Library in Dublin in 2001. He lives in Co Cork.*

Edna O'Brien, London 1971

Laurie Lee, London 1991

William S. Burroughs, London 1989

George Mackay Brown 1995

IN EUROPE'S DEBATABLE LANDS (1950)

—

Hubert Butler

—

From the Irish Archive, one of Hubert Butler's uncollected essays.

1. YUGO-SLAVIA

The relations between Yugo-Slavia and her neighbours change rapidly. Looking over some notes of a visit I paid three months ago with a delegation, with which I was unofficially associated, from the National Peace Council under the leadership of Lord Boyd-Orr, I find that this particular mission, although it did what was required of it, has not much present relevance.

It is only our incidental experiences that still have interest. We were invited in order to testify to the falsity of the Cominform allegations, for it had been said in their press and on the wireless that Yugo-Slavia was making warlike preparations against her neighbours and had handed over bases to Britain and USA.

We were not, I suppose, expected to make any impression on the Coninform Press. It was thought we might do so on the domestic Communist in Britain, who felt that Yugo-Slavia was being used as a bridgehead for an Anglo-American assault on the Soviets. Whether we changed this view at all I don't know, but even if we had had no military experts with us, the facts were self-evident. We studied the allegations closely, and went to all the reputed British or American bases, except one, the island of Vis. We planned our own routes and timetables. We visited the Albanian, Bulgarian, Rumanian and Hungarian frontiers, the aerodrome of Nish, the Belgrade to Zagreb highway, the Kossovo Polje and the island of Korcula.

The assurances we received from the heads of the Orthodox, the Roman Catholic and the Moslem communities, as well as from Mr. Moshe Pijade and many Yugo-Slavia officials, convinced us of Yugo-Slavia's desire for peace. But more convincing still were our encounters with the ordinary people in the streets and cafés of provincial towns. We wandered where we liked, and those of us who could not speak Serbo-Croatian usually found some other common tongue. We met no one believing in preventive war, or any war.

Peasant Gaeity

When we got within fifteen miles of the border, a Yugo-Slav officer accompanied us, so that we should not be treated as spies, but nobody interfered with us. We spent several hours, for example, in Dmitrovgrad on the Bulgarian frontier. (Dimitrov has been made by the Bulgarians a posthumous hero of the Cominform so it is exasperating to them that the anti-Cominform Yugo-Slavs dissent from this view of him, and still think it an honour for this little border town to bear his name.)

In a café there we found some refugees from Bulgaria. One, who called himself "a stomatologist," had jumped off a boat in the Danube and swum ashore. Like many others he had secured a job in the town. It was a feast day of the Blessed Virgin, but the dancing, which usually took place in front of the now locked church, had been transferred to the market square. From a balcony overlooking it in the new Dom Kultura, a sort of civil center, we looked down on a mass of shifting colours as the country people, mostly Bulgarians, in their gorgeous clothes whirled round in the kolo, the national dance.

The town has a population of only 2,500 but the hall in the *dom* had room for fully a quarter of them. There is a library there, largely Bulgarian and not oppressively "tendentious," and several recreation rooms. The rather anaemic murals of idealized peasants and the effective frieze of country scenes, moulded in cement, were the work of a couple of local artists.

These frontier journeys took us through the regions where racial minorities exist. Today Bulgarians, Albanians, Macedonians, and the others have what they never had before, encouragement to publish in their own languages and cultivate their own traditions, as far as these can be fitted into the rigid Marxist framework. I saw a number of their literary quarterlies, in which the extremes of internationalism and parochialism meet and try to mingle. The experiment, a not unusual one in many western countries, can seldom have been tried in such difficult circumstances.

Frontier Delilahs

But we had to do our duty by the Cominform charges. The Orient Express passes through. Dimitrovgrad is on the way to Sofia and Istanbul, so the frontier post outside the town has some importance. Two soldiers came out to meet us from a customs shed of white-washed mud, on which an old dog sat upon some firewood. One of the soldiers was the hero of a recent frontier episode, which he recited with much pride. He had been, according to the practice of the railway, in the habit of travelling with the express across the frontier to the next station in Bulgaria, Dragoman, and back again to Dimitrovgrad. It was a reciprocal arrangement. But after the Cominform resolution the Bulgarian officials on the train had started to bully him, taunting him with Yugo-Slav treachery. Once they had pushed him off the train.

Another time they had said: "Curse your Serbian mother" (a terrible oath it would appear) and flung his red star away. There must have been a Bulgarian soldier traveling on the express too, but it was not until after that it occurred to me to wonder how he fared when the train crossed into Yugo-Slav territory, so this delicate issue was never raised. Now neither Bulgarian nor Yugo-Slav soldiers pass the frontier with the express.

There were stories of aimless but provocative shootings across the border and of Russian officers clearly seen mixing with the Bulgarians. So too at the other frontiers. At the Rumanian frontier post, near Bela Crkva, below the Carpathians, an officer produced from the guard room a large log book, in which every "incident" since the "Resolution" was carefully dated and recorded. The most startling of these had happened three weeks before. A party of schoolchildren on an outing had been paddling in the boundary river and had unwittingly crossed into Rumania. They had been arrested and no word had yet been heard of them. Further back in the log book the officer blushingly drew our attention to another entry. The Rumanians had one day, by means of female fascinators, tried to entice the Yugo-Slavs on the opposite bank to neglect their duties. In vain.

Stalin Eclipsed

What is the significance of this continuous series of incidents, each one of which might be inflated into an act justifying war? Are they really inspired from a higher quarter, as the Yugo-Slavs appear to think? I do not believe it. Closed frontiers are a source of provocation in themselves. The guards have infinite leisure on their hands to imagine they are being insulted and to think of ingenious retaliations. The uniformed peasants, whom they see moving about on the opposite bank, are probably of the same stock as themselves, but they become mysterious and sinister through being unapproachable. Their gestures, their shouts, their laughter are all put down conscientiously in the logbook. It is not necessary for the Russians to manufacture hatred and suspicion. They grow of their own accord.

Some of us expected to find that the rupture with the Cominform would have led to a retreat from Marxism, but there was no sign of this. On the contrary, Marx and Lenin have grown in stature as Stalin has shrunk. Similarly, after the Reformation the authority of the Bible grew as the authority of the Pope dwindled. When we suggested to Mr. Moshe Pijade, one of the great figures of the Government that the sacred books of Marx and Engels had loss some of their significance he drubbed us severely.

Yet, in practice, there are signs of a much greater freedom and flexibility. The professor in Marx has become more important than the prophet, and professors can be criticised.

After the supreme blasphemy of rejecting Stalin had been committed, "theological" Communism, as the Yugo-Slavs call it, has been severely shaken. In two directions the effects of this are apparent; there is a drive towards decentralisation. Belgrade has taken over all the prestige of Moscow, but has shared it out with Skopje, Zagreb, Cetinje, and the other republican capitals. Stalin has shrunk but Tito has not, I think, appreciably swollen. In civic buildings, where portraits of the two once hung side by side, Stalin has been replaced by unglamorous figures, provincial secretaries and presidents. There are far fewer slogans, banners, processions, neon-lit exhortations. There is more criticism and reflection. The breach with the Cominform has had another notable effect. The difficulties of meeting and talking with foreigners are now slight. It is possible for a citizen to invite them freely to his home and to chat with them in the street or in hotels. Unless there is some special reason for constraint, it does not exist.

Hunger, Pride

Some people saw a happy augury for the future in the Yugo-Slav hostility to their neighbours. We did not all feel this. The kind of peace that is based on an equilibrium between several sharp antagonisms is never reliable. Yugo-Slavia's alienation from Russia might bring her into the Western camp, but such an alignment would be based on strategy, not on sympathy. It would be precarious and unreal.

The Yugo-Slavs are, on the whole, proud of their desperate isolation. The world, they say, is divided into East, West and Yugo-Slavia. The longer they can keep their independence uncompromised the better it will be for everyone. At the worst they can now offer a forum where capitalist and Communist can meet without constraint or hostile intentions.

There is now one thing that obsesses their minds, far more than the fear of war. They are desperately hungry and dread a famine. Not for political reasons, but for Christian reasons everything possible should be done to bring them relief.

2. DUBROVNIK AND CAVTAT

I went to Dubrovnik in a captured German aircraft, on whose dark walls some Canadian soldiers had scribbled their names and addresses. I had bought a large map so as to trace our passage over the mountains of Bosnia and Herzegovina, but I found that it was only by kneeling on the floor, with my elbows on the seat, that I could catch an occasional glimpse of a mountain.

The aeroplane pitched and rolled. The small windows were mostly of opaque glass and only one or two had clear centers. When I gave it up in despair a soldier promptly picked up the map and started a lively description of his experiences in the Partisan war. The passengers all left their seats and crouched round him, peering through the portholes for the landmarks he described. We swirled over the peninsula of Pelleshatz. I thought I caught a glimpse of the Mestrovic Mausoleum on the promontory of Cavtat, and then the aircraft came down in a field 18 miles north of Dubrovnik.

It is the only flat space on that rocky coast, and a poor aerodrome at that, a swampy piece of land without concrete runways. It did not need an expert to see that neither Yugo-Slavs nor Americans were converting it for military purposes. A cottage on the highway above served as an air terminus. It was draped with a big banner, on which was written "Long live the Ninth Chess Olympiad of Dubrovnik".

Peasant Grace

A group of people crouched over the papers reading the latest chess result, for chess is to the Slav what dog-racing is to the Dubliner. I soon learned that Yugo-Slavia was leading over the other sixteen competitors. As we were talking a girl, in the dark Dalmatian costume, wearing a large straw hat on one side, came gracefully down the hillside, leading a mule whose two panniers were full of purple grapes. She passed by gravely smiling, like a figure on a frieze, while we offered to buy some of her grapes. "No, they're for the chess-players" she said, and all our pleading was in vain. The bus arrived, and as we sped along the lovely road the driver, in reply to a question of mine about the Olympiad, replied: "Oh, no, the Russians didn't turn up. They only come when they're sure of winning".

I do not think that even the Cominform had declared that Dubrovnik was an American base but we were encouraged to go there, not only because it is the port for Korcula, but so that we should see how peacefully and happily the Yugo-Slavs were entertaining themselves. In addition to the chess there was a literary congress, with delegates from many countries. The Dubrovnik Festival was also in progress, with musical entertainments every night and plays by Ragusan authors of the fifteenth and sixteenth centuries. (The old name for Dubrovnik was Ragusa). There were several exhibitions, historical and marine. For a small seaside town, this does not seem bad.

Madame Comrade

I searched the 200 pages of the beautiful Festival Book to discover any reference to Marshal Tito or Communism. There was none. Nor did I see in the streets the red stars, slogans and banners which unusually decorate a Communist festival. Dubrovnik is the most conservative and urbane district of Yugo-Slavia. Its citizens naturally shun what is crude, and their Communism is polished and polite. I was told that it was a long time before they could accustom themselves to saying "Comrade". They said "Mr. Comrade" and "Madame Comrade".

Although Dubrovnik was occupied by the Italians it was never, like the north Dalmatian coast, annexed to Italy. It belonged to Pavelitch's Croatia, but Pavelitch was never seen there. So the Italians did not, as in Split, make efforts to Italianise the place. (Actually there were only about ten Italian residents.) All that they did was to remove the Mestrovic stone carving of King Peter of Yugo-Slavia from the town walls and in other ways destroy traces of the old Serb and Yugo-Slav kingdoms.

The Italian garrison adapted themselves quickly to the pleasant life of the town. They did not bully, and as they were short of wine they sold their revolvers and equipment. After the fall of Mussolini they were replaced by Germans, and everything changed. I do not believe there is any spot in the world where nature and art combine in such loveliness as at Dubrovnik. The old city, inside the town walls, is undamaged – the Rector's Palace, the Mint, the churches, monasteries and old town houses are treated with reverence. Dubrovnik is being preserved as a museum of Dalmatian history.

It is too early to expect complete objectivity, for the Croatian contribution is over-emphasized while the influence of Venice is insufficiently stressed. But this is an inevitable reaction from the exaggerated claims of Italy. Scarcely 1% of the population was Italian before the war, but in the University of Padua, I once saw a students' hall decorated with frescoes of half a dozen Dalmatian towns, represented as outposts of Italy. Mussolini was constantly declaiming about "Dalmazia nostra," and every time he declaimed some Croat patriots would destroy an emblem of Venetian rule in some Dalmatian town.

Great European

The Lion of St. Mark over a town gate would lose a head or a tail, or an Italian fountain would be mutilated. That was before the war. Now there is no more declamation or destruction, but a certain evasiveness is still evident in the potted history of the guide books.

The town itself is the cool grey colour of the Dalmatian rocks, but outside the ramparts there seem to be more flowers than stones. Cascades of purple bougainvillea cover the walls and every kind of exotic shrub flourishes in the gardens. The caper plant, already shedding its long pale flowers, grows from crevices in the walls. There are pale blue plumbagos, giant heaths, lemon-coloured daturas.

The naval yacht, which was to take us to Korcula, was delayed so we spent the afternoon on a visit to Cavtat. Mestrovic's Mausoleum was built in memory of our members of the Racic family, wealthy and cultured ship owners, who died of influenza in 1918, and the monument is considered one of Mestrovic's masterpieces. The sculptor is still in America to which he escaped from Patelitch's Croatia; his house at Split, which he built for the display of his sculptures, is empty. Another large collection of his works preserved by an old friend at Zagreb awaits his return. He is eagerly expected in his native land, and I believe there is a chance that he will return before long.

Few artists have ever exercised so great an influence on their country as Mestrovic. He was a Croat, an ardent Yugo-Slav, and a great European. He and his friends believed that the whole of humanity is one spiritual family, but he was no shallow internationalist. He wrote: "I knew that it was my duty to do whatever I could to sow a few seeds on the wasted soil of my own country." That is the way people thought in the new countries of Europe after the First World War.

On the way to the Mausoleum we were hailed by a purposeful old woman with a large key. She insisted on showing us over the private gallery of the 19th century painter, Vukotitch, a revered native of Cavtat. Some Yugo-slavs who came with us stood entranced in front of the glossy academy portraits, identifying the son who went to the Argentine and Mrs. De Bont's brother, and so on. Eventually the high priestess of the shrine, became bored with their enthusiasm and we escaped. This corner of Dalmatia has its own small local gods who dwarf the stature of the national heroes. Neither King Alexander nor Pavelitch was ever regarded with favour here, and it is going to take Tito all his time to make an impression.

Fragrant Land

When we got back to Dubrovnik three naval officers were waiting for us, drinking wine on the terrace under the olive trees. The journey to Korcula takes six hours, but although it was nearly 10 p.m. we decided to start at once and sleep on board the naval yacht. The vessel was built for comfort rather than combat, and we guessed that its builders must have had in mind some Austrian archduke, who would hover importantly on the fringes of battle. There were four berths, and the rest of the party reposed in the chairs and settees in the saloon.

We were comfortable enough on board, but at early dawn I went on deck to watch the grey coast of Korcula. We went the whole length of the island, and as we came closer I caught the unmistakable fragrance of Dalmatia. It is a smell of myrtle and juniper and rosemary, and all the evergreen shrubs which grow on thin rocky soil. It seems to be sealed into their hard dry leaves and does not vary with the season.

Now and again we passed a small sea port of high grey houses with tiles of mottled umber. The windows in the lower storey are always small, for they keep their stores and wine there in cool dark rooms. Above, the large windows of the bedrooms have green wooden shutters. We went so close to the coast that we could see the early risers looking after their vines. At times, the coastal islands are so bare that it is hard to see what reward there can be for building that network of small stone walls to protect a few tufts of grass in a waste of grey rock.

When at last we landed at Vela Luka, the town was already fully awake. Some of us did the routine job of visiting the Harbour Master and seeing his records of the incoming vessels and their cargo. As usual, we found him perplexed, but polite. An odd Italian trading boat had come, but when we enquired about Americans he simply laughed.

Quick Wits

We were followed by an interested crowd, chiefly of young people. Why is there such a disproportionate number of the young in Yugo-Slav towns? Perhaps it is because the war destroyed so many of their elders. I have seen as high a figure given as 3,000,000 dead out of a population of 16,000,000.

The children and young people of Korcula are mostly fair-haired, unlike the Serbs, with fine feature and quick wits, They are well dressed and if we had not known it from other sources, it would have been hard to guess that they were under-nourished. I escaped from the crowd down a side street and saw an old man leaning against a leather shop. "Have you ever seen any Americans on the island?" I asked him after a chat. "Yes, a bunch of them," he replied promptly. "When was this ?" "They are here now!" he said conspiratorially and beckoned me to follow him.

We went up one of the narrow staircase streets with which the island is honeycombed. At the top the old man drew me behind the shelter of a Venetian fountain. From the terrace we looked down over the sunlit quay and saw John Lawrence and a couple of our party talking to some fishermen. "There" hissed my guide triumphantly. Pointing to the group, he said proudly, like a naturalist who has added a rare butterfly to his collection, "Americans."

3. ON KORCULA

When we got a chance we visited the schools wherever we went. We did this partly from curiosity (we had a British Professor of Education with us), but partly because a school is an admirable centre of gossip. There are children there from all surrounding districts. If an American had been seen in this village or that, some child would be ready to chatter about him, for Yugo-Slav children are seldom tongue-tied.

The class at Vela Luka on Korcula was no exception. We broke in without shame, totally disorganizing the lesson, which a plump, pleasant young woman was conducting. John Lawrence stood by here desk and told the children why we had come. "So have you seen any Americans?" he ended. "No" they cried all together, but as this answer seemed so bleak the livelier ones tried to embroider it. "Yes, yes" one small boy waved his hand furiously. "I've seen Americans." "Oh have you? Where? Tell us." "In Africa".

It appeared that during the war he had been moved to the Yugo-Slav camp on the Suez Canal. Then another boy, with a black eye waved his arm too. "Yes, yes, I've seen Americans." "Oh where?" "On the films." He was the school jester and there was a roar of laughter at this. One of his school mates explained that he had got his black eye because he had visited an American film called "Gentleman Jim" and had started to behave like one of its heroes. We seemed to be following this particular film round Yugo-Slavia, in Montenegro, Macedonia and in Croatia. "Dzentleman Dzim" was on all the hoardings, corrupting the young Marxists with his flagrantly bourgeois ethic.

War Paradox

Korcula had a fairly peaceful history during the war. It became a refuge for the Jews, who had fled from the Nazi persecutions in Zagreb, and the Italians, who were in command there, had treated them with relative kindness. The Italians hoped to annex the greater part of the Dalmatian coast. Because of this, their relations with the Croats, who formed 98% of its population and yet were supposed to be allies of the Axis Powers, were often uneasy. Although Pavelitch, the "Leader" of Croatia, had offered the throne of Croatia to the Italian Duke of Aosta and agreed to cede to Italy much of the Croatian coast, most of the Croats were furiously resentful. The result of this was that the Italians frequently favoured the Serbs, who were their enemies, against their allies, the Croats. When the Croatian Ustashe (the followers of Pavelitch) had started on the extermination of the Serbian Orthodox in Croatia and Bosnia, the Italians had sometimes intervened on the side of the Serbs. This throws some light on the complicated story of Mihailovitch, whose commander on the Dalmatian coast was given a state funeral by the Italians, his avowed enemies.

There were small regional wars going on, in which, as in whist drives, the partners were changed. It was warm and lovely when we sailed back from Vela Luka to the town of Korcula, the capital. The dolphins played around the boat, and once a flying fish landed among the deck chairs. There was a staff officer on board, whose job it seemed to be to watch in some obscure way over the crew. He was dignified, and one of us tried to thaw him out with jokes through the interpreter. "You're the spy, I suppose?" was the first well-meant joke, but it didn't translate at all well. In frigid tones, the officers replied that "he only served his country and did his duty, as any British sailor would." There was a click of heels and he vanished, with the interpreter after him interpreting madly. That was not the last British joke that misfired. They went on being made with wonderful perseverance.

Departed Glory

Korcula is one of those enchanting medieval cities in miniature, whose survival is hard to understand. A period of great prosperity must have been followed abruptly by centuries of stagnation. Just enough energy remained to keep the noble palaces, archways and churches from crumbling away, but nobody had replaced anything or destroyed what was useless. Near the Cathedral there was a huge pile of recent rubble, in which the heads and legs of Venetian lions could be distinguished. But the inhabitants were not responsible for this vandalism. It was the result of two British bombs.

The future of these beautiful islands is not rosy. Their prosperity coincided with the prosperity of Venice, when each island was a stepping stone on the southward and eastward path of a great maritime power, a store-house or port of call, which gave access to the interior. But apart from such a little fishing and some special crops such as the rosemary of Hvar and the pyrethrum (for flea-powder) of Mljet, they have few means of subsistence. There is no water in Korcula, and it has to be stored in tanks or brought from the mainland in barrels. There is a large hotel being built outside the town and, perhaps, it is as holiday resorts that Korcula and the other islands will survive.

As we walked back to the boat we met, facing the sea, a large white wall, on which successive occupants of Korcula had stenciled their slogans. There was a scar on the plaster, where a blunt human head, that must have been Mussolini's had peeled away. Under it a few letters of "Duce, Duce," were discernible. Fading away below it was a slogan that had been superannuated, rather than repudiated: "While Tito fights, the King gets married." And another, which I noted gratefully, was fading also. It read: "It is the duty of every honest man to unmask traitors."

Wall News

When I got back on board I hunted round for the wall news. It has always seemed to me one of the customs of Communist life most worthy of imitation. Three years ago they could be found in cafés and schools, and in railway stations and barbers' shops. They were often lively and revealing. But the wall news in the yacht was hidden by a pile of packing-cases, in front of which sailors were playing chess. The sheet was full of stereotyped platitudes about duty. I contrasted it unfavourably with the wall news I had seen on a less ostentatious passenger boat. There had been a long poem about the crew, which I spent a happy half-hour putting into English to amuse the captain. It had begun:

> The little Rab goes on its way,
> Though seas be calm or tossing,
> While comrade Janko cleans the decks,
> And Captain does the bossing.
> While Bozho Baltich cooks the meals,
> And Antun waits at table,
> The passengers sit round and eat
> As much as they are able...

And so on, through all the members of the crew. There were also in that wall news many obscure private jokes and the usual exhortations to co-operation. It was not very original, but clearly it was an attempt to give expression to the friendliness that must grow up between men who work together. A Dalmatian who was with us told me that the wall news, like so many other importations from Soviet Russia, was falling into disfavour. So too were the voluntary labour corps and the discussion groups, which every citizen was supposed to attend. None was bad in itself; indeed, voluntary labour corps are said to have been first advocated by "A.E." and adopted and applied by a friend and admirer of his in Bulgaria (though I note that Sean O'Casey denies "A.E.'s" authorship). The idea has its good points, but in its application there had been much petty tyranny. Still, the compulsion was not as irresistible as its opponents have claimed.

Pay in Kind

One morning I was in a café in Dubrovnik listening to six strangers rejoicing over the abandonment of this intolerable burden of pseudo-voluntary labour. One of them suddenly asked: "Which of you has ever done any?" It turned out that one of them three years before had spent three weeks helping with the harvest on an abandoned German farm in Slavonia. He had been given a pair of boots for the work, and he said: "Yes, I must admit it was one of the best holidays I have ever had. And at my job it would have taken me a fortnight to earn the pair of boots".

The others admitted that they had never been obliged to go on one of the voluntary labour shifts at all, not even once in four years. The excuses had been various: old age, illness, or that they could not be spared from their jobs and so on.

The Croats, who have been for centuries a subject and insubordinate people, have always grumbled with such ingenuity that it is impossible for the foreign visitor to discover what are the genuine grievances and what are not. This is particularly unfortunate today, when it is obvious that real hardships abound.

4. MONTENEGRO

Geographically, Montenegro begins at the Dalmatian coast town of Hercegnovi, though all round the Bay of Cotor, which lies south of it, the people are chiefly Catholic Croats. There used to be a big emigration from these parts to America. We were reminded of this by a yellow bus which met us on the outskirts of Hercegnovi. On it in large letters was inscribed, "School Bus. The Gift of the Montenegrins of California to Their Brothers." It is known locally as "schoolbus," and is a proof of the friendship between the Yugo-Slavs of America and the home country which politics has not yet destroyed.

We stopped at the large Boka Hotels, in which ten years ago all the members of the British colony of Yugo-Slavia were detained before they started on their two months' journey through Italy to Britain. In the garden we found a large table laid out for a meal. We were met among the palm trees and the bougainvilleas by the President of the Odbor, or local council of Hercegnovi, and by the Finance Minister of Montenegro. He is a big affable fellow, who was given a curious recommendation to me by a middle-class friend in Belgrade: "Yes, he's an honest man, he was always a Communist, not just a post-war opportunist." There was also Canon Lukavich, a Catholic priest, who was also the local historian and a scholar of repute. The President of the Odbor had spent a long period of the war in Dachau. He had been elected to the presidency on his return. He seemed an able, thoughtful man, with a smattering of foreign languages.

Vendetta's End

After the meal, John Lawrence and I, because we could talk with them in Serbo-Croatian, went for a drive with the Finance Minister and Canon Lukavich. On the Canon's advice, we stopped at several places. One was the Orthodox Monastery of Sveti Sava, where a fine collection of silver reliquaries and fifteenth-century MSS still survives. Later, we stopped at Risan, where an amateurish excavation of the old Roman town was being conducted by the local art master. We parted from the Canon on arriving at his parish in Cotor. He was an amiable and intelligent old man; he had taken no part in the fighting, but had organized help in food and comforts for the Partisans. In recognition of this he wore a Partisan medal and had a small post in the Montenegrin Cabinet.

I do not know of any other place like the lovely Bay of Cotor and its little towns, Cotor, Dobrota, Perast, Risan. These have huge palaces, where Venetian merchants once launched trading vessels to the East from the quays at the end of their gardens. They have all, except Tivat, the naval base, been dead for centuries, and today they seemed more dead than ever. At the entrance to one town we saw a sign: "Go slow. Blind People". Another town seemed full of cripples. Budva has hospitals and a hostel for the writers and journalists of Montenegro. The whole coast is becoming a place for convalescence, repose and recreation. Its prosperous, aggressive past is gone beyond recall.

I knew this district fifteen years ago. In the mountains above Cotor I attended the last *izmerenje* or reconciliation ceremony to take place in Yugo-Slavia. It was Easter, and the two families to be reconciled were the Bauks and the Orloviches, who had a vendetta because of a murder committed six years before. The murderer, a slim city clerk, had sheepishly gone through the ceremony of being adopted in to the family of the Bauks. He had had to creep down a long lane formed by a hundred Bauks, confronted by a hundred Orloviches, all in their splendid Montenegrin clothes.

At the end of the lane he had been raised to his feet and embraced by the brother of the murdered man. Then there had been mutual embracing between all the Bauks and all the Orloviches. After an address by the priest the complicated ritual had ended in a banquet in the churchyard, at which the Orloviches waited upon the Bauks. It was a moving ceremony, but the life was even then going out of it. One or two of the gorgeous Montenegrins exchanged *sotto voce* sarcasms in American slang. There was a journalist present, but a cine-camera operator who should have arrived missed his bus, and the murderer had only the traditional humiliations to endure.

Palace Beauties

The long, winding road up Mount Lovcen took us to Cetinje. We ended the evening in the hotel at a big table from which we looked down the hall, on some fifty young holiday-makers dancing a kolo and singing a strange litany, of which I could only pick out a fragment of the refrain:

> O, Central Committee, we reject the lies, the slanders of the Cominform!
> Where were you, Anna Pauker,
> When Tito was defying the enemies of our people?

These prosaic words, when sung, had a gay and exotic effect. While we listened an archaeologist from Sarajevco took his place beside me. I found we had a mutual friend, an archaeologist in Ireland, to whom we sent a joint postcard. He was supervising a new archaeological survey conducted by the Montenegrin Government.

The Palace at Cetinje, which we visited the next day, contains sumptuous but not tasteful furniture, and rooms full of weapons. There are many photographs of nineteenth-century royalties, for the handsome princesses all made great alliances. Upstairs are the relics and pictures of the great Montenegrin poet Prince Njegosh. A member of the Petrovich dynasty, a huge, dark fellow, with a startling resemblance to the portrait of one of his ancestors, hovered round us politely. Apparently he still lives in the palace.

There is a monastery near the palace. While we were exploring its library, the Curator exclaimed: "Do you know the bishop is in town today- I expect he'd like to see you." Soon afterwards we were chatting with the Metropolitan Arsenije in a small, book-lined room. He was a fresh-faced old man, with a grey beard cut like a spade; and we found him jovial and talkative. He is a great dignitary of the Orthodox church. He was acting Patriarch for a time, and was thought to be a likely successor to the late Patriarch Gavrillo.

Gestapo's Choice

He answered our questions briskly. "No, religion was taught in the churches only now. In theory it could be taught in the schools, too, but...". He gave a gesture which we had seen often before and whose meaning we understood. Conditions varied from place to place; there was a real conflict between Christianity and Communism, but, on the whole, it was being waged with less ferocity than might have been expected.

He talked to us more freely about the days of the war. In 1940, as Vicar to the Patriarch, he had received a deputation of three English Bishops whose names he could not remember. (Stuart Morris, who was with us, was of the opinion that he was referring to the visit of the Bishops of Chichester and Gibraltar.) They had come to discuss the possibility of a closer union between the Church of England and the Orthodox Church.

The discussion had been friendly, but conclusive and non-political. The Gestapo heard of it when the Germans had reached Belgrade, and it aroused their deepest suspicions. So Arsenije found himself at the Gestapo headquarters in a room with two doors. "That way to freedom. It depends on you which you leave by." Then he sternly asked what the English Bishops had discussed. Arsenije at last convinced the officer that they had been debating exclusively doctrinal differences, "One of our principal causes of disagreement is the doctrine of the Real Presence."

"And did you come to an agreement about it in the end ?" the Gestapo man asked searchingly.

"No, I'm afraid we did not succeed," Arsenije had sighed.

"You didn't? Hooray!" Here Arsenije, the narrator, jumped out of his chair, mimicking the Gestapo man's delighted exclamation. With a smile he led Arsenije to the door for freedom.

The Metropolitan said that the Germans had reproached him for giving a Christian burial to the Communist Partisans. He then explained to them that every Serb of Montenegrin was an Orthodox Christian until he signed a written declaration to the contrary. "I'd give them all Christian burial, if I was asked," added Arsenije.

He had been in Croatia before moving to Montenegro; and we asked him what difficulties existed now in a mixed religious community. Was the *Ne Temere* Decree a source of bitterness?

Exiled Bishops

We asked him about the Ustashe massacres and the compulsory conversion campaign. He had been in Croatia after the liberation, and gave us a horrifying account of the devastated villages and wrecked churches he had seen. There had been, he said, 240,000 compulsory coverts and half a million people had been massacred. We asked him about the Stepinac trial. He did not answer directly, but said instead, with conviction, that the conversion campaign could have been stopped, if the Roman Catholic Bishops in Conclave had at the beginning issued a proclamation denouncing it.

I asked him about Pavelitch's establishment of a Croatian Orthodox Church, after the murder and exile of all the Serbian Bishops in Croatia and Bosnia. It has been explained by Archbishop Stepinac's champions as a sincere attempt to stop the massacres. A Russian émigré bishop, Germogen, had been appointed head of the artificially constructed Church in replace the imprisoned Dositej in Zagreb, and an unfrocked Orthodox priest, Mifka, had taken the place of the murdered Bishop of Sarajevo.

I had heard about the Germogen previously. Before the war he had lived in retirement in Yugo-Slavia until the Albanian Government desired to form an autocephalous Orthodox Church which, according to Orthodox tenets, is impossible. The Albanians wished to consecrate as Patriarch an Albanian bishop, but could find no other bishop to carry out this sacrilegious task, so they sent for Germogen with an aeroplane and twenty thousand dinars. Germogen had complied. He had performed the act of consecration, and then returned to do penance in the monastery of Hopovo, which he had left only to become the head of Pavelitch's Orthodox Church.

Mr. President

"But our problem was Mifka," said Arsenije: "just before the liberation we had a meeting of our bishops and the question came up, what in the world are we to do with Mifka? And I said to them 'Don't worry. We won't have to do anything, the Partisans will cut off his head.' And sure enough they did."

Before we left we were told that the President of Montenegro would like to see us. For half an hour or so we sat at a long table opposite a row of Ministers, some of whose faces were familiar to us from their portraits in Montenegrin hotels and cafes. As usual, there was an awkward beginning and a friendly, sociable end. One of the Ministers spoke English, and questions and answers flashed backwards and forwards.

First we disposed of the business of Anglo-American military aid and then we talked of schools and theatres, the management of factories, decentralization of control, the food situation, and the minorities. It would be out of place to touch here on these vast and complicated subjects. I can only say that any question we asked was freely answered and no one made light of difficulties and failures.

5. MACEDONIA

Slav endurance is a wonderful thing. At one extreme there is the most civilized patience in the world, at the other end, the most abject submissiveness. We chiefly met the patience. To carry out our programme we had many times to change our plans, but we never met with irritability.

Mrs Vilfan, whose husband was one of the delegates from Yugo-Slavs at Lake Success, and our other Yugo-Slav companion, Petar Knezhevich, were telephone-minded, so that whatever place we chose to visit we found there a reception committee. When we reached Skoplje at 2 a.m. there was still a tired secretary drowsing over a banquet of roast port and grapes; two Ministers of the Macedonian Government had been waiting for some hours and had gone to bed. It was friendly and flattering but at 2 a.m. bed is better than banquets.

Our three chauffeurs, Rade, Yanko and Pero, were the chief sufferers from our vagaries, for often we had to keep them driving for hours on end. Once at midnight in Kossovo Polje, the great plain where the Serbs fought their last battle against the Turk in the 14th century, Rade turned quietly into the roadside, and went to sleep. The other two cars drew alongside and waited twenty minutes. Only the passengers were wakeful, listening to the snores of the chauffeurs and the distant barking of dogs. After a time all three awoke simultaneously and soon we were off again.

Not Etiquette

From Skopje after our usual investigations, we traveled towards the Albanian frontier. On the road we passed the local train on its way to Tetovo. It was going at about ten miles an hour. The little engine had something like a fire screen on top of its funnel. In a truck behind there was an oddly domestic looking assortment of objects like bellows, shovels, scuttles and watering cans. But most remarkable of all was the train itself, for out of every window on the running board, on the roof, passengers were crowding and the rear was brought up by a flat, sideless tray, on which there gravely squatted forty Albanians in white skull caps. My companion, Joseph Lauwreys, had a camera, and when we were a couple of hundred yards past the train he slipped it on and jumped on to the embankment. The others also stopped, and the train puffed slowly past us to the clicking of cameras and delighted English exclamations.

It was not until we had started again that we realized from the grim faces of the chauffeurs that we had been guilty of a breach of good taste. "Why did you take that photo?" Rade asked Joseph. "Oh, because I thought it would make a nice picture."

"It is a nice picture to see a lot of poor people crowded and uncomfortable?" Joseph made desperate efforts at appeasement. He talked of the crowds on the London underground and he added, "We want to see the old as well as the new that is replacing it. It is your fight against poverty that we admire."

"And why so?" Rade pursued inexorably. "It is riches we are fighting against, not poverty."

We plunged deeper and deeper into misunderstanding. But when we left abstractions behind, we seemed to leave our disagreements with them. Rade, like other country Serbs, had the gift of saying simple things so that they did not seem banal. When we sounded him about Russia and the Cominform, he said, "There are good Serbs and bad Serbs, good Russians and bad Russians, good English and bad English. I do not prefer one nation to another. I like good people."

Simple Faith

He said this without a hint of smugness. It had been the same that night on Kossovo Polje, when Pero, looking at the stars, advanced some theological arguments which would have sounded trite, even in the gas-lit days of Bishop Herber; but here, in these strange, lonely surroundings, they had an appealing freshness.

"Why Pero, you must be a believer,"Yanko laughed.

"Yes, I am," Pero said easily.

There is little talk about religion in Communist Yugo-Slavia, but, if you hear someone speak openly about God, or immortality, it is a real voice talking, not a routine echo of something obligatory. There are few political implications or overtones. Rade did not seem to have been troubled one way or the other by the religious conflict in which Yugo-Slavia was plunged. I asked him if he was Catholic or *pravoslav* (Orthodox). "I am *pravoslav*, of course, anyone who is not a *pravoslav* is not a Serb".

We noticed in all Yugo-Slav drivers a callousness which has nothing to do with the decay of religion, but much to do with the rapid mechanisation of a simple people. When bullock-carts or pedestrians came in the way of our cars, they were driven remorselessly into the ditch, and when we protested, we were made to feel unmodern.

On the road to Tetovo, in a village where the tobacco leaves hung in racks outside the cottages and the maize straw was stacked in the branches of pine trees, we met a touching funeral procession.

A child's coffin, covered with a Bosnian carpet, was borne on a wagon pulled by two oxen wreathed in flowers. The priest, walking ahead with a platter of bread and wine, was preceded by a man bearing a wooden cross with a circlet of marigolds where the shafts intersected.

Dickensian

The busiest shop in Tetovo was the large, new bookshop. I do not think it possible to exaggerate the significance of the rapid growth of literacy in Yugo-Slavia. Where will it lead to? In England, in late Victorian times, there were great Presslords ready to take advantage of the newly-won literacy of the masses. They captured their public by studying its tastes, but the contents of Macedonian bookshops are painfully austere, with few concessions to frivolity or crime or sex, or even light entertainment. Reading is still the pursuit of the earnest, the priggish, the ambitious.

There has been a big purge of the Marxist manuals since the split with the Cominform, and the gap is filled with the books on electrification, viticulture, political speeches and translations from the classics. A small crowd gathered round us in the bookshop, led by a lively Macedonian boy. We were asking for the poems of a Skopje professor whom we had met in the morning, but the boy said: "No, don't read that, it's childish. Read Veliki Ochekivanja." I puzzled over this: "Big Waiting?" Then he brought the book. It was *Great Expectations*, by Charles Dickens.

How will literacy be used in this backward Republic, from which Alexander once set out to conquer the world? Almost anything might happen. A friend, a theatrical producer from Zagreb, who was transferred to Skopje, was astounded at the contrast between the enthusiasm of the unsophisticated Macedonian audiences and the blasé destructive skepticism of his native town. As the Marxists relax their grip on culture – and this seems inevitable – will Hollywood step in ? The bookshops now enjoy more prestige than the cinemas but a closer intimacy with America will alter the balance.

Toleration

One of our tyres was always puncturing, and to the ensuing delays I owed several curious conversations in remote places. In a Serbian Village I talked to a peasant with a German name. He pulled out of his pocket a crumpled photograph of a son whom he had lost in the war and also an official notice in German describing the youth's death on the field of honour. It was signed by the commanding officer and stamped with a swastika seal. There was also a neat map of Central Bosnia with an arrow showing the spot where the young solider had died.

I wondered at the innocence of the old father, at the perfection of the Nazi charity machine, at the wisdom of the Yugo-Slavs in tolerating among them this unsophisticated old traitor. The son must, I think, have been fighting in the Prinz Eugen Brigade, which was composed of Yugo-Slavs of German descent or sympathies.

Another time, at midnight, a peasant overtook us with a wagon load of grapes. He shouted at us in German. He had been taken to do farm work in the Luneberge Heide. The farmers had treated him well. "Gute Leute" (good people), he had said, "Gute Leute." There must be many Serbian peasants who never in their life-time sort out the extraordinary mixture of experiences which they have undergone.

Humour

Once or twice Yanko diversified our night drives with sport. In the plain of Leskovac the car started to leap from side to side of the road for fifty yards.

There was a sudden bump, a squeal of pain, and the vehicle stopped. He got out with a smile of triumph, and picked up a big hare which he had been chasing. That was our longest drive.

A little later we began once more to bounce from side to side. I listened for the squeal, but instead we heard the horn of the car behind. We stopped and Pero came up. "Yanko is going to sleep. Mr Knezhevich is going to sit beside him as he talks more than you do".

I changed over to the other car, but soon Pero began to fall asleep. So he opened the window beside him and kept his head stuck out. "It keeps me awake," he said, "if the wind blows my eyelids open".

We reached the city at 4 a m. A wag, who was less drowsy than the rest of us, played a cruel prank when we arrived. He got out first and roused us up. "Quick," he said "the Minister of Finance is upstairs. He has been waiting for us for hours with grapes and roast pork".

6. CROATIA

The massacre of the Serbian Orthodox in 1941 was one of the most terrible events in the history of Christendom. In 1943 the exiled Orthodox Church in America published an account of it, *The Martyrdom of the Serbs*. The book stated that in its cruelty and in the number of its victims this massacre of Serbs by Croats far surpassed anything that happened in the French and Russian Revolutions. Although the book was sponsored by the Archbishop of New York and had contributions from General Mihailovitch and the heads of the Orthodox Church, it is now almost forgotten. The facts it contains are too painful and disturbing for journalism, and the time for a serious historical study has scarcely arrived.

When I was in Zagreb, I found that one of the most important of all the documents relating to this period had never been published in Yugo-Slavia, far less translated into English. It was a long letter, dated November 1941, from Archbishop Stepinac to Pavelitch, the quisling leader of Croatia, protesting against the barbarities of the campaign of compulsory conversion to the Catholic faith which Pavelitch had begun. The letter contains extracts from the memoranda of four other bishops.

Counter-Denials

I spent a couple of days in Zagreb translating it and some other documents, and published them in *The Church of Ireland Gazette*. The authenticity of this letter is beyond a doubt. Why has neither faction used it in the bitter controversy about Archbishop Stepinac? I think the reason is that one party has hotly denied that the compulsory conversion campaign ever developed. The other party has asserted equally emphatically that Mgr. Stepinac backed the campaign unreservedly. This letter gives lie to both parties.

The regions in which the massacres and conversions took place are not easily accessible to the ordinary visitor. While I was still with our group, I only once, by accident, found myself in a village which had suffered from them. Something had gone wrong with our car in the middle of a flat northern plain and I had walked on until I came to a broad village street in which the large cottages each stood in its own field, like a farmhouse. It was dinner-time and the street was empty, except for a few long wooden carts laden with maize and driven by peasant. I was overtaken by a man dressed like a clerk. He asked me if I was looking for someone. I asked if he could show me the Orthodox priest's house. When we reached the door the priest came out in his shirt-sleeves. His beard was grizzled, his clerical clothes stained and worn. After taking me across to the church, the priest shut the door and assured himself that he could not be overheard. He then began to tell me of the miserable state of the Orthodox Church under Communism, no money, no rights, and the people afraid to come to worship. He asked me had I seen the carts full of maize going by. "Yes, I had."

"They are requisitioned by the Government. The peasants are raging about it," he explained. He said that he had been imprisoned by the Germans in Belgrade for more than a year. The church had been locked, except for a short time when a Catholic priest from Djakovo had taken services. "He was a good man," said my informant. Most of the people of the Orthodox faith, it seems, had run away from the village. Those that remained had to be converted, but their conversions by the kindly priest were purely nominal to save their lives; he did not plague them to give up their beliefs and traditions, as they were plagued in other places.

"It was far worse round Nashitse, to the north of us," said the Orthodox cleric. "Often they were massacred even after they were converted." He would like to have gone on talking, but I was afraid I might delay the others, so I had to leave. I was later to find that he was true to type and that the Orthodox bishops had a more conciliatory spirit than the average parish priest, both towards the Communist Government and towards the Catholic hierarchy of Croatia – or perhaps, they were more diplomatic in expressing themselves.

A few days later in Zagreb, when I was by myself, I drove from Krizhevtsi, where the Greek Catholic Church has its headquarters, to Bjelovar, and to several other villages near by. I chose the route from the maps and arranged where to stop. I was glad to have a Communist, Miss Jovanovitch, with me, because otherwise I might have found myself under suspicion. She was helpful and intelligent, and understood that I should sometimes wish to pay my calls alone.

Hunted Out

To choose one of my many encounters, when I was at Narta (in East Croatia) we found the Orthodox priest, Father George, at home, a jolly friendly fellow, with a red face and white skullcap. He said he had only been there since the previous priest had been hunted out into Bosnia in 1941, and had died here, and the whole village had been compulsorily converted. He (the new priest) had come from Serbia, but when he got there first the Communist organizers blamed him for the slow progress their propaganda was making in the village. He was then imprisoned for a year. "But now I'm back again," he said cheerfully, "and they don't interfere with me, and I can usually get the village council to do what I want."

He took us into the church which adjoined his garden. After the village had been converted the church had been adapted to Roman Catholic usage. This meant the removal of the icons and the iconostasis, the large screen which divides the Sanctuary from the body of the church. He showed me the newly-erected iconostasis, a temporary affair of brown paper and laths. He had attached to it several icons that had been badly battered, but it was being restored, and he told me that he was doing this out of his own funds.

"I gave 20,000 dinars myself," he said. "I've only a wife to keep, and I can afford it. The villagers can't."

"How many come to church on Sunday?" I asked him.

"Oh, none," he said, surprised at the naiveté of my question. This raised a number of other questions but I could only ask the crudest, "Where do you get your money from then?"

"Well, they are not frightened to come on Feast Days, so I make a bit then on candles and other things like that. I managed to collect about 1,200 dinars a month."

"Do you get something from the State, then ?" I asked in surprise for these sums are very small. Foreigners can spend as much on a hotel meal.

"Nothing. I am allowed to charge 200 dinars for baptisms, 300 for marriages, but the peasants can't usually afford it, and I don't ask them. Then we have to give about 200 dinars to maintain the Bishop of Zagreb."

He took us to his house through his well-kept garden with its rows of aubergines and cabbages, and green and red paprikas. He told us that he had 12 acres. Inside the house he led us to a long bare room with a big table, which looked as if it was used for vestry meetings. Out came the inevitable bottle of silvovitsa brewed not from plums but from his own black currants. He started a good-humoured attack on Miss Jovanovitch: "I have nothing against the Communists as such," he said to her, "but we Christians ought to be much better Communists than you are. We say that if a man has two shirts, he should give one to his brother. Did Karl Marx ever say that? And, do you know," he added, "there is a great deal more graft now than there used to be. In the old days the Secretary of the Obdor (the village council) took at least fifteen years to save enough to build himself a house, and the present fellow's done it in a year and a half."

This was the first time I had met with such free speech, but he obviously knew what he was about. No perfunctory tribute to the regime could have done it so much credit in my eyes as the free candidness of Father Georges' criticism.

Free Speech

The only Christian leader whom I met in Yugoslavia, who seemed to accept the new order with something more than resignation was the Evangelical pastor of Zagreb, Dr. Edgar Popp. There are historical reasons for this. Until nearly a century ago, Protestants were barely tolerated in Croatia. As late as 1820 Protestants were still, by imperial edict, forbidden to settle in the frontier zones. A little while previously the authorities had driven out the Quaker Kukfuss. Even under the Yugo-Slavia state there had been some prejudice against them because of their foreign affiliations. (They are called the German Evangelical Church).

At the time of the German occupation, Zagreb was full of Protestants. Bishop Popp, Edgar Popp's father, found his congregation much increased and a serious problem facing him. It was too hard for him to solve. He did not manage to prevent his church from being implicated in the campaign against the Orthodox, since the forced converts were given the choice of four religious communities into which they might be received, the Roman and Greek Catholic, the Evangelical and the Moslem.

I learnt that Edgar Popp's father had for humanitarian reasons received in Zagreb 420 "nominal" converts; their names had been entered in a book, but they had not been baptized. Because of the pressure of his German and German-Yugoslav congregation, the bishop had been inveigled step by step into the quisling camp and had accepted from Pavelitch an Order "with star" for "sincere collaboration with the Croatian Government." When the partisans reached Zagreb, he was executed.

Dr Popp was not at home when I called first at the offices of the Evangelical Church, so I went to the picture gallery at the end of the street. It was built before the war by the sculptor, Mestrovic, but had never been used for its intended purpose. Pavelitch, who favoured the Moslems against the Orthodox, had, on his arrival, changed it into a mosque and added two minarets, which have only just been pulled down. An exhibition of "Zagreb under Pavelitch" was being held.

The walls were covered with posters acclaiming Hitler and denouncing Serbs and Jews, and public notices about the execution of those who had resisted Pavelitch. I recall, in particular, the death sentence on the cook at the Esplanade Hotel, who had harboured an enemy of the State.

When Dr. Popp returned he was wheeling a new bicycle and was loaded with parcels. He had been to the station to receive goods from Protestants in America. The bicycle was to help him on his calls in his wide and scattered parish.

He was a vigorous, cheerful young man. His community, which once had 400,000 members, had shrunk a lot with the death, deportation or flight of many German Yugo-Slavs who had favoured Pavelitch. The remnant could not be considered an alien minority. I think the Communists were following the policy of King Alexander and all authoritarian governments, who are confronted by hostile groups. It is their practice to support the smaller against the larger one. Because of his policy the bulk of the Croats consistently opposed the monarchy, while the Protestants in Croatia were more favourable to it.

Hubert Butler (1900-1991) was twentieth-century Ireland's most distinguished essayist. He was the author of four collections of essays assembled in the last decade of his life and published in Ireland by Lilliput Press: Escape from the Anthill *(1986),* The Children of Drancy *(1988),* Grandmother and Wolfe Tone *(1990) and* In the Land of Nod *(1996). He lived in Zagreb for three years in the mid-thirties and wrote frequently about Yugoslavia. This essay describes his second visit to postwar Yugoslavia in September 1950. It is published here for the first time since its appearance 51 years ago, courtesy of the Butler estate.*

UNFINISHED IRELAND: HUBERT BUTLER'S CONTEMPORARY RELEVANCE

Neal Ascherson

History's poxy ironies.

I begin this talk with a quotation not by Hubert Butler, but from an article written in Vienna in November 1914 about the outbreak of war.

> What is the press? Only a messenger? One who also importunes us with his message? Torments us with his impressions? Insists on adding to the fact he brings us his conception of it? ...
>
> No, [the press report] is the event. Is it discourse? No, it is life. It not only claims that the true events are its news about the events, it also brings about the uncanny identity that makes it come to seem that deeds are first reported and then done ... Thus it is that I don't mind being told that I am for ever exaggerating the importance of the press. It is no mere messenger – how could a messenger demand so much and get it too? – it is the event itself...
>
> Once again, a mere instrument has got the better of us ... With many years' practice, (the reporter) has reduced mankind to such poverty of the imagination as to make it possible for man to wage a war of destruction against himself. (from *Das Weltgericht*, Vienna 1919)

Much can be drawn from those sentences. One point is that it took half a century before these ideas reached the anglophone world. A second point is that Hubert Butler seems always to have understood about messengers who are the event themselves. He was fastidious about words to the point of being laconic, often, and he knew from long experience that the reporting of an event can be more momentous, and can require more critical energy, than the event itself.

The writer of those words was Karl Kraus, the – what shall we call him? – culture-critic of late-Habsburg and wartime Vienna. Any label understates his many-sided anger. There is a peculiar plaster statue of him which occupies what may well not be his old table at the Café Central, and it was proposed that a plaque should be put up inscribed: "Here Karl Kraus sat every day, reading the newspapers he loathed". Some people have suggested that Hubert Butler and Kraus had much in common. I think that this is only true up to a point. Chris Agee has written that Butler's most characteristic literary or polemic form can be described as the parable, something for which Kraus seldom had the patience. It's fair to say, though, that both men excelled at what in Central Europe is called the *feuilleton*, a particular kind of intellectual journalism which is witty and biting, elegant but piercing, and which reveals deep learning lightly borne. The *feuilleton* writer (I am quoting here from my own Foreword to *In The Land of Nod*) is "interested in the epiphanies which make currents of social and political change visible through the lens of some small accident of absurdity".

Café society in Vienna may seem a long way from Bennettsbridge. Maybe so, but for me the difference between Kraus and Butler is one of sophistication. And here I want to turn the easy assumption around. It is Kraus who was the provincial visionary, and Hubert Butler who was the man of the world with a much broader grasp of international politics and human motivation. Butler does not approach Kraus's quality of apocalyptic satire, or his nervous, dialectic brilliance at turning clichés inside out. He could never have written *The Last Days of Humanity*, and I think he could never have treated those around him with the unpredictable, inconsequent nastiness of which Kraus was capable. But he was as tough and obstinate as Kraus in the fight with his adversaries, and rather more consistent.

Adversaries are not simply the censors and the gendarmes, of course. Both men, the Austrian Jew and the Irish Protestant, had to cope with what you might call aggressive emollience, in shapes peculiar to their societies. For Kraus, it was the fatuous good nature of the Viennese, who assumed that this tense little chap could be disarmed by asking him to dinner and by the suggestion that it would all be the same in a hundred years. Butler, for his part, had to cope with what he unforgettably called being "up to the neck … in this soft sweet-smelling porridge that has everything in it and tastes of nothing". The editors, for example, who would print mendacious attacks on him and then somehow just fail to publish the letters he sent in reply; challenged, they might send an affable, intimate note suggesting that it had all been set up in type but somebody went off with the proofs on holiday and forgot to tell somebody else … you know how it is here! The subtext here is the warning that to persist carries penalties: not arrest or confiscation but exclusion as an unclubbable, sad outsider. Both Kraus and Butler ignored the penalties. They pressed on.

Kraus never really went anywhere. Butler, as we have heard, lived in many foreign countries, often in times of extremity or crisis, and he experienced them in depth by living among their ordinary inhabitants and learning their languages. He, not Kraus, was the cosmopolitan intellect. Kraus, not he, was the metropolitan intellect. What was Sub-Carpathian Ruthenia to these two critics? Kraus, if tidings of any kind reached him from Uzhhorod or Mukachevo, would have simply milled them to extract radioactive particles which might have meaning for humanity in general or for the Habsburg state in particular. Butler, in contrast, actually knew something about what he called "Carpatho-Russia". He had spent much time listening patiently and respectfully to Carpatho-Russians as they told him their own feelings about their small country.

In New York, he became a friend of the exiled Sub-Carpathian politician (or church diplomat) Alexei Gierowski. His knowledge of Yugoslavia helped him to grasp the significance of Orthodox Christianity in that luckless territory and to appreciate the unexpected fact that "Carpatho-Russia" was in the Orthodox see of Sremski Karlovac in Serbia. In this, there was not a trace of that "English" stamp-collecting glee about the possession of obscure knowledge which is so patronising, so repellently metropolitan. Why is it thought sophisticated to dismiss the arrangements of small, far-off peoples as faintly comic? As the Auschwitz survivor said to the Red Cross when they asked him why he wanted to settle so far away in New Zealand: "Far away from what?"

Hubert Butler took other nations, other societies, on their own terms. He instinctively respected their sense of priorities, and did not attempt to distort them through a lens "made in Dublin" or London or anywhere else. (Only the very best of foreign correspondents take this approach now, and they exasperate their news editors by doing so). He understood that allegiance to Karlovac and to Bishop Dositheus, an ethnic Serb, was a serious thing for the Orthodox community trying to survive the policies of Benes, Hitler and Stalin in "Podkarpacki Rus", comically exotic as it might seem to strangers in the West. When Dositheus died of his injuries, kicked and beaten to death by a Catholic mob in Zagreb, Butler was one of the very few foreigners who could hear the distant, manifold resonances across Eastern and Central Europe of that small tragedy.

I am supposed to be discussing Hubert Butler's relevance to the 21st century. Before talking about how his thoughts may make an impact on this knock-kneed young millennium in its pimply first decade, it's worth pointing out that Butler was not primarily a prophet. Butler did not sit down in Kilkenny and write a work entitled "Ireland: Testbed for the End of the World". That was the sort of thing Kraus did, because Vienna in his time really was such a testbed, or at least a range on which all the explosives to be used in the Nazi cataclysm were already being tried out. Butler, in contrast, abstained from cosmic pessimism about the future and concentrated on diagnosing the present. But that was worrying enough to him, and he expressed some terminally gloomy views about the landscape he eyed.

For instance, he was fond of saying that something was "dead", by which he often meant that it had lost its memory. From time to time, in the days when this country was perhaps Celtic hedgehog rather than tiger, he would claim that Ireland was dead. This was almost always a reference back to passages of history when Ireland lived more energetically and dangerously, for example when people sought to live under "the common name of Irishman". But he could also recognise corpsehood in entire professions. "Unlike archaeologists", he wrote in 1984, "anthropologists have shown themselves ready to admit that their science is dead." This too is a puzzling observation, taken on its own. Anthropology is flourishing, while archaeology in Britain or Ireland or the United States has more practicants and a bigger public than ever in its history. But he was talking about the heartlands of Europe, as he often did: not just about the monstrous abuse of those two professions by Hitlerism – with the enthusiastic assistance of most of their scholars – but about the postwar refusal to admit the truth about that past. "I think myself that archaeology did not really die until all international scholars decided that it would be wise and generous to let bygones be bygones." The new generation of German archaeologists under 40 would know exactly what he meant by that, and they have decided, 50 years on, that the only way to resurrect their discipline is indeed to dig it up and display the remains in the hope that life will return to them again.

He thought that any intellectual surrender to any state brought with it the risk of moral death. This opinion was part of his hostility to the very specialisation of learning itself. Hubert Butler preserved a view which can now seem archaic: that learning, to survive, had to be universal, "an integral part of an educated man, transfusing everything". What he called "departmentalisation" cut off the moral view, and left the scholar defenceless against the powers who coveted his or her skills in order to abuse them. "In this way archaeology, which had been born beside ruined abbeys and whose purpose has not been knowledge but to keep alive in a small community the sense of the past and the continuity of history, became one of the whore sciences whose poxy favours can be bought by any government prepared to pay for them".

This is one of my favourite Butler passages. But isn't this merely the nostalgia of the last country gentleman, whose ancestors went on the Grand Tour, acquired "polish" and flourished before the intellectual division of labour? And what has this reckless, Gothic declaration of love for amateur antiquarianism got to do with professional scientific archaeology? What is the contemporary relevance of any of this?

More than might at first appear. To start at the narrow end first, the re-humanising of archaeology is now proceeding fast. While few would agree that its purpose is not knowledge, "post-processual" archaeologists would now agree that their discipline has to be "multi-vocal" – including the voice of the small community which uses the material relics of the past to enhance its "sense of the past and the continuity of history". This voice cannot be patronised away by the claim of a professional trained élite to superior knowledge. In the United Kingdom, museum strategy is reluctantly coming back to the idea of the local museum, or at least to returning many objects from capital-city vit-rines to the localities where they were found. I don't know that Hubert Butler ever wrote about it, but I assume that he would have disliked the strongly cen-tralised and authoritarian streak in the Heritage boom, the element which sim-ply imposes on all citizens a list of sites or monuments which they are ordered to cherish on trust for posterity. What he would certainly be welcoming are signs that the monolithic version of Heritage is now beginning to break up, and that local people – farmers, teachers, shopkeepers, contractors, New Age wiz-ards, even men with metal-detectors – are now able to contest the uses to which a scheduled cultural landscape can be put.

He believed in the priority of local communities; he believed in small nations. But not just because he was an apostle of smallness for itself, like Leopold Kohr. Butler was a nationalist, with a steady faith in the virtues of national statehood and independence. It has already been asked, the obvious question: would the post-1989 disasters in south-eastern Europe, the Yugoslav wars, have made him change his mind? After Vukovar, Srebrenica and Racak, can small-state national-ism be regarded as anything but a ticket to the fiery furnace?

The reply must be a double No. Butler understood, as the English still find very difficult to understand, that nationalism is never entirely good or bad, "civic" or "ethnic", but – as Tom Nairn famously taught, with his image of the two-faced nationalist Janus – always contains elements of both. The point is in the proportions of the mix. For Hubert Butler, who had seen independence struggles, successful or doomed, all over Europe from the Baltic to the Adriatic, the modernising and liberalising element was inherently stronger. He condemned "the new passionate racism – the disease of the twentieth century". But he did not shy away from the self-assertiveness of nationalism, so long as it was not distorted by xenophobia. "Germans were ejected from the Tyrol and Slavs from northern Italy. What has this to do with nationalism, which is comprehensive and based on neighbourliness and a common devotion to the land in which you live?" Looking at the struggles for Jerusalem or for Sarajevo, you might ask: What have they to do with anything comprehensive or neighbourly? Here Butler, uncharacteristically, was twisting language to suit his purposes. He was trying to redefine nationalism so narrowly that the word excluded bad behaviour. The brutality of General Mladic, he might have said, disqualified him from the honourable title of nationalist.

Hubert Butler, as we have heard, admired Wolfe Tone for his inclusive patriotism, open to all who lived in the land whether they were Catholic or Protestant, Irish, Scottish or English, but not invoking the overseas diaspora. This especially appealed to Butler, who felt that "diaspora nationalism" was akin to racism. On this point, he differed from President Mary Robinson, whose open-hearted outlook in certain other ways resembled his own (indeed, she was the first public figure to show obvious Butlerian influence in her official pronouncements). I wish that he could have lived to savour the intriguing commemorations of 1798 and of the Famine, with their subtle re-inventions of public memory. Mary Robinson, as you will all remember better than I, expertly steered the Famine recollection away from thoughts of mass graves, Trevelyan or "soupers" and endeavoured to re-brand the occasion as a festival of the Irish diaspora. I cannot think that Hubert Butler would have liked this, although it might have made him laugh.

There is, in short, nothing dated about Butler's interest in the small free nation – in or out of a supranational confederation of states. Nationalism may be out of fashion in London and Washington – when has it ever been anything else in those capitals, except during the brief flowering of President Wilson's Fourteen Points? But the comfortable little polity grows more and more attractive in the age of globalisation, attractive both to ordinary people and to global corporate investors. Most members of the UN are small, and a great number of them are micro-states with tiny populations, whose independence would have been dismissed as a joke only a few decades ago. Meanwhile nationalism, with all its faults and crimes and failures, still remains the vehicle onto which most oppressed people in the world load their hopes for a better life and for justice.

And there is nothing dated, either, about Hubert Butler's dislike of rhetoric about broad horizons, higher unities and unanimities, "global communities" and all the sub-Hegelian verbiage which Prime Minister John Major, in his own neck of the woods, used to refer to as "Eurocrap". Butler was not in the least insular. But he had a passionate loyalty to the "real" world which he loved as a permanent jostling of small or large differences and contradictions. He agreed with Alexei Gierowski, the Carpatho-Russian, that ecumenists were on the wrong track. "We have to venture out from the well-kept museum of symbols on to the junk-heap of cast-off clothes, broken crockery and maggoty corpses which is history". (Günter Grass has written much the same). He wrote with affection about the New Ireland Forum in 1985, but gently sent up its high-mindedness: "The Forum failed of its effect but left a lingering sweetness in the air. The desire for unity and harmony is something like the desire for sleep". What mattered was the reality of physical neighbours, not distant fantasies. There was nothing Hubert Butler could do about the power of modern communications, but it worried him that even letters (for he was worrying long before email and the mobile permeated our homes) encouraged us to ignore the neighbour who lived a few yards away. In a well-known passage he complained: "Christianity was born in a small community … Today the idea of neighbourly love has been diluted until it covers all humanity. We grieve for distant events and people with sympathy as thin and ephemeral as the newspaper in which we read about them. We suffer from a disease so widespread as to seem incurable. Yet where the diagnosis is obvious, the cure cannot be for ever beyond our reach".

The writings of Hubert Butler help to dissolve the ill-defined fuzz of anxieties and advertising that we call globalisation. He is not always helpful. For example, Butler's doubts about a "diluted" neighbourliness which covers all humanity do not accommodate the shrinking of distance by cheap air fares and new media of communication, changes which allow a growing number of genuine "neighbourships" to be established in other continents. But I think that he would identify the vanity of the "globalisation" word, seeing that this was only one more attempt to bluff good people into an illusion of impotence. After all, the Reaganite or Thatcherite appeal to "world market forces" amounted to only one more suggestion that unemployment and crushing foreign debt are also – in Butler's phrase – "a disease so widespread as to be incurable".

What remains for me a puzzle is what Hubert Butler would have thought of the universal "culture of human rights" which is now arising. He might have detected a sort of blasphemy in the assumption that everything that goes wrong must be somebody's fault, requiring compensation. That sue-for-all society creates its own piggish dependency, running quite contrary to his notion of "the Right of Private Judgement" which he trusted to be the heart of Protestant ethics.

But I am sure that he would have been delighted by the coming of something like a universal criminal jurisdiction, in the matter of crimes against humanity. His special intimacy with Croatia allowed him to see what hypocrisies, what spiritual betrayals of trust are required before a Christian society can bless its sons and send them out to butcher innocent men, women and children of other faiths. What frightened him at least as much as the crimes of the Ustashe was his discovery that those crimes had provoked hypocrisy and spiritual betrayal in his own country as well. I count "The Artukovic File", the story of his investigation into how and why Ireland came to hide the chief organiser of sectarian genocide in Yugoslavia, as one of the most enthralling true tales of detection I know. But it is a sad tale as well, sad and humiliating about Irish real or feigned ignorance of what went on in the world. This is why I feel certain that Hubert Butler would have rejoiced to see the emergence of international Tribunals like those at The Hague, whose warrants run all over the world, or the Lex Pinochet which means that no government will ever again be able to shelter an Ante Pavelic or an Artukovic by pleading ignorance.

Lastly, Ireland. Or to put this more tactfully: lastly, Europe and Ireland-in-Europe. Hubert Butler wanted a proud and easy intimacy with Europe – with all of Europe, and not just its West End. He wanted to live in a society which was in every way open to the outside world. But just suppose something entirely improbable – that Síle deValera had invoked the thoughts of Hubert Butler when she made her recent speech in Boston about political union as a threat to Ireland's "unique identity, culture and traditions". Could she legitimately have appealed to passages in his political creed?

After the Union of 1707 between England and Scotland, the Scottish Whigs were quite certain that enlightenment, modernity and prosperity could only flow in from the south, from London. To keep the inrush going, they were prepared to let it wash away a great deal of native identity, culture and tradition. The Scots Tories, like Walter Scott, thought differently, sometimes for good reasons. The division of opinion about Europe in Poland today, a vigorous but in some ways highly traditional society, is between radical urban reformers and conservative rural patriots. Reading "Brussels" instead of "London", it reminds me of those old Scottish arguments about England and Empire. So do the arguments I read in *The Irish Times*, in which enthusiasm for Europe sometimes reaches a Whiggish, new-broom intensity.

Hubert Butler's works warn that a debate about whether Ireland should become American or Swedish is missing a point – his point. Beware of enthusiasm for distant abstractions, at the cost of close and familiar details. Never mind America and Sweden: Ireland has not yet become Irish, until the alienation between majorities and minorities has been overcome in a new sense of community. There is a world to win. But there is also a family of neighbours down the road, and unfinished business with them. Hubert Butler enjoyed history's poxy ironies. But not that Irish history should now repeat itself inside out: that one part of Ireland should again march away and sign up under the flag of some vaster identity – and leave the other part forgotten in the rain. Yes, there is a threat to Ireland's "unique identity" – but it's to the identity which has not yet been created.

Pleanary Address
Hubert Butler Centenary Celebration
21 October 2000
Kilkenny

Neal Ascherson is a jounalist and columnist with The Observer. *His most recent book is* Games with Shadows *(1998).*

THE SECRET LIFE OF DEATH

—

Ivo Zanic

—

In the Balkans as in Ireland, the dead have their uses.

I

On 9 January 1992, at the Sarajevo Holiday Inn, the self-appointed Assembly of the Serb Nation in Bosnia-Herzegovina was in session. (It was actually made up of the deputies elected as candidates of the Serb Democratic Party – SDS – to the Assembly of the Socialist Republic of Bosnia-Herzegovina, in the general elections held in the autumn of 1990, and who left it a year later in order to proclaim themselves an independent Serb legislature.) At the end of the day they announced the establishment of the Serb Republic of Bosnia-Herzegovina (SRB-H) and issued a Declaration to mark the event, which (according to the report in *Vecernji List*) stated: "On the territories of the Serb autonomous regions and counties, as well as other Serb ethnic communities in Bosnia-Herzegovina, *including those in which the Serb nation has become a minority due to the genocide carried out against it in the Second World War*, on the basis of the plebiscite held on 9 and 10 October of last year in which the Serb nation declared its wish to remain in one state, Yugoslavia, the Serb nation rightfully proclaims the republic of the Serb nation in Bosnia-Herzegovina."

The news could not fail to bewilder many readers, because it unequivocally revealed that the authors of the Declaration were including in the total number of the population in the given area their dead co-nationals too – as being really present, actively and not just symbolically. Their presence was equated with the presence of the living at one important level at least, that of statistics: all the more important in that it had a real legal and political effect, since it gave them legal and political subjectivity. If only the living were counted, certain territories (which, and of what size, is of little importance here) clearly could not be claimed by the new state formation; with the dead counted in, however, these territories become part of it.

II

At first glance this use of the dead appears as only one among many cases of *politically* unfinished or *politically* incorrect deaths, which must therefore be remodelled as soon as the opportunity arises.

In 896 Pope Formosus, eight months after his death, was dug up from his grave, dressed in papal robes and placed on the papal throne in the Lateran Basilica, so that he could be put on trial for proclaiming himself pope in con-travention of the canons. He was asked direct questions, to which his repre-sentative nominated by the court replied; and when the trial was over and the accused found guilty, the papal robes were stripped from him, the three fingers he had used for benediction were cut off, and his body was thrown into the street. There is also the case of the Spanish woman Ines de Castro, who was secretly married to the Portuguese Crown Prince Pedro, but his father King Alfonso IV had her executed because he did not wish a foreigner to become Queen of Portugal. Three years later, as soon as he ascended to the throne, Pedro had her dug up from the grave and her skeleton crowned as queen, with full ceremonial.

Both cases can be described as retrospective interventions into the social – hence, also political – meaning of death: for the self-proclaimed Formosus had died with a status that was higher, and the ill-fated Ines with a status that was lower, than the one to which they had a right and which was socially theirs. It might appear that the authors of the Declaration on the establishment of SRB-H were using the same procedure in relation to their deceased co-nationals. However, whereas the alteration of the political content of the Pope's and the Queen's first death was effected through their second death – apparently sym-bolic, yet truly only then properly real and fully realized, because final also in political terms – the spirit of the Declaration implies no such change. The dead of whom it speaks are not recalled to the world of the living for their status to be changed, but on the contrary for it to be confirmed: shown to be truly unchangeable, because determined by national identity as an axiomatically per-manent category.

The Declaration, in other words, recalls them not in order to finalize their death – not in order to give that fact merely a different form, without howev-er denying its content – but precisely in order to deny the very fact itself: not just once and exceptionally, but permanently and as a matter of principle. Having once been recalled, they can be recalled again whenever they are need-ed. Once legally validated, their statistical – or demographic – presence can be validated as far back as you like, since death once denied is denied forever.

Such ontological pretensions were not claimed, however, by those who tried the self-proclaimed pope or those who crowned the ill-fated queen: they simply took them – borrowed them for a while – from the world of the dead, in order to finalize as necessary the *form* of death upon their *body*, by disfiguring or embellishing it, by debasing or elevating it to the right degree.

What the Declaration is talking about might also appear comparable with another form of a political alteration of death, different insofar as it does not require the actual presence of the body that was necessary for the posthumous coronation or for the corporal punishment of the condemned person – something that the Declaration does not imply either. I am referring to posthumous admission into a political party, which is what happened to Alexander Nevsky in 1942 when he became a member of the Communist Party of the Soviet Union, in the context of Stalin's intention by renewing Russian traditional values to mobilize all social forces for the war against the Axis. However, neither Alexander's admission nor that of Pushkin (which happened in the same year and for the same reason, additionally motivated in the poet's case by the hundredth anniversary of his death), nor any other such recruitment to membership in the rich history of political parties, changed or reconceptualized in the slightest the fact of death as the irrevocable and real absence of the person who was being admitted. It merely restated and instrumentalized it at a level that remained quite banal and mundanely political. Alexander's death was in no way altered or finalized, elevated or debased, but simply included – with its complete symbolic meanings – in the semantic domain of the living (one of the latter in particular), in order to change and finalize *them*.

When in other words, in the context of his ritual admission into the CPSU, they evoked the complete life of the great Prince Alexander Nevsky who in 1242 had defeated the army of the Teutonic Order and thereby halted the German drive into Russian lands, they did not mean that he had been resurrected exactly seven hundred years later to repeat his deed. No, he was left to the dead, exactly as he was at the moment of his death with all his accomplishments and his single life, while the ruler named Stalin – faced likewise, after so long a passage of time, by the contemporary version of that same German danger – was actually altering his own life, by arraying himself in the robes of a great prince and so, while still alive, revaluing and thus denying his future death. This, of course, is a ritual of quite a different kind: transparent, wholly secular and calculated. There is no trace in it of that atmosphere, as morbid as it was solemn, that was present at the trial of the dead pope or the coronation of the dead queen. Finally (and this is far from unimportant), in this ritual too – as at the trial and the coronation – it is quite clear who are the living and who the dead. In a state, however, in which the dead exist together with the living and among the living – a state that is being established by the joint labour of the dead and the living – this is not clear.

III

Louis-Vincent Thomas, in his *Ethnologie de la mort* writes with reference to Black African and Western societies of two types of civilization, differentiated precisely by their attitudes towards death and the dead. The former is a *symbolic civilization,* in which the living and the dead form a single, united, integral community; the latter is a *civilization of discontinuity*, in which death is perceived as opposed to life and separate from it, so that a dialogue between the two worlds – let alone a fusion of the two worlds – is inconceivable. For a member of the former community time is a *continuity,* a reiterated repetition; for members of the latter community it is a discontinuity, a separation. And while the member of the former civilization lives in an organic unity with past, present and future, happily united with his ancestors and his descendants in a wholly undisturbed togetherness, the member of the latter has driven away his dead and made a rift in time in order to prevent them from constantly turning him towards the past and thus spoiling his future.

In the former civilization death is close, intimate and accepted; in the latter it is surrounded by a void, isolated, repressed and forbidden.

In the *society of continuity*, the dead retain such importance that death does not really exist. The living do not separate themselves from the dead; the dead are truly present in everyday life and ties with them are carefully maintained, either by bringing them gifts or by visiting their dwellings. The purpose of keeping ties with the dead is mutual support, because the deceased do not cut their ties with the living either but, depending on their attitude, help them or harm them. The dead return favours to the living in such ways as they can – affecting their health, the fertility of their fields, or the multiplication of their cattle. The precondition for healthy functioning of such a society is precisely the permeability of the border between the two worlds, or rather its non-existence – so that, as the folk tale has it, a blood-brother can rise from his grave to be groom at his blood-brother's wedding and, having thus fulfilled his duty, return happily and with a clear conscience to the grave. In such a society a crisis arises only if someone prevents the dead from sharing social life with the living, or the living from maintaining through ritual the presence of the dead: in other words, if someone attempts to separate two otherwise inseparable worlds, sever their communication.

In the *society of discontinuity*, where the difference between the realm of the living and the realm of the dead is deep and unbridgeable, a crisis is heralded by the loss of this difference: by the mingling of two otherwise separated realms. If the frontier between them is nevertheless erased, this can be done only under strictly defined conditions, clearly delineated in time and space, with a purpose that is unambiguously defined and, if socially undesirable, at least tolerable. Otherwise, understandably, deep structural and functional disturbances appear.

The trial, coronation and party admission mentioned above thus indubitably belong to the civilization of discontinuity and monologue, the world in which the living are stronger than the dead, because none of the dead were invited back to the world of the living permanently, for the sake of dialogue or some joint endeavour, but only very briefly: for as long as was necessary to complete some unfinished business from the world of the living, according to the latter's rules and finally by its means. Not for one moment did the two worlds actually meet or understand each other, nor was there ever any intention to create such a relationship between them.

The difference between these cases and what we begin to perceive in the background of the Sarajevo Declaration becomes clearer, when the institution of social death too is taken into consideration. One example coming from Gabon is mentioned by Thomas, while the other from Brazil was reported in *Vjesnik* about ten years ago. In Gabon the law allowed the head of state to commute the supreme punishment by proclaiming the person condemned to death to be "socially dead". This meant that he would not be shot or hanged, but cut off from society, isolated in a secret place, deprived of all family, civil and citizenship rights, and entered in the register of the dead with the date when his sentence came into force as the day of his death. The *social death* of the condemned was thus a substitute for his *real death*.

In Brazil the treatment was applied only once, albeit on that occasion to a sizable social group: namely, 1509 marine officers who, because of their opposition to the military coup of 1964, were dismissed from the army, had their names erased from all the records and military documents, and were also proclaimed officially dead – though they were not in any other way persecuted or harassed. Since, however, without documents they could neither find employment in the country nor leave it to look for employment elsewhere, their wives – finding themselves without any means of support – began legal proceedings in order to be given at least the military pension which, seeing that their husbands were officially dead, was legally theirs. In June 1967 the military government, caught in a trap, did indeed begin to pay these wives the regular pension:

as "widows" they were indeed entitled to their deceased husbands' pension, though it was frequently the same dead husband who opened the door to the postman.

This small inconsistency on the part of the Brazilian authorities, who (whether from impetuosity or fear of the possible consequences, or whether from an inadequate grasp of the border between the two worlds) stopped half-way and, unlike their counterparts in Gabon, permitted the condemned persons to remain physically present in the world of the living, albeit functionally expelled from it – this grotesque situation in which the living were not really alive and the dead were not really dead, since neither could fully be so as long as they were intermingled – nevertheless does not change the essential nature of their decision. Though less perfectly implemented than the one in Gabon, its intention was still quite unambiguous. In both cases the institution of social death could act as a substitute for real death, because a clear and irrevocably drawn border was assumed between the world of the living and the world of the dead: a border leaving no ambiguity or possibility of mutual contact whatsoever. In other words, the necessary precondition for such an institution to be available at all is an awareness of the discontinuity between the two worlds: an acceptance of the fact that the class of the living and the class of the dead are separated and demarcated.

Once a person crosses the border between them, he remains forever on the other side, absolutely and irrevocably absent. But this is precisely what is contradicted by the spirit of the Sarajevo Declaration. For in Gabon and Brazil we are dealing with people who are allowed to remain physically alive, while their death as members of society is insisted upon. The Declaration of the Bosnia-Herzegovina SDS, however, rests on opposite assumptions. Here, the essential thing is for the authors' co-nationals to be socially alive, while it is quite secondary whether they are physically alive as well, since that has no effect whatsoever upon the authenticity and credibility of their presence in society: nor, as a consequence, upon the historical, political and legal quality of the state in whose making they too participate – its legitimacy and reality.

IV

The way in which a dead co-national, in the Declaration, is functionally equated – as a member of society, *zoon politikon* – with one who is alive is comparable, at the level of poetic procedure, with folk myths about the ideal ruler who is sleeping under a mountain or who has temporarily gone somewhere, but who will surely return one day to bring deliverance to his suffering nation.

He could equally well be the Russian Prince Ivan, the Slovene King Matjaz or the German Emperor Frederick II Barbarossa. The folk imagination always counts on their arrival at the decisive moment, either in response to a call sent them from the world of the living, or as a result of their own decision reached in the secrecy of their hideout that the moment of Return has arrived.

The co-nationals of whom the Declaration speaks are simply sleepers awaiting the call, a sign that the moment has come, just as Prince Marko is not dead but asleep with his half-drawn sabre by his side, and when some supernatural or subterranean force pushes it right out of the scabbard the sound of metal will rouse him and he will emerge into the light of day; and just as Matija Gubec sits beneath the ground with his captains round a stone table bearing glasses filled with wine, and his beard curls around the table and when it encircles that table for the ninth time then the mountain above him will split asunder, and he and his army will awake again to win freedom for the Croats, emerging from the underworld, in Tommaseo's exultant words, "strengthened by the centuries-old dream, full of ancient memories, like a river swollen with water made plentiful by its long journey from a distant land".

For neither have these co-nationals been written off as social actors – at least not in the popular imagination – and it is precisely as social actors that they return, because it is above all as such that they are needed. They are here to organize society, restore justice and avenge injustice, in true cooperation with the living. Those who drafted the Declaration know this, speak about this, and call just for this. Their sleeping co-nationals are returning at the moment of the state's creation: not, to be sure, as splendid heroes from the folk epics, settling their debts with the sword in battle, but (as befits the time and conditions) as citizens with electoral rights, and with voting slips in their hands. They are participants not in a real but in a symbolic (though no less authentic or important) battle called a plebiscite – "but a true one", as Vuk Draskovic warned (*Nedjelja*, 26.8.1990), in which "all the mass graves, all the camps, and all our unborn descendants from those mass graves" will be voting – at the fateful moment (for only then will they return) that Danko Popovic announced, at the end of 1990, as the moment of an inevitable re-arrangement if not break-up of the state: when "Serbia takes back what it brought into Yugoslavia", after which the next step will be to "pose also the question of plebiscitary declarations by the remaining provinces in which Serbs live, but in a way that enables also those Serbs whom the Ustashe murdered to declare themselves" (*Duga*, 6-20.12.1990).

That we are dealing here not with empty rhetoric or a metaphor, but with real, genuine voting, was testified to by a journalist who, at a Sarajevo polling station in November 1990, during the plebiscite that the Declaration was to invoke two months later, noticed that some people were voting several times in the same place using the same identity card, while others even spoke quite openly about having already voted at twenty different places. He asked for an explanation from the woman sitting at the official table, who had heard and seen everything but had clearly considered it quite lawful. She replied briefly and clearly: "Those are the votes of Serbs murdered in Ustashe camps, or in Tudjman's" (*Nedjeljna Dalmacija*, 14.11.1991).

Since both this reply and the formulation in the Declaration come from within, from the categories of the civilization of continuity, they reinforce each other to form a robust, internally consistent, conceptual and cognitive framework. This was all in any case indicated well in advance, for example by Vuk Draskovic's statement that: "The Croats should know in advance that the break-up of Yugoslavia would also invalidate the AVNOJ and Brijuni borders, so at that moment Jasenovac and Jadovno and all our mass graves would acquire the right to vote" (*Start*, 20.1.1990); or when he said that the referendum of Serbs in Croatia, held in late summer 1990, was "merely a continuation of the referendum held in Croatia between 1941 and 1945", when "every Serb executed by the Ustashe voted for all time against the Ustashe state". All that was now required was "to garner these new votes" – i.e. add the votes of the living to the votes of the dead (just as his co-nationals in Bosnia-Herzegovina would actually do in their plebiscite a year and a half later) – "and then we shall see the outcome. It is possible that we shall confront international public opinion with the astonishing fact that there are more Serbs than Croats living in Croatia today. For we do not write off our dead" (*Nedjelja*, 26.8.1990).

To refuse to "write off" the dead – refuse to exclude them from the totality of the national community – really means to deny the conception of death as failure: hence, indirectly to negate the opposing civilization of discontinuity, to take away all its credibility and even its right to exist. Death, which was once very close to human thought and did not frighten anybody, as Philippe Ariès wrote in his *Western Attitudes towards Death: from the Middle Ages to the Present*, became disturbing not only in itself, but also because of its connection with the concept of failure (of a programme, a plan for the future). The same thing was alluded to by Elias Canetti in his *Crowds and Power*, where he emphasized that what the living most fear is the envy of the dead, which is why they try to propitiate them by bowing down to them and offering them food, providing them with everything they need for their journey to the land of the dead, so that they will remain far away and never return to make trouble and torment the survivors: so that they will accept being written off (to use Draskovic's phrase).

V

This, however, is not enough to deflect fully the anger of the dead, since they do not begrudge the living objects that can be produced or acquired, but life itself. When Canetti says that "every dead man is someone who has been survived", this is valid only for the civilization of discontinuity, but not for the one built on the opposing principle of continuity – which precisely provides the anthropological foundation, the anthropological source, for the discourse of Vuk Draskovic, Danko Popovic and the Declaration proclaiming the Serb Republic of Bosnia-Herzegovina. For in this latter civilization the dead are not consumed by any passion to get hold of the living, since they are already together and intermingled: not just living in peace alongside one another, but also collaborating harmoniously in the great national project. "The dead Serbs, whose energy did not turn to ashes and dust because energy is eternal, are today helping the living Serbs to establish their spiritual, cultural and national being": that is how Jovan Raskovic explained the nature of the relationship (*Duga*, Special Edition, June 1990).

In this civilization, the dead are not the kind of dead who suffer because they failed to stay alive; nor are their living co-nationals the kind of living who are terrified of death, and in whose eyes everyone who is not alive has suffered a terrible defeat – the defeat that comes from the fact that others have survived him. The dead are neither rejected nor useless. On the contrary, "the dead Croatian and Bosnian Serbs murdered by the Ustashe" – or rather their skulls, since "skulls are far better at foreseeing the future death, part violent, part silent, of the Serb nation in diaspora ghettoes, should they opt for 'life' in the planned confederation" – are "the secret advisors of Mr Raskovic, as unchallenged leader of the SDS": that is how the *poetics* of this political discourse and the *anthropology* of this political activity were explained with the utmost clarity by Vladimir Srebrov, president of the SDSB-H youth organization founded under the name of *Mlada Bosna* (*Nedjelja*, 12.8.1990).

What is involved here is another kind of death, namely a death that is not a failure; and another kind of dead, namely dead who are not resentful surviving losers but wise and contented advisors to the living. What is involved, therefore, is the choice of another anthropological code, one that alone can express the meaning of a compact according to which the dead will vote in the way and at the time that best suits the living, and in return will forever participate in their state as equal citizens. It was quite logical that the Serb para-state in Croatia formed and structured itself in the same fashion as that of their co-nationals in Bosnia-

Herzegovina. As the president of its assembly Mile Paspalj said at a meeting in Montenegro: 'The Serb Krajina Republic has one million and two hundred and fity thousand citizens, because we include among our citizens also seven hundred thousand Serbs from Jasenovac: we are of the same birth and make.'

At the same time, moreover, with their death declared not a failure but rather a manifest success, the life of their enemies suffers a qualitative alteration: viewed in the light of the former's revalued death, instead of being a success it now becomes a fateful failure. The roles are fully reversed, so that the ascent of the seemingly dead into the world above takes place simultaneously with the descent of the seemingly alive into the world below. In this unbreakable mutual causality, the success of one side necessarily becomes the failure of the other. The spectacular ascent of the peasant leader Matija Gubec through the sundered mountain is nothing but the proof that Count Tahy has suffered defeat. If the sleeping or exiled hero did not at some point return, it would mean that the enemy had profited from his misdeed, from genocide; just as, according to Danko Popovic, "without the votes of those whom the Ustashe slaughtered" – i.e. without their political and legal immortality, or at least equality with the living – "the Croats would enjoy the fruits of their crime" (*Duga*, 6-20.12.1990). It is precisely this return, this organized mass appearance at the voting booths – "in accordance with the principles of historical and natural right, sticking to the ethnic map of 6 April 1941" – which guarantees that "in the event of a final separation from Serbia ... neither today nor ever in the future can or will the Croats and Muslims be allowed to draw any advantage whatsoever, and especially not any state advantage, from that great crime", as Draskovic shouted as far back as February 1988, at a public meeting on Yugoslav constitutional changes organized by the Serbian Writers' Association (V. Draskovic, "*Koekude, Srbijo*" ["Whither, O Serbia"], 75-6).

VI

Draskovic rightly suspects what is likely to happen when he speaks of international public opinion being confronted with "astonishing facts", because the part of it belonging to the civilization of discontinuity – and he seems to feel this includes the whole outside world – will simply find such facts inconsistent with its conception of death and incomprehensible within its cognitive categories. It will indeed be astonished by them. To those who inhabit the civilization of continuity, however, everything will be quite natural and comprehensible: in its terms, this part of the Declaration is no tasteless rhetorical figure, but a straightforward political, legal and every other kind of reality that can be proved with valid voting papers.

When in June 1992, less than two years after that interview of Draskovic's in the Sarajevo weekly *Nedjelja*, his insurgent co-nationals in the Dalmatian hinterland asked for the so-called "pink zones" too be included in the territories under UN protection (UNPA), they motivated their application on the grounds that in that area – around Vrlika, in the municipality of Sinj – "more than 50,000 Serbs used to live". The journalist Toni Pastar was indeed astonished, as Draskovic had predicted he would be, but not too astonished to try and make a joke of it and, by playing along with the grotesque claim, derive some sort of meaningful explanation for a statement in collision with all existing statistical data. So he wrote (*Slobodna Dalmacija*, 30.6.1992): "They did not say whether they meant all Serbs who had lived in the area since their initial settlement, i.e. over hundreds of years. Using the same measure it could be claimed that millions of Croats have lived in the same area, but what would be the point?"

The journalist was perhaps not aware that, by analysing the figures *ad absurdum,* he had actually hit on the truth. Yes, they did indeed mean "all Serbs who had lived in the area over hundreds of years". The applicants did not particularly stress this, because it was self-evident. And no, it would not be possible to unearth millions of Croats and counterpose them to those fifty thousand Serbs. To begin with the two communities inhabit substantially different temporal categories – one historical, the other mythical – so cannot be compressed into simultaneity. In the second place essential, qualitative differences – differences of value – are involved, which make addition of the categorial apples and pears impossible. Thinking and writing from within the civilization of discontinuity, the journalist behaved consistently and his joke was pertinent – a logical next level of development within his conceptual system. Those whose claim so amused him, however, were not joking at all, nor did they think there were any grounds for the levity exhibited by the journalist.

VII

To adopt another type of discourse, the historical, political and even legal relationship between the Croat and Serb nations can basically be interpreted in terms of the two types of eschatology of which Philippe Ariès writes. In the first centuries of Christianity a collective eschatology was in force, inspired by the vision of the Revelations of St John, that was in total contrast to the one offered from the twelfth century on by the new iconography inspired by the Gospel of St Matthew. The former is represented iconographically by a scene from a seventh-century French bishop's tomb, in which the Elect stand upright with arms raised and invoke Christ, who at the end of Time returns in all His glory. The spirit of the latter is embodied by scenes of resurrection or separation of the saved from the damned, by the word *judex* on Christ's aureole, by Christ sitting as a judge or St Michael weighing souls. In the former case there is neither trial nor judgment, everything is based on miracle and on evocation of the Great Return; in the latter the idea of judgment dominates – along with that advocacy, since the Mother of Christ and St John kneel as intermediaries on each side of Christ the Judge – and each man is judged in accordance with the balance of his life, the sum of his good and bad deeds divided between the two pans of the scales.

The former of these scenes would obviously fit the statements by Draskovic and the others almost perfectly, as a pictorial or iconographic expression of their spiritual essence, since it too derives from a conception in which there is no place for individual responsibility or the weighing of good and bad deeds, but everything is decided in advance at the level of the collectivity. On one side are the Good – the dead who belong to the right community, the right Church and the right Nation – who have merely fallen asleep, slipped into a peaceful dream, and will stay like that until the Day of the Second Coming, the Great Return, when they will all wake up in the heavenly Jerusalem, in paradise – i.e, in the Serb Republic of Bosnia-Herzegovina. Standing opposite them are the Evil Ones, the dead who do not belong to the right Church or the right Nation so cannot survive their own death: who will never awake, but will be left behind in non-being.

It is precisely the irrevocable death of the Evil Ones that guarantees that the adversary – i.e, the Croat national community – will in no way be able to prevent the final Serb victory. Neither the Croats nor any other rival dead can rise again, and their co-nationals who survive them cannot summon them up as effectively as the Serbs can their own. Draskovic's insistence that the Serbs do not write off their dead implies, after all, that the other side does do so. For in the civilization of continuity the purpose of life is not just maintenance of one's own power by unifying the class of the living and the class of the dead, but also the permanent annulment of such power in hostile or rival communities. The proclamation of one's own power simultaneously negates that of the other. The resurrection of Draskovic's co-nationals is a variant of Christ's resurrection, since through it death loses all power over them, while the one who had the power of death – the Devil, i.e. the Ustashe, the Croat – becomes impotent.

The creation of the Serb Republic of Bosnia-Herzegovina thus proceeds through the joint work of the dead and the living, in total accord with Danko Popovic's words that "the earthly Serbia has never won a single authentic victory without the presence of the heavenly Serbia" (*Svet*, 11-24.7.1990). The poetics of communication between these two worlds corresponds typologically to the poetics of the folk epic, in those of its scenes where the border between the dead and the living disappears. When Nikola Jankovic, in the epic poem "The Duel and Wedding of Nikolica Jankovic" from the Jukic-Martic collection, kills his father's killer the Udbina *barjaktar* Nukic, he knows that this is pleasing to "his father's bones in the grave", because his contacts with the world of the dead are not formal but intimate and real. In "The Revenge of Bojcic Alija" from the Hörmann collection, the hero complains that "the Vrljika *ban*" harasses him even in his grave, constantly challenging him to a duel; since "dead legs cannot fight a duel" and "dead arms cannot wrestle", he sends a message by way of a fairy to his brother Osman to confront the challenger in his place. Osman does so and kills the *ban*, so that Alija can finally rest in peace. The structure and meaning of this scene is not hard to recognize, literally transposed, in the act of the dead voting in the so-called "plebiscite of the Serb nation" in Bosnia-Herzegovina. Since "dead legs cannot fight a duel", the dead empower their living co-nationals – indeed demand of them – to create a state that will finally bring peace to both. They can do this because, in the civilization of continuity, as Draskovic says, "the dead are stronger than the living" (*Nedjelja*, 26.8.1990).

VIII

The poetics of the Serb Republic of Bosnia-Herzegovina is, on an anthropological level, the poetics of the folk epic, the poetics of an archaic pagan consciousness. The state recognizes and implicitly defines its own genesis as a *call* or *summons to ancestors*, just as in moments of great danger – e.g., on the occasion of a sudden assault by the enemy – an appeal for help is issued to comrades, or to a whole village or clan. Researching the phenomenon of such summons (which concerns living as well as dead heroes), Veselin Cajkanovic has collected a mass of evidence testifying to the fact that what is involved here is no outburst of momentary excitement, but a custom, a rule, that is always repeated, as it were in every battle – hence, also at such all-important moments as plebiscites determining a nation's fate – and whose origin is lost in the mists of ancient, pre-Christian beliefs. The victory thus achieved is a shared victory of the living and the dead, the fruit of their joint endeavours, just as the state that comes into being through a summons to ancestors is, thanks to their response, not merely a shared achievement, but also a shared homeland: form of the final and permanent unification of all the dead and all the living.

IX

Finally, the profound difference between the being of the civilization of continuity and that of the civilization of discontinuity also engenders different conceptions of war. For the former, war is not necessarily tragic, since to die – to cross over to the other side – involves no loss for the surviving part of the community either, given that it does not write off its dead; and the same is true for the individual in question, given that he retains the power to influence the life of the community and even directly participate in it. For the latter, by contrast, war is deeply painful, since its members are conscious that the crossing over, should it occur, will be irrevocable and total; here war is by definition a loss, even if just one of its members should die, and peace a gain – both qualitative and quantitative – by virtue of the very fact that no one is lost.

Dobrica Cosic's maxim about the Serbs being "winners in war, but losers in peace", inconceivable in the civilization of discontinuity, can be properly understood precisely if viewed as a true expression of the civilization of continuity. For this civilization cannot lose in war, because in it the dead are guaranteed a full social life even after death. When in the middle of 1993 President Clinton announced a military intervention against the Serb army in Bosnia-Herzegovina, the Association of the War Invalids of Serbia wrote a protest letter which spelt out with exceptional clarity the basic concept of such a worldview: "There is probably not a single Serb living today who has not already been killed in one of his ancestors." (Serbian television, daily news of 13 August 1993). True, the first layer of meaning says that the living are only seemingly so, because death was already in them, and this would have to be the reason for a feeling of historical tragedy. However, the second layer of the message, or the other side of the truth, says that the dead are also seemingly so since, to put it crudely, if this was not so there would be no one to write this letter. This is what is essential and what the reason is for a feeling of historical optimism: each individual is a participant of both worlds, exists simultaneously in both kingdoms, but in this substantial unity it is not death that subjugates life but life that subjugates not only death but also the historical time itself. Hence in the final meaning the letter to Clinton was not written by a desperate person confronting defeat but a victor announcing his invincibility. The civilisation of continuity cannot suffer any loss if even just one of its members survives, since he is sufficient to be the link between the two worlds; the means through which the political will of his dead co-nationals will be credibly expressed; the deputy who, after the fairy tells him that his brothers cannot find peace even in their graves, will hold a plebiscite and legitimately vote in the name of them all. Given that the dead and the living form a unity, their sum – and this is all that matters – never changes, under any circumstances whatsoever, so long as the principle itself of that world survives:

so long as, at least through the life of a single member, the survival of that principle is guaranteed. The final derivative of a political culture with such a basis is the message pronounced (as the punchline) on the occasion of a visit by the Knin Folk Group to Belgrade at the end of 1990. Purportedly taken from a church document entitled "The Revival of Blood Brotherhood", the message was: "A Serb, if only one remains in the world, is a nation!" (*Svet*, 28.11-11.12.1990).

This is true, however, only as long as war – real or symbolic –– lasts and a condition prevails in which awareness of death disappears: when societies, as Edgar Morin writes in his "L'homme et la mort", become petrified and frozen in order to pass every test and win; when even civilizations of discontinuity can temporarily lose their being. As soon as peace returns, that sole survivor will realize that he is hopelessly alone, left in desolation and terrified by death: hence, that he has lost in peace what he had won in war – which, among other things, can be defined also as the possibility of endless self-multiplication. Hence, the only salvation and escape is a renewal of war, its continuation in perpetuity, either at the level of reality or at the level of symbols.

1993

Translated, from the Croatian, by Branka Magas.

Ivo Zanic is a novelist, essayist and anthropologist. He teaches at the University of Zagreb.

POEM

—

John Montague

—

GRAVE SONG

Too many deaths
Wear the heart away
Or grind it to a halt
A while, to start again
In a different way:
Having lost for a time
Its sense of itself,
The unique burden
Of a particular life.

But the form
Is solid enough, sound
As an old churchbell
And a tune picks up
Deeper, stronger
That does not deny
The somber sunken message
Of that burial ground:

Where the grave lay open,
Yes, but to the open sky.

John Montague's latest volume of poetry is Smashing the Piano *(The Gallery Press, 1999).*
He lives in Co Cork.

TWO POEMS

—

Medbh McGuckian

—

THE SELF-CONCEALING

Now, now, words for it,
The eyelids of those eyes,
The eyes' blue school,
Whose school is the school of heaven.

To where could we step back
From this destiny of denial
Whose fourfoldedness
Encircles the globe?

Not only through a ringing out
Of its voices,
But with the greatest difficulty
Can we hear the silent voice

Of this joining. The name flows
From the naming,
And more willingly
Beauty dwells on earth, but spares

Its appearing, as its ownmost self.
The earth replies by its own
Movement, the ray of light
That meets the newborn,

With the old saying of their togetherness.
Insofar as death comes, it vanishes,
And whether it comes from afar,
It is also a life.

HAND RELIQUARY, AVE MARIA LANE

God knows that there is no proof
That part returns to wholeness
Simply because miracles happen
At a single church-going.

Her verdant branches labelled
With the names of the five senses,
The garden not ours, she prayed
For her illness to last beyond the grave,

And be the unsealer of that tree.
She might have been dead for a week,
Though she went on with her deep
Dying, her womb a transparent crystal

Turning into a brown relic
Even before her death. The blinding
Beauty of her hood opening
Acted upon me as my own ghost

Would do, sounding silk,
As with a lifting gesture
She tore off flesh from her hand,
Driving wide her middle finger

Into the palm of the other.
Till being a vessel, Christ appeared to her
As a dish filled with carved-up bread
So unnaturally sweet, so lightly crushed,

She could quench the tall language
Of his image in her mouth,
Which was the breast-wound, always on the point
Of being taken, in his female side.

Medbh McGuckian teaches creative writing at The Queen's Univerity of Belfast. Her last collection of poems was Shelmalier *(The Gallery Press, 1998).*

JESUS AND RESURRECTION

—

Andrew Furlong
Dean of Clonmacnoise

—

The Church of Ireland has convened its first ecclesiastical
court for heresy in over a century.
Why? The Dean puts his case.

Preamble

The Court of the General Synod of the Church of Ireland is its highest authority for hearing a charge against one of its clergy for his or her beliefs. The judges consist of three bishops and four members of the legal profession. A sentence might be the loss of one's job or removal from holy orders. Among a number of charges put forward against me by my bishop, Most Rev Richard Clarke, is the charge that I deny the divinity of Christ. Members of the clergy, at both their ordination and their institution to a new post, make declarations of assent to historic formularies of the faith. I was called to a hearing of the Court on 8th April 2002 at which the trial was adjourned to 10th May 2002.

To my mind, all religious traditions are pointing to the ineffable and the indescribable and are asking questions about meaning and purpose (the meaning of both our own lives and that of the universe); they all evolve over time and contain much diversity of thinking and believing; they are continuously in need of re-interpretation. The historic Creeds of Christianity, as well as the documents that came to form the New Testament, were formulated in thought forms that belong to a very different age to ours. In both my articles and in media interviews I have been trying to express, in contemporary language, the meaning of faith from within the perspective of an evolving Christian tradition. I have joined a discussion and a debate that has been going on since our modern era began, in which there have been many conflicting viewpoints expressed.

The Shoah (the Holocaust), as well as the assumptions on which our modern scientific understanding of the world are based, are commonly cited as reasons for not believing in an interventionist God. Does this mean, therefore, that it does not make sense to understand, in a literal way, the story of the Son of God being sent from heaven to be the Saviour of the world? Does it mean that we cannot rationally take this story to refer to something that happened as a historical event? If it is not true as a historical fact, can the story be true in some other way?

Two other issues concern me, which relate to life both in Ireland and throughout the world. It seems to me that the implications of believing in a non-interventionist God affect dialogue between members of the Christian faith tradition and those of other faith traditions. In the past Christians have seen their tradition as having a superior position, in relation to others, because of their doctrine of the Incarnation (for which belief in an interventionist God is required). Secondly, the image of God in the Christian tradition comes across as primarily male (think of the doctrine of the Trinity: one God, Father, Son and Holy Spirit, or of the Lord's Prayer: "Our Father"). While there have been female images of God in Christianity's evolving tradition, they have never had a sufficiently important place, to my mind. As the implications of believing in a non-interventionist God are worked out, it seems to me that there can be much greater emphasis put on the notion that God transcends gender and is not to be thought of as primarily male. I believe we need many more symbols and images that come from the feminine world, as well as to hear more frequently the female voice speaking to the world, in both compassion and fury, in the name of her God.

The Jesus of History

The Enlightenment, usually dated from circa 1650-1780, saw the end of the pre-scientific medieval worldview. Beliefs such as volcanoes and avalanches being acts of God, or famine and disease being punishments from God, or a person being capable of wielding supernatural powers belonged to that old world-view. So did belief in an interventionist God. The Enlightenment heralded the new age of Reason. Since the 17th Century both the understanding of history and the methods of historical investigation have developed very considerably and continue to do so. It has put theology and the "beliefs of the faithful" into crisis. For theologians it has meant trying to distinguish between the "Jesus of history" and the "Christ of faith". "The distinction between the two figures is the difference between a historical person who lived in a particular time and place and was subject to the limitations of a finite existence, and a figure who has been assigned a mythical role, in which he descends from heaven to rescue humankind and, of course, eventually returns there" (Robert Funk, *The Five Gospels*) . The ground-breaking work of scholars such as Hermann Samuel Reimarus (1694-1768), David Friedrich Strauss (1808-1874) and Albert Schweitzer (1875-1965) has been built upon by scholars from around the world too numerous to name; Irish scholars, such as Sean Freyne, have made significant contributions. It has been called the quest for the historical Jesus.

"The question of the historical Jesus was stimulated by the prospect of viewing Jesus through the new lens of historical reason and research rather than through the perspective of theology and traditional creedal formulations" (Robert Funk). It was seen that the documents of the New Testament, and other Christian writings of the same era, contain the stories of the "Christ of faith"; and that it requires considerable "detective work" to find the "Jesus of history" behind and within some of those stories. The vast range of differing interpretations of Jesus, and of his significance and meaning, that has emerged over the last 250 years has been affected by the stages to which modern historical methods and self-understanding had reached and by the current dominating philosophical climate of the day. It has also been influenced by the socio-economic-political and cultural backgrounds of the scholars, and by a variety of other factors that relate to hidden assumptions and motives, values, personality and gender differences, and psychological and spiritual development.

The search for the historical Jesus has been aided by new knowledge about the socio-economic conditions under which he lived, the extent of Hellenization in 1st century Palestine, and the nature of provincial life in that part of the Roman empire. The discovery in the 20th century of the Dead Sea Scrolls and the Nag Hammadi manuscripts (including the Gospel of Thomas) have also contributed to a fuller understanding. However, to my mind, the major factor has been the methods developed to assess the probability of the words of Jesus, as recorded primarily in the gospels, being his authentic words. One fellow of The Jesus Seminar, founded in U.S.A. in the mid-eighties, estimates that 50% of the words ascribed to Jesus in the Synoptic gospels (St. Mark, St. Matthew, St. Luke), St. John's Gospel and the Gospel of St. Thomas are not authentic words of Jesus. Each age and culture, no matter how modern the techniques of historical investigation used will, though, to some extent find its own "Jesus of history". A range of criteria have been developed and refined over the last two hundred years to aid scholars find the words most likely to have been said by Jesus. If he only spoke in Aramaic, then the best we have are the Greek translations, with a few exceptions, of those words. These criteria fall into a number of main groups: it is possible to see how one writer has altered the text of another writer (for example, the authors of Matthew or Luke have changed the text of Mark's Gospel); Jesus used a distinctive language and oral style found in aphorisms and parables; sometimes the needs and problems of the church were addressed by words of Jesus put on his lips by the church; the beliefs of the church about the significance of Jesus were expressed by Jesus himself through constructing sayings and speeches and putting them on his lips. This is but the briefest summary of a complex area of scholarship over which there is diversity of opinion.

The Christ of Faith

There are differences as well as similarities between my current thinking about the Jesus of history and that of the Jesus seminar and their founder, Robert Funk. They would see Jesus as a wandering sage (or teacher) and John the Baptist as an eschatological prophet. While I, too, see Jesus as a wandering sage, teaching through remarkable parables and unusual aphorisms, I also see both Jesus and John the Baptist as "end-time" prophets who expected a supernatural intervention by God to restore the fortunes of their nation, giving back to them both independence and peace in a kingdom ruled over by their God. We agree in thinking that the first generation of Christians thought that Jesus would return, within their lifetimes, to usher them into a new kingdom, now envisaged as being in heaven.

The ancient community of Israel was a small nation by comparison with the much bigger ones who dominated life in the Middle East over the period of a thousand years before the birth of Jesus. The members of this community believed that their God was intimately involved with their history, out of his love for them as "his own people"; and they developed a way to understand their defeats and misfortunes as expressing both the anger of their God and his punishment on them for their disobedience to him and his laws. After their experience of exile in Babylon (beginning in 586 BCE) and in the centuries following, some of them developed a hope that some day their God would drive away for ever their enemies and that their fortunes as a nation would be restored (see, for example, Daniel, especially chapters 7 and 12).

For this strand of Judaism, theirs was a nationalistic and religious utopian vision. Their God would reign in power and glory. This new kingdom which would follow on after the resurrection of the dead and the judgement of all was thought by a variety of groups in 1st century Judaism to be around the corner. The Essene community living at the Dead Sea expected it at any moment, and John the Baptist saw it as his mission to warn people about it. The judgment would be fearsome according to John the Baptist. The group called the Sadducees, who did not believe in the resurrection of the dead, would not have agreed with this vision.

What some Jews presumed, at this time in the evolution of Israel's religious tradition, were several beliefs. First of all, they did not think of people when they died as going "straight to heaven" to enter an eternal dimension of life. Rather they thought of their dead as waiting in some shadowy existence below the ground for the arrival of the judgment day. Before the exile they had not believed in an afterlife at all, it was a relatively recent belief for some to have adopted. Secondly, they seem to have thought that God would appoint an agent for the task of bringing in the new kingdom (a messiah or several messiahs? Or a Son of Man figure? See Daniel 7 and 12). Thirdly, they appeared to believe that there would be a time of tribulation and trial before the day that the new kingdom would dawn (see Daniel again and the Gospels).

Whether Jesus of Nazareth was a wandering sage or rabbi, or whether he as an "end-time" prophet like John the Baptist, his aphorisms and parables are part of his continuing legacy. Pontius Pilate probably sentenced Jesus to death because he appeared to be looked on by some of the volatile pilgrims, who had arrived in Jerusalem for the Passover festival, as a messiah. Neither Pilate nor the Jewish leadership wanted civil unrest fired by deep religious beliefs and nationalistic hopes.

While we will never know for certain what triggered the disciples' claims that God had raised Jesus to new life beyond the grave, one thing to my mind must be clear. Believers in God agree that the existence of God cannot be proved, although in the Christian tradition attempts have been made to do so by many distinguished theologians, through the centuries, such as Anselm and Aquinas. If God's existence cannot be proved, then it follows, I consider, that the disciples needed faith to believe in Jesus' resurrection; for only God could bring back to life someone who had died. If the disciples met Jesus, after his death, in a way that did not require faith, then his resurrection would be a proof of God's existence. So this means, for me, that Jesus' resurrection belongs to the faith stories that emerged about him after his death, a point not always (I think) clearly appreciated. These stories belong, therefore, to the "Christ of faith". We have noted already another related belief: that he would come back again (see 1 Thessalonians 4) to usher in the new kingdom. This kingdom very soon after Jesus' death ceased to be thought of, by his followers, as an earthly one; it became a heavenly kingdom. In fact, Jesus has not returned as they expected, and the world has continued on its way.

The various interpretations of the meaning that the first generation of Christians found in the death of the Jesus of history also came to form part of the faith stories of the "Christ of faith". The Jewish scriptures (the Old Testament) were hugely influential in the task of drawing out the meaning of his life and death as they were now coming to perceive it. He was believed to be the one who had destroyed human death, which had come into the world as a result of sin. Secondly, they believed, he had borne, through accepting death, the punishment which should have been faced by the rest of the human race (those already dead, those who were alive and those not yet born). Thirdly his death was believed to have been a sacrifice made to God.

Many people (though not by any means all who subscribe to the Christian faith) recognise difficulties in these interpretations of what Jesus' death was believed to have meant or achieved. Some of their objections are the following. From science, we know that death is a natural process and not (as traditionally believed) a punishment for sin and a power needing to be defeated. (See, for instance, Romans 5.12: "Therefore as sin came into the world through one man and death through sin, and so death spread to all because all men sinned."). From ethics, we know that an innocent person (claimed to be Jesus) should not bear the punishment of the guilty. (See, for instance, Romans 5 and 6). From theology, to require for the forgiveness or salvation process a human death and sacrifice suggests divine sadism. (See, for instance, Hebrews 9.11-14: "But when Christ appeared as a high priest of the good things to come, then through the greater and more perfect tent {not made with hands, that is, not of this creation} he entered once for all into the Holy Place, taking not the blood of goats and calves but his own blood, thus securing an eternal redemption. For if the sprinkling of defiled persons with the blood of goats and bulls and with ashes of a heifer sanctifies for the purification of the flesh, how much more shall the blood of Christ, who through the eternal spirit offered himself without blemish to God, purify your conscience from dead works to serve the living God").

Whatever one may think of these objections, it is clear that for the first generation of Christians the Jesus of history became in their faith stories a Saviour and a Mediator. The Christ of faith was growing in meaning and significance for them. The faith stories – whether they be his birth stories or the theological discourses put on Jesus' lips in St John's Gospel – all help to portray who the Christ of faith was for Christians of the first century CE. Some of the stories would speak of him as God's pre-existent Son and of the Word made flesh ("and the Word was God": St John 1.1).

Theologians today examine the Mediterranean world of this 1st century in which the gospel was formulated and preached. They know of its many other religions, especially those that speak of a dying and rising god. It was a world very different to ours in 21st century. People then believed in interventionist gods; in some of the stories they told, these gods might procreate children of human and divine parenthood (think of the stories of Greek mythology). In Acts 14. 11-13 we read that some of the people of Lystra could say of Paul and Barnabas: "The gods have come down to us in the likeness of men!" and "Barnabas they called Zeus, and Paul, because he was the chief speaker, they called Hermes. And the priest of Zeus, whose temple was in front of the city, brought oxen and garlands to the gates and wanted to offer sacrifice with the people'. It was a world where, for worship, animal sacrifice was common, such as in the Temple worship of Judaism in Jerusalem. It was a time when the Roman emperor was sacrificed to as another god; a world where there was a strong belief in the supernatural, and where many miracles were believed to have happened. It was held that special people could perform supernatural actions.

The Jesus of history believed to be risen and alive, believed to be the Saviour of the end-time, was now being interpreted and believed to be a divinity as well. (See 1 Corinthians. 8.6: "To us there is but one God, the Father, of whom are all things, and we in him; and one Lord Jesus Christ"). The title "Lord" suggests a belief in divinity. The Christ of faith and the stories of what was believed about him continued to grow in the centuries leading up to the formation of the historic Creeds of the early church especially those that related to doctrines of the Incarnation and of the Trinity. All of this was taking place in a pre-scientific world in which interventionist gods were believed to be continuously at work. It was possible to believe in a person who was both fully divine and fully a human being at the same time in such a world; it is very difficult to do so in the 21st century. This is a part of the controversy in which I am engaged.

History and Faith

What are the connections, as I see them, between the Jesus of history (whose story lies behind and within the stories of the Christ of faith which are found in the New Testament and in other early Christian writings), and those stories of the Christ of faith, and the mysterious God we reach out to, seeking to adore and serve? I referred briefly to the parables and other sayings of the Jesus of history. In these he speaks of his belief (as a member of the ancient community of Israel) that God can be trusted to be both infinitely loving and endlessly forgiving. The Christ of faith, believed to be both Saviour and divine, embodies these values of love and forgiveness. There would have been no Christ of faith if there had not been, first, a Jesus of history. However, if the stories of the Christ of faith are not to be taken in a literal and historical sense, they can still have another sort of truth.

The Christ of faith points to the mysterious God of infinite love and endless forgiveness, whom both Jesus and his followers had believed in, and who is still believed and trusted in today. The stories of the Christ of faith are saying that we are found loveable, forgivable and reconcilable by God. This is what is believed to be true. It is this same truth of faith that is metaphorically referred to in the Pauline saying "in Christ God was reconciling the world to himself" (2 Corinthians 5.19). The stories of the Christ of faith telling of his birth, death and resurrection are metaphors of faith that transcend the literal and point us to realities beyond our normal range of knowledge.

Confusing the stories of the Jesus of history and the stories of the Christ of faith has caused immense trouble for the churches. It has not been easy for many people to make the distinction between them; particularly since the Christ of faith stories (about the coming and return of a Son of God as Saviour, Mediator and Divine person) are intimately connected to the stories of the Jesus of history, the man from Nazareth. One example would be the stories of Jesus' resurrection appearances. Many Christians would still see them as historical reports, albeit of an unusual and unique event. Mary, so the faith story goes, met the risen Christ and saw him with her own eyes; here was the man she had come to know and love over the last few years and who had been put to death by crucifixion on the previous Friday. The disciples had a meal with the risen Christ; again he is the same person that they had shared supper with on the previous Thursday evening. As was noted earlier, only God can raise someone back to life after he or she has died. If the resurrection stories really were descriptions of historical events, then it would prove the existence of God, which believers do not accept to be possible. We believe God exists, we do not know it. So this means, to my mind, that the resurrection stories are faith stories and belong to the Christ of faith stories, stories whose truth is not dependent on these stories being taken literally, as descriptions of historical events, but rather is dependent on a metaphorical and symbolical interpretation; pointing, as they can, to what we believe to be true about God and his love and forgiveness. Indeed, even to speak of historical objectivity is to use a post-Enlightenment concept and, therefore, to introduce a reverse anachronism to the 1st century. Many scholars consider that 1st century writers were primarily concerned with expressing meaning rather historical literalism in the modern sense.

I believe that Jesus would be both amazed and horrified if he were able to come back and meet us today. As a practicing Jew, he would have had no idea that a new religion had been founded in his name, nor of the beliefs formulated about him, nor of the forms of worship in which his name and his story figure so prominently. He would feel very remote from our world and culture. Yet despite all the differences, he shares some fundamental values with those who in one way or another sense that they have some significant things in common with him. His religion was that of ancient Israel, of 1st century CE Judaism, and in Temple or in synagogue, he found vehicles to use to convey his worship of Israel's God. These vehicles may be quite different from those used in Christian worship, but what they transport is much the same: praise and gratitude, penitence and remorse, bewilderment and pain, trust and rage, dependence and responsibility. Many of the ethical and spiritual values of ancient Israel's faith are found in the Christian way of life too: peace, forgiveness, justice, compassion, hope, accountability, freedom, dignity, worth, love, and co-operation. He believed that we live in a moral universe and that ultimately we are accountable for our lives to a moral God. It is in this sense that we should understand the traditional image of the kingdom of God.

Silence and God

Is there a way to understand the Incarnation which takes us away from having to use the Greek and Latin philosophical concepts of the first five centuries CE which suggested it was plausible to believe that in the one "person" there could be both a human person and a divine person? I share with others a belief that the church is in transition as it continues to move from a pre-scientific supernatural world in which its creeds were formulated into a modern world. Space needs to be provided for fresh thought that may not appear to be orthodox, but may be a bridge leading to a new orthodoxy. This is how the church's intellectual life has progressed in the past. There are many examples of how, over differing issues, some members' thinking went ahead of the "corporate faith" of the church as an institution, and then later on the "corporate faith" caught up with its membership.

Karl Barth described theology as rational wrestling with mystery. Theologians do their work of thinking about God, as do "ordinary believers," by using a range of different analogies, metaphors and symbols. Two of the ways in which the relationship between human beings and God have been imagined involve thinking in both personal and non-personal analogies. Using a non-personal analogy we can think of God as like an ocean; and we, and all the rest of her creation, are the waves on the ocean. Speaking like this, we can state a belief that we live in God or say that God is in everything. Using the images of ocean and wave poetically we can say that God (as ocean) knows the life of the wave from the inside, God is in the wave. Here is a way to express that the divinity of God was intimately connected with the humanity of the Jesus of history, that God knew human life and experience from the "inside", by being so connected to Jesus. Clearly, however, such a connection is unique only in the sense that each human being's life is believed to be unique.

On the other hand, to use personal analogies is to think in terms of an "I-Thou" relationship, as Martin Buber described it. Here God is thought of as like a person. We stand before such an all-embracing God and are found to be loveable, forgivable and reconcilable. We also stand before such a moral God as beings who have been created as moral beings, who are held accountable and responsible. We are created in love, for love, and by a God of love.

While a considerable number of members of the Christian churches no longer find it credible to believe in an afterlife and might interpret concepts such as "resurrection" in terms of this life's experiences; I find myself still believing in life after death. To believe in life after death is not something that I can prove, any more than I can prove the existence of God. However, because I believe that we are infinitely precious to God, and loved and valued beyond our imaginings, I still find it plausible to believe that there is meaning beyond death in a new moral universe, which we cannot begin to conceive. It is highly mysterious; but, such is the goodness of God, that I believe and trust that all evil will finally be vanquished (but in that deeply demanding way of "overcoming evil by doing good").

We are social beings whose humanity is significantly dependent on our relationships not just with each other, but with the cosmos and its Creator. I find it appalling that so many of us, particularly in the so-called developed world, go on daring to live lifestyles in painful contradiction to our professed beliefs and values in a global village full of the horror, humiliation, and neglect of others' basic needs as people. The sociologist, Francis Fukuyama, in his book, called *The Great Disruption*, on the transition from an industrial age to an information age, wrote that he thinks that the mainline religions will see a decrease in the importance of the creedal aspects of their evolving faith traditions. A religious tradition is sometimes described as having four components: creed, cult, code and community. He has suggested that people will go on joining the mainline churches for several reasons. They will want to belong to a community with a value system (a code) that their children can be brought up in. They will want a community with rituals and resonance that connect deeply with the past. He believes that there will be more emphasis on ortho-praxy (right practice) and much less on orthodoxy (right belief), as has his-torically been the case in both Judaism and Islam; and the creedal aspect of religious traditions will be recognised for what it is: a rational wrestling with mystery where there can legitimately be considerable diversity in the specu-lation undergone.

Increasingly, stories both of the Jesus of history and of the Christ of faith will almost certainly function like the great plays of someone like Shakespeare. For generations, people have found that a production of *Hamlet*, *Macbeth* or *King Lear* has spoken with power and meaning to them and has helped them understand a little more of the mystery of what it means to be human. So too, in all probability, the Christian stories will continue to speak with power and meaning to our human condition.

Even in the pre-scientific age of interventionist gods people were aware of the hiddenness, silence, and mystery of such gods. In our modern age, this hiddenness, silence and mystery are more apparent. It is as if God presents herself/himself as an absent God. In the aftermath of the Holocaust, the sense of the silence, absence, and unknowability of God has pervaded the modern era and fills the work of a poet like R.S. Thomas and was reflected upon deeply by Simone Weil. It raises the question of who are we in the face of such mystery.

Conclusion

I have written of religions, elsewhere, as being like motorways which are constantly in need of another lane. In other words, I am saying that it is nor-mal for there to be much diversity within an evolving religious tradition. Some will travel along a conservative lane, some down an evangelical lane, some down a liberal or radical lane. As new understandings and interpreta-tions emerge, more lanes are required to accommodate those journeying with fresh ideas. Ultimately to live with faith is admit that we do not know for sure about God nor indeed about the rightness of our ethical commitment. God may or may not exist. We remain problematic to ourselves, and life retains its mysterious quality. Part of our identity, wrote John Caputo, is that we do not know who we are. W.H. Auden thought that one good way to live with this sense of the mystery of who we really are is by laughter, which is both a protest and an acceptance.

The broad church that I believe is important to maintain will continue to contain diversity of thinking and believing as the stories of Christianity, preserved and interpreted within the Christian community, are passed on to the next generation. In particular, the understandings of the Christ of faith stories will to, my mind, continue to require to be received with tolerance, broadmindedness, generosity of spirit and mutual respect, as believers remain mindful that nobody knows for certain when it comes to the things of God. I hope the seven judges of the Court of the General Synod of the Church of Ireland will have these things in mind when they sit to deliberate and decide on their judgment.

Andrew Furlong studied theology at Trinity College Dublin and Cambridge University. He worked as priest for many years in Zimbabwe and now lives in Trim, Co Meath.

FIVE POEMS

—

John Burnside

—

AT MENNO-HOF

I kept getting lost on the way,
though the roads were straight
and the land around me
close to featureless,

but why would one barn
stand out from the rest:
the Hutterites and Amish in their
black-varnished, horse-drawn buggies

slowing the traffic;
their butter-coloured lanterns lit
at crossings, like a history of warmth
upheld against the year's first wave of snow.

Only a flurry of sleet
when a band of deer
broke from the woods that morning
and shied away,

but thick and fast enough by afternoon
to slur the roads, erasing signs and fences,
reducing settlements and homesteads to a blur
of smoke and light.

Surely it made more sense
to miss the place,
that single farm the faithful set aside
for visitors, to keep the cameras

and tourist buses from the Amish homes,
making a museum of their lives
to separate the holy
from the charmed.

Was this the only way: to live apart,
to tend your fields and bring your children up
in righteousness, and let the world outside
go straight to hell?

I would have asked, but everyone I met
was too polite,
the history they told so well-rehearsed
I never quite believed that they believed

it mattered: not
the founders, or the exiles for their faith,
not God, or Scripture,
only what they had

to hand: the light machinery
and grain stores,
or the fields for miles around
tended and blessed.

My guide, a youngish woman in a cap,
would answer any questions I might have
during the tour.
I tried to think of something that would let her

wander from the script and say the words
she never spoke aloud, but all she did
was smile her practised smile
and move me on.

She'd set herself apart
from me and mine
and nothing I could ever do or say
would touch the wider life that she had learned

from Gospel
and the farming catalogues,
the names of cultivars and types of feed,
the miracles, the Sermon on the Mount.

Yet later,
on the drive back to Detroit,
I thought of her awake, and sitting up
beside a window, quiet in the dark,

less certain than she'd seemed, or less prosaic,
her dead loves brushing the glass like migrant birds
and all she kept apart – a name, a song –
gone missing, in the first storm of the winter.

UKSA*

i.m. Nils-Aslak Valkeapaa

I dreamt I was in a house that was not mine;
and in that house there was a single door
blue as the sky reflected in standing water:

a door that was neither death, nor the life to come,
but something like a puzzle, or a game
that children play, on snowbound afternoons,

edging towards a silence on the stairs
or some high window, where a copper bowl
is filling with that gleam cast by the snow,

that pool of light, empty of wind and time,
where souls begin again, naked and bright,
and blue as the sky reflected in standing water.

The word uksa *in Sami is equivalent to the English word* door.

DUNDEE TENEMENTS IN WINTER

Where nothing is, or nothing but new snow
falling between the buildings like the space
behind the scenery, the lit backstage

where actors vanish, written from the plot
as accidental deaths, or passers-by
walking away from the action, no longer required,

there is a gap through which the mind could slip
as smoothly as out downstairs a neighbour's cat
slips through a gap in the fence and disappears

where nothing is, the angels of the yard
filling with snow, the empty drying green
a theatre of absence where our lines

remain unspoken, though we say the words
the way they were rehearsed, turned to the house
and missing one another, as the script

dictates: our sole and obvious concern
the witnesses we never hear or see
silent beyond the lights, where nothing is.

FOXGLOVES

If there is any miracle in things
it comes so fine and inexplicable
that nothing shows at all beyond the smoke
of twilight, when I come into the room
and leave the lamp unlit, the curtains drawn.

The room is still and empty in the glass
where foxgloves turn to darkness as the evening
thickens; and my face is not a face
but light and texture, greenleaf, sparrowsong,

the anything and nothing of a world
where home arrives from nowhere over years
of pause and sidelong glance and looks away,

the lovers we might have been, out in the dark,
not looking back to see the light go on,
or out beyond the pale of leaves and grass
the place where shadows touch: guiltless, unwitnessed.

THE WOUNDED ANGEL

after Hugo Simberg

Later, they would lie about the angel.
The older boy, a lad with cropped blond hair,
saying he hadn't found it; the other
constantly changing his story, a tale
of joy transformed to something like a kill,
the blood thick on his hands, a cry of fear
that might have been his own.
                              Nothing was there
when he led them back to where he'd heard the fall
as heartbeats, whimpers, memories of snow:
how, suddenly, it shudders from a roof
and blocks your way – and how you always know

that something else was waiting, some bright grief,
waiting and long-expected, almost known,
inches away, and just ten yards from home.

The angel could fly but won't. It could
also look around but keeps its eyes glued
to the ground. It wants to be helped.

Marjatta Levanto

It wants to be helped.
           Think of the birds
that flutter in at windows: pigeons; starlings;
a swallow, one bright afternoon, whose wings
threaded our bedroom with flight, then disappeared.
They come to us, as angels sometimes come
from fields or riverbanks, or some blank yard
we know from childhood, come to be restored
with skill and love. They are what we resume
when darkness falls: the selves we scarcely dream
for fear of losing minds still half-possessed,
still tenanted by daylight and our own
accomplished fear; ourselves when we are blessed
with wounds no hand can heal; ourselves alone;
inches away, or just ten yards from home.

for Kirsi Korhonen

John Burnside's most recent volume is The Locust Room *(Cape, 2001). He lives in Fife,
Scotland.*

AUTHENTICITY

—

Deirdre Madden

—

A chapter from a new novel.

This is why Julia thinks she became an artist: because of a game she used to play with her father when she was a child. He devised it himself to occupy her on winter evenings. He would show her a picture, usually from an old greetings card or an outdated calendar, for a short, fixed period of time, and then she would have to describe it to him in as much detail as she could recall. She was good at this game. Her mind became quick and sharp; it was difficult for her father to find images complex enough to challenge her. She remembers one in particular, an old Christmas card, with a scene of men and women in old-fashioned clothes, skating on a frozen river, and wonders now at her father's patience, sitting peering at it as she reeled off as much as she could recall. From time to time he would ask her leading questions to nudge her along. "The man you mentioned on the left, skating between the two women: can you describe how they're dressed?" How vexed she was when she said that both the women were in scarlet dresses and her father said no, it was the man who was wearing a red coat.

When she was too familiar with the image to have any further use for it in the game, still she liked looking at it. The painting had a peculiar atmosphere, frozen, golden, wistful, that drew her into the world of the picture in the way a photograph could never have done. She used to stare and stare at it, and imagine that if she looked at the picture long enough and hard enough, she would be able to break its spell. Then she would be able to see into that lost world, and the diminutive skaters would begin to move across the ice. Some of them would slip and fall, and those who were shown as having tumbled over in the painting would pick themselves up, and wobble away on their bladed feet, and the vanes of the icy windmill would turn, and the tiny crow would fly from the tree.

Her father noticed that she got enormous pleasure from the picture, and what he did next was a stroke of pure genius: from a barrow of second-hand books in a street market he brought home a large book full of colour reproductions of old-master paintings. They used it for the memory game, and even she felt that she had met her match in Bruegel's proverb painting: the running egg! The roof slated with fruit tarts! But afterwards, she was quite happy to sit on her own and leaf through the book, looking at the pictures and entering those other worlds, as she saw them, where things were similar to the world she knew, but different too, in a way she found impossible to define but which she knew to be real. In this frame of mind, it was not the most detailed pictures that interested her, but the still life paintings. A wooden platter of curled, frail wafers and a bottle of wine sheathed in wicker. Lobsters and oysters, a cut lemon, its pared peel hanging off the edge of the table. A streaked tulip, translucent grapes and a songbird's nest. She stared and stared at these things, wondering how it was that they seemed more exact, more true, than the apples that grew in their orchard, than the cakes and biscuits her father provided for them. Her beloved father! He acted from the purest of motives; did not wish her to "get on" in life, was not covertly trying to educate her. He had handed her the book with the words, "You'll enjoy that."

But even this was not enough. He led her on, further and further, like a blind man leading his companion to the very gates of a palace. "What do you like so much about these pictures?" he asked her one day, glancing over her shoulder. "The things in them are realer than real things," she replied, which she knew her father would not challenge or ridicule, even though she didn't expect him to understand. He nodded gravely and continued to stare at the page for a few moments before pointing to one particular picture and saying, "Just imagine someone sitting down and painting that."

It was a casual observation but she took it as an instruction. For days afterwards, she studied intently the painting he had been looking at when he had spoken. Two chased silver vessels, two drinking glasses, one long, ribbed, upright and full; the other elaborate, fluted and empty, lying tilted on the table-top; and two plates, one of which bore an elaborate fruit pie and the spoon which had broken it up to serve it. The other plate held the portion that had been served, and stood at the edge of the table, so precariously positioned that it looked as if it might at any time fall forward, spilling the pastry and fruit on the floor. (Because there was a floor, there had to be a floor, didn't there, even if she couldn't see it.) What else? A few scattered hazelnuts and walnuts, a few shattered nutshells and a knife with a bone handle; the whole bathed in a rich buttery golden light that made much of the curves of the tilted fluted glass, and the soft lights hidden in the silver vessels.

The artist had set all these things out on the table, spent a considerable peri-od of time arranging them to pleasing effect, and then begun to paint. She thought of the concentration it must have required, of how he would have stared at the things to get to their essence, but how he then managed to trans-late that to the canvas in paint was beyond her understanding. She could imag-ine, though, his thrill of satisfaction when the work was complete, in that short interval when the two existed together: the arrangement of objects on the table and, a few feet away, the painting that would preserve them for ever, per-fected. And then the painter would have broken that link between the objects and their image, by leaning over and lifting up the tall ribbed glass, and the plate that contained the portion of pie. She imagined that he topped up the glass of wine, and perhaps served himself a more generous portion of the dessert. Maybe he took the silver spoon with which to eat.

She knows that he went out into the garden of his house, for by now she has entered so fully into his world that she can feel how stiff his fingers are, and his eyes are strained. For all that, he has the deep satisfaction of work well done, done as best he possibly could. She can feel the sun on his neck and shoulders, taste the short pastry and the sharpness of the apples and blackberries that the pie contained. She imagines him chewing, drinking, wiping the back of his hand across his mouth and lifting his face to the sun, its power and heat.

So deep was her pleasure in the scene she had conjured up that she decided to share something of it with her father. "I like to think," she said to him, "about how, when the painter had finished this picture, he ate the pie."

His response knocked her flat."Maybe there never was a pie," he said. "Maybe the painter made it all up."

For a moment she literally couldn't speak, so extraordinary was the idea. "What do you mean?" she said at last. "How could there not have been a pie?"

"Maybe he just imagined one from all the pies he had seen and eaten in his life. He might have painted it from a sort of picture he had in his head, rather than from a real thing. If he was as good a painter as all that he probably just made up what he painted, having in his mind all the pies — and glasses and knives and tables and silver cups — that he had ever seen in his life. Don't you think that's possible?"

She didn't know. The idea had never occurred to her. She only knew that what he said destroyed at a stroke the pleasing image she had cultivated in her own mind, of the man with paint on his hands and crumbs on his lips, sitting in the sunshine, as delighted with himself and his work as she had been. But the man she was left with now, taking his ease having finished making a pie out of nothing but paint and imagination: that someone could do that seemed more extraordinary still. That night she couldn't get to sleep for thinking about it, and she raised the subject again with her father the following morn-ing.

"You remember this picture?" and she pointed it out again in the book. "Are you sure it's as you say?"

"I never said I was sure of anything," he replied. "And what does it matter? There's a pie there now made of paint and canvas, what more do you want? What do you mean by real, anyway?" He leafed through the book. "I don't know why you like those ones so much," he said. "They're too ordinary. I never see the sense when people go on about something being lifelike in a painting. Where's the point in that? This is the sort of picture I love," he said. He was pointing at a picture of a bearded man suspended in midair, and she could see what her father meant when he said he wondered if the angels who were clinging to him, his legs gripped firmly in their arms, were trying to carry him off into the sky, or if he had wished to ascend to the heavens before his time was due and the angels had been dispatched to haul him back down to earth where he belonged.

"You're not going to tell me that's real," he said, "that it all happened in front of the person who painted the picture."

"How do you know?" The idea of just such a scene delighted her, and seemed to her mind no less likely than the painter of the still life having no objects before him to copy. She loved the thought of the painter working at his easel with the group of figures floating before him, beams of light coming through the ceiling to illuminate the scene, a light breeze keeping their vivid draperies in an exact, billowing arrangement.

"So what happened then when the painter stopped painting?" her father challenged her.

"They floated down to the floor of the room and rested themselves. And then all of them – the saint, the angels and the painter – sat down together and ate a fruit pie that didn't exist."

Deirdre Madden's most recent novel is One by One into the Darkness *(Faber, 1995).* Authenticity *will be published by Faber later this year. This extract is published courtesy of the author and publisher.*

DEPARTURES, RETURNS

—

Bruce Allen

—

Time near a Japanese pond.

MARCH 12

Four-thirty in the afternoon. Dusky cold. Just-visible shades of amber in murky gray clouds threatening rain. Though I was busy and should have been glad to say inside, something called me away from my desk work, out of the house and down to Shinobazu Pond.

I didn't hear the call so much as I felt it. Something was in the air.

I know such talk bothers some people. Secret callings. Presences and vibrations – it smacks of the pseudo-mystical. And yet, my tutored scepticism about such things notwithstanding – quite forcibly I was called to stop my work and get outside in the dank late winter dusk.

I'd been sensing that it was probably nearing the ducks' migration time and I didn't want to miss their departure. Getting ready to leave Tokyo on a long flight of my own. It's likely that my senses have been somehow pre-tuned. Sceptics will argue that such callings are just the workings of unseen yet rationally-explainable cues often internally produced. Perhaps subliminally-noticed sounds had been reaching me in my house a mile away from the pond. Over the din of city arteries filled with rush hour trucks and cars.

Approaching the park I could feel the airborne tremor of eerie high-pitched vibrations increasing yet the first section of pond was almost completely deserted. Had I arrived too late ? It still seemed too early – still too cold here, let alone up in Siberia, Mongolia, Alaska or wherever the ducks might be going. Where were they ? The energy in the air built up as I walked closer to the farther reed-covered section of the pond.

And then a wave shot by overhead – a wave, or phalanx, or squadron.

These were not the same ducks I had been watching through winter. No longer those plodding, waddling ducks I had been feeding – those tame city-dwellers who almost got stepped on as they sauntered along the pavement – these were beings suddenly united by some tremendous force, moving amidst a unified field of energy. As I came closer, the sound that I had been feeling, yet barely hearing, became more distinctly audible. It was a high whistling trilling, energizing and electrifying, different from any sound I had noticed previously from the ducks, as if expressing a will to allow only the minimum loss of energy in flight, yet at the same time unable to repress a secret of primal joy.

The passing V-forms of ducks are now barely visible overhead in the fading light. A hundred or more crows, normally the bosses of the pond, wingling along in their loping, prepossessing sort of flight, are suddenly dumbfounded by this new phenomenon. Barely able to evade the rushing, oncoming phalanxes, they stall out in mid-air, falling away clumsily.

About fifty ducks wing by, and then another group, and another. As thirty minutes or so pass, a dozen squadrons of ducks make their final great arc about the perimeter of the pond, as if to take one last look; perhaps to lock the image and location of the pond into their deepest memories, or to implant them in the genes of a generation yet to be born. Then they gather speed, crying out their whirring farewell calls as they go, and are off to the northland.

The pintails' take-offs are strikingly different from what they have been all winter. Before, they left the water with slower, scooping wing flaps that lifted them quickly into the air. Today, they remain closer to the water, flapping with shorter, faster wing beats. Wings tripping along the surface of the pond for forty meters or so before gaining altitude, almost bumping the heads of swimming ducks, they rise in an act of coordination and fierce gracefulness. A deep sounding of *tiii-tiii-tiiii-tiiii-tiiit-tiiii-i-i-i-tt* surrounds the pond, as if issuing from a giant tympanum formed by the water. The sound follows them, higher and higher, farther and farther, until it gradually fades away far off in the north.

At least two thousand ducks remain on the pond now; probably less than half the number of a week ago. A deep stillness settles, and in the gathering darkness the remaining ducks – pintails, tufted ducks, and a few shovelers – are dark shadows among the lotus and reed stems, made visible only by the reflections of the bright electric blues, reds, yellows and greens, of the neon signs circling the park. The carnival-like luminescence lends an oddly-fitting contrast to this timeless ritual unfolding deep within the city.

MARCH 15

I'm caught up in two departures: that of the birds, and the one I will soon be making. With twenty-five minutes to spare before catching the train to the airport, I check my bags at the station and go out to the pond for a few minutes. Brilliant first spring sun plays on a few early-blossoming cherry trees. Of thousands of ducks, only a few hundred are left. Mostly I see the black and white markings of tufted ducks, and the reds and greens of a few pochards and shovelers.

With most of the pintails now gone, the ranks of the other birds appear to have swelled. In the past few weeks the greens, chestnuts and iridescent overtones of the shovelers seem to have sharpened. Among the tufted ducks, their royal purples and magentas have deepened. Similar changes have brightened the chestnut-maroon-mahogany tones of the pochards.

Perhaps the heads of the tufted ducks are bobbing with a little added perkiness, yet this could come just from the good spring weather, which lends a similar energy to people walking around the park. But something important must be going on within their consciousness, sub-consciousness, blood, muscles, genes – a combining of molecular changes, cellular ripenings, muscular sharpenings and mental focusings – all serving to marshal the commitment for their departure.

Since I was a young child and first rode on an airplane I have loved watching from the windows of planes. Today, I have the luxury of gazing out over the vast, melting, snowy Siberian plains, crossed and re-crossed by endless loops of meandering rivers and lakes. I wonder if this is the land the pintails are heading for. They spend their winters in Tokyo on a small pond crowded with thousands of other ducks and surrounded by millions of people and their vehicles, buildings and all – and then their summers up here amidst millions of acres of tundra. How can they handle such transitions and extremes?

As the plane gains on the sun, midday slowly unfolds. Seen from above, Siberia appears as a huge dreamscape wilderness. Countless rivers wend their contorted ways across the seemingly endless flatlands. The records of millions of years are written in thousands of doodling loops and oxbows. Strangled and stranded, and then rebridged, only to be breached again and re-broken; billowing and contracting, they coil and uncoil upon themselves. Here the secrets of fluid dynamics are written in large strokes across the face of the earth, following the slightest changes in elevation.

I imagine that in the early years of air travel, passengers used to be more interested in, even awed by the views out the windows. But today, with in-flight movies to entertain us, we are requested to keep the blinds shut. We are encouraged to buy at the duty free time and watch videos and sleep on time.

Looking out of the window has become marginal, distracting and even ill-mannered. What only a hundred years ago was a sight reserved for the gods has become something taken for granted. A vision we might look on with a trepidation similar to that of the ancients who feared to pronounce the name of the Divine.

What lies outside the window of the plane is an intimation of the entire history of the earth. Some of its parts move by as fast as the air, clouds, winds and jet planes – all whisking by in an instant. Others move more slowly; as liquids, seas and flowing rivers. Others move as lumbering, semi-liquid fields of snow and ice; sagging and melting in the spring sun. Still others remain more in place; as semi-solids and forms slowly disintegrating. The rock solid mountains too are crumbling and flowing organisms. Their tell-tale streams of dust and debris are signs, marking the snows in sepia, gray and rust. They stain first slope, then stream, then river, then lake and oceans. Time itself is revealed and recorded in the footprints of water, ice, rock, dust and silt.

OCTOBER 24

Cycles and circles are the universal rediscovery of all people who watch the seasons. This seemingly simple – at first even trivial – idea turns within us and grows in complexity as we age. And as we become more aware of this complexity, strangely we are also drawn back to simplicity. In circles we find ourselves belonging more closely to the world.

Though the cycle of the year has no universally designated point of beginning or end, the return of the ducks marks a major turning point in the life of the pond. After half a year's absence, as the plants fade in color and settle into rest, the ducks bring new life.

When I first arrived at the pond today I had been thinking that not many ducks had returned for this time of year. The pond and sky seemed empty. And then, far in the distance, something that first appeared like a swarm of tiny gnats slowly grew larger, until they finally became distinguishable as a group of ducks, fluttering wildly and straight toward me. Then another group approached. And then a third.

Watching, I sense among the ducks a nervous reluctance to settle down on the water right away. As with their departures in spring, it appears they prefer to touch down at dusk, during the transition between day and night. They circle around again and again, apparently confirming that this is the right place, though they must be bone-tired after their long flights, and eager to rest.

I jog around the pond's perimeter, shivering in my sweaty running clothes, hoping to see more birds touching down. It gets too cold and dark to stay longer, and I leave for home with most of them still circling above. But with the ducks returning, somehow I feel relieved and reassured. I cannot help but feel myself taking a small part in the year's turning.

Developing feelings for cycles and circles takes time, in part because it requires that we have gone through a number of them ourselves. The feeling for the turn of the year comes not from lectures, sermons, or reading, but from being outside, watching and anticipating. The resonance comes from the ground and from the sky.

When I am able to focus my attention more fully on the cycles of the seasons I feel there is something different about my thinking and perceptions – a sense of release, of recognition and connection, a hint of the way our ancestors thought throughout most of our long, body-and-soul-forming past. Thinking our lives through circles changes the way we perceive the world, particularly because it alters the way we consider the nature of time. Our linear conception is, at least for a moment, shifted back toward the circular time understood by people in earlier ages.

In modern civilization's brief instant of cosmological time, we have learned to see ourselves as living largely outside of the returning circles of time – outside the cycles of seasons, crops, weather and generations of life and death. Although at least some of our clocks still follow a circular pattern, and our calendars repeat fairly regularly every twelve months, our understanding of time follows more what we see on a time-line chart of history, or on a digital watch. We have come to think of time as running perpetually forward, without ever doubling back on itself and offering us return. We see ourselves as bravely striking our ways forward – rarely considering that we may sometimes be treading our own tracks.

A linear time orientation may be necessary for the functioning of modern technological and commercial society. But if we think only in terms of linear time, it becomes easy for us to ignore the underlying cyclical nature of life. Although it is difficult for us to shed our culturally assimilated sense of time, we can sometimes shift ourselves into, or at least borrow from, a more circular conception of time. These "circular moments" are when we feel most at home in the world.

The ecologist and philosopher David Abram has written extensively on the relation between our changing conception of time and our loss of vital contact with the natural world. He speaks of the world perceived by people who live in circular time as a "sensuous cosmos." People living in such a world feel the natural elements of the earth as being alive and as communicating with them, even for those of us who live in modernized societies. Watching and participating in the cycles of the earth allows us to return to a vibrant, communicative, interconnected cosmos. In doing so, our looking at nature becomes not just a moment of relaxing, but one of re-living and re-creating.

———

"From a cosmic point of view, the velocity of human thought is more or less fixed – attuned in sometimes useful ways to the velocity of an apple falling from a tree, to the rate of the earth's spin, to the leaping speed of a predacious coyote, to the gentle passing of the seasons, to the wavelengths of visible light and audible sound. We are defined by these velocities, among others. You could imagine species living on quite different timetables. In fact, you can see them: bumblebees and bristlecone pines, inhabiting temporal planes that barely intersect our own. Careful though. Speed is not who you are."

James Gleick, *Faster*

Bruce Allen lives in Toyko. This extract is from a work-in-progress, Shinobazu: Notes from the Urban Wild.

THE SOUND OF THE PAST

———

Tim Robinson

———

The first fractal of a new work-in-progress...

A small concrete cross stands by beside the road that follows the Ballynahinch River to the sea. The proprietor of The Angler's Return, two bends of the road and the river farther on, tells me it marks where one of the gillies fell dead of a heart attack. "Wasn't it good that he died looking out at the river he'd worked on all his life?" she added. But from the time of the tyrannical Tadhg O'Flaherty, who forbade fishing in the lake by his castle, to the fish-ins of the Gaelic Civil Rights Movement in the sixties, the fisheries of Connemara have been occasions of class resentment. Perhaps the man died cursing the river that had brought him a lifetime of midge-bites and the condescension of the rich.

Whatever the burden of the gillie's last breath, it was dispersed into the air to be degraded by the hiss of rain or eroded molecule by molecule in the Brownian fidget of drifting pollen-grains, and captured, a little of it, by the tilting, spilling, cups and saucers of the water surface, dissolved, hurried under the old bridge at Tuaim Beola and added to the sea. So one can imagine it infinitesimally present in, and persuasively interpreting, the sough (which however is not a sighing) of the Ballynahinch woods, the clatter (not a chattering) of the mountain streamlets, the roar (not a raging) of the waves against the shore.

These indefinite but enormous noises are frequent in Connemara. Sometimes from my doorstep on a still night, I become aware that the silence is set in a velvet background like a jewel in a display case, a hush that, when attended to, becomes inexorable. It is compounded of the crash of breakers along distant strands, variously delayed, attenuated, echoed and re-echoed. A frequently falsified but never quite discredited forewarning of gales, it is an effect that, from our perspective here, precedes its cause: a depression moving across the Atlantic and advancing its concentric rollers towards our coast. By the morning, perhaps, a tumult of air will be battering the windows, all its wavelengths, from the vast heft of gusts over the hill that half shelters us, to the spasms of the garden shrubs and the fluting of a dry leaf caught between two stones, merging into one toneless bulk noise. Going here and there in thought through the pandemonium, only the most analytic listening can disengage its elements: shriek of sedge bent double out on the heath, grind of shingle sucked back by the reflux, slow chamfering of a stone's edge by blown sandgrains.

Such vast, complex sounds are produced by fluid generalities impacting on intricate concrete particulars. As the wave or wind breaks around a headland, a wood, a boulder, a treetrunk, a pebble, a twig, a wisp of seaweed or a microscopic hair on a leaf, the streamlines are split apart, flung against each other, compressed in narrows, knotted in vortices. The ear constructs another wholeness out of the reiterated fragmentation of pitches, and it can be terrible, this wide range of frequencies coalescing into something approaching the auditory chaos and incoherence that sound-engineers call "white noise": zero of information-content, random interference obliterating all messages, utterly dire, a metaphysical horror made audible, sometimes dinned into prisoners' heads to drive them mad in the cells of their brains.

Similar too is the sound of the past, the wreck of time's grand flow in tortuous passages. It is not the sound of history, though. History has rhythms, tunes, sometimes even harmonies; but the sound of the past is an agonistic atomicity. Sometimes, rarely, a scrap of a voice can be caught from the universal damage, but it may only be an artifact of the imagination, a confection of rumours. Chance decides what is obliterated and what survives if only to be distorted and misheard. Of the gillie who died by the river, I know nothing more, but may yet find out something. But who, for one of the crowding shades besieging my book, was Cuach na Coille, the "cuckoo of the wood"? I hear of her from a single source only, and only this: that she was a beautiful horsewoman, who lived in Derryclare Wood. I fear that nobody living can tell me more. Even in the ancient forest itself, where slender shafts of sunlight look almost material enough to cast a greenish shadow, and sometimes in the restless canopy a cuckoo claims to be "here/there", the mysterious horsewoman does not appear, tantalising with her untold tale. Hers, with his, may stand for all Connemara's abolished voices.

Tim Robinson, cartographer, naturalist and writer, lives in Roundstone, Co Galway. His two-volume Stones of Aran *(Lilliput Press) appeared in 1986 and 1995.*

TOP OF THE TIDE

Michael Viney

Together on the beach.

My ashes, I like to think, would settle with instant self-effacement into the beach at the foot of the hill, flying perhaps like a skein of wind-blown sand, then sifting invisibly among the fragments of other worn-out lives.

At the middle of the beach, on a plateau, there is a drift of broken shells that gets richer the closer you look: tiny scallop fans in pink and orange, minute cowries like rolled-up finger-prints; curved tiles from the broken domes of sea urchins, violet and rose. Here, I imagine, a broody ringed plover might nestle down to lay her eggs, enfolding crumbs of my skull into the warmth of her white breast-feathers.

The beach has had twenty-five years of my life – our lives – back and forth along the tide-line. Our window-sills have silted up with a sandy bric-a-brac of shells and seeds; driftwood and coconuts pile up in the corners; segments of whale, stone-grey, stand mossily about in the garden.

When the hillside was thick with human settlement – thatched cabins, swirling turf-smoke – the strand, too, was familiar and domestic, shell-sand and seaweed a dressing for every potato-ridge. Now, abandoned and grassed-over, the ridges catch the winter sun like swathes of green corduroy, and shell-sand leaves the beach in tractor-loads. For ten months or more of the year, tyre-marks and distant hand-waves are our only human contact on the shore.

There are other sorts, sometimes sublime. Otters, free to hunt by day, emerge from the breakers with flapping fish and run up into the dunes to eat them. We have met, on occasion, but, like the fox that sets its trail a head of us along the morning tideline, the otters prefer to leave us messages in morse code. They cross the tracks of seabirds, fieldmice, beetles: the small print and footnotes of a privileged communication.

What the tideline has to talk about is chance. Of my being there at all, of course, among all possible destinies, pacing an edge on the Earth that is never in the same place twice; and of the chance in all the other lives remaindered among the tumbled kelp in a flotsam of calcium and gristle. Some of these confront the soul with such monstrous evolutions of chance that the horizon rears up like a tsunami, blotting out all hope of heaven. Two of their species may even touch down, gently, on the same tide.

The beautiful violet sea-snail, *Janthina*, arrives from warmer waters, and only exceptionally in one piece, its emptiness a whorled and fragile thimble of gentian light. It is an ocean drifter, a snail suspended upside down from the mirror of the ocean surface and borne along by a silvery raft of bubble-wrap it has manufactured, one bubble at a time, by trapping wind in a skin of exuded mucus.

By-the-wind sailors, *Velella velella*, often arrive in thousands at the tideline, a glistening shipwreck of rainbowed oval discs a few centimetres across. On each, a tiny, diaphanous sail is set diagonally, mostly (in the Atlantic) NW–SE but also NE–SW. Thus, propelled by the same wind, some will sail leftwards and others to the right, dispersing the species according to prevailing winds instead of being massed in doldrums and tangled in Sargasso weed.

The cast-up discs are all that is left of the deep-blue jellyfish that were once suspended beneath them, feeding on young fish and pelagic organisms caught by its stinging tentacles on its random passage through the sea. The jellyfish, on the other hand, are the particular prey of *Janthina*, a gastropod drifting to the same random compass. They meet by bobbing blindly against each other, like toy boats on a park pond, and one eats the other.

In our decades of beachcombing, Ethna and I have found just two *Janthina*, resting within a pace of each other and delivered by the furthest wavelet of the same slow spring tide. That we found them together and together seemed some reassurance of special favour, against all odds.

Michael Viney writes a weekly column, "Another Life," for The Irish Times. *His month-by-month journal of life in County Mayo,* A Year's Turning *(Blackstaff Press), appeared in 1996.*

ON THE MORAL RIGHT TO PUBLISH

Eileen Battersby

A rare moral grandeur.

Sudden death is never fair but it has seldom been more cruel than in the case of German writer W.G. Sebald, thinker, artist and creator of a small, though magnificent, body of work. Dead at 57 following a car crash last December, his is a case of human loss being matched by an artistic one. In a society in which everyone assumes all answers, Sebald was a true original possessed of curiosity. He saw questions and also examined the connections and coincidences of which a human life is made.

Austerlitz is both an individual search for identity and a profound exploration of the horrors of war, most powerfully of the Holocaust. It is also elegy and testament, and true of all his work, a meditation. In this work the familiar Sebald narrator, ever embarking on relentless intellectual quests, now assumes the role of listener, become the confident of the restless central character, Austerlitz, an architectural historian. On its publication last October – Sebald was no longer a secret – the German and English editions appeared almost simultaneously. There were those who, on discovering this wonderful masterwork, went on immediately to read his other books. Aside from the beauty of his writings, there is a powerful realisation that here is a writer with something valuable to say.

It was there all along, a rare moral grandeur. *The Rings of Saturn* (1995: English translation 1998), is a majestic quest narrative and confers endless possibilities not only on the reader but on fiction itself. It is the story of a journey undertaken on foot through coastal East Anglia. The narrative begins with the question of the whereabouts of Sir Thomas Browne's skull, mentioning en route that Browne was the son of a London silk merchant. Just short of 300 magical, inspiring pages later, it closes, again recalling Browne's father, the silk merchant. In the course of the travels described within these two points is an extraordinary variety of apparently random fact and fancy, the real and the invented. For him erudition and imagination walked hand in hand.

His love of details conferred depth and layers of meaning. That brilliant use of the random was already apparent in *The Emigrants* (1993: English translation 1996). Hailed in Germany on publication as the work that had finally addressed that country's history with a heartbreaking and profound honesty, it has a strange, haunting eloquence. It reveals the power and the grief contained within the most calmly elegant of word pictures. *The Emigrants* juxtaposes four apparently independent stories of lives lived in the shadow of war and, in combining them, recreates forgotten worlds of exiles and ghosts. As the narrator joins up diverse pieces of information, lives and (with them) various lost souls, emerge.

Vertigo, the first of his collage narratives published in Germany (1990), was the third to be translated into English, appearing in 1999. Also written in four parts, it is another quest, part thriller crisscrossing the trail of two murders, as well as the wartime adventures in Napoleon's army of a young soldier who becomes the writer Stendhal. It also contains a remarkable autobiographical sequence.

Sebald's books are ones you carry about in your head forever. Aside from his undisputed, elusive genius, and laconic wit, Sebald brought an enormous integrity to the business of writing. It is a quality sadly absent in our tacky era of celebrity fiction, with comedians busily publishing overly hyped, embarrassingly unfunny narratives.

Many, many books are published, a disturbing number of them are poor; very few have anything of real value to say. Even fewer appear to have anything to do with literature – that most elusive goal. Much the same, of course, will be said about poor standards in commercial cinema where the art has been lost in special effects and film-makers see their audiences as idiots in search of movies that don't require much thought. After all, in a junk food culture, what's good for the body clearly suits the mind. As pampered First World Man and Woman are confronted with ever-increasing amounts of leisure time, what are loosely described as the arts become more than caught up in entertainment – they are supplanted by it.

Of course, any alert social historian will already be pointing out that the 19th century English novel evolved as exactly that, entertainment, and was perfected by none other than Dickens himself. Yet somehow there is a vast gap between 19th century entertainment with its bedrock of Victorian morality and the level to which we have perfected the mindlessness of entertainment as a concept, or a perverted life code.

No doubt those same social historians are busily trying to identify what went wrong with 20th century English fiction post-Evelyn Waugh. Aside from a handful such as Golding, Pritchett, a cult prophet like J.G. Ballard, Graham Swift or Ian McEwan (whose beautifully poised *Atonement* has restored to the English novel much that has been lost), fiction as written in England has entered an ad man's limbo of twenty- and thirty-somethings frightened of growing up. Surely there is more to English fiction than Nick Hornby's extended journalism masquerading as fiction? It is as if within every chatty "this is how I live at the weekends, isn't it a scream?" newspaper column there lurks yet another crummy novel just waiting to be snapped up by a publisher and endorsed by famous friends good for a quote and ripe for a laugh. Not that David Lodge with his tired sit-com variations of the campus novel are any better.

The Irish cannot afford to sit back and smirk, either – judging by much of the work being offered by a generation of writers who have enjoyed the wayward largesse of British publishers who apparently feel simply being Irish is sufficient proof of quality. It is time we looked beyond what is fit to publish and consider instead what is even morally worthy to be even called a book, a narrative, a text.

Of the under-fifties currently at work, few appear to be approaching writing with intent – never mind intelligence. It is not too difficult to see why Eoin McNamee's languidly choreographed murder mystery *The Blue Tango*, or Sean O'Reilly's *Love and Sleep*, an angry European odyssey into self-hatred and fear, should stand head and shoulders above the rest. Having just come off judging duty for an Irish fiction award, I have to say the poor quality of the entries left one feeling more bewildered than insulted. Notions of story appear to have become lost, while narrators stumble out from the pub, juggling gags.

Writing does not have to be intellectual, but it does help if it is intelligent. Perhaps the real problem is not that the writers are untalented; rather the blame lies with the reader. The lazier we became mentally, the easier it was for writers to stop thinking as well. The result is what we see around us – words with little meaning and less relevance. Irish fiction in the main can still look to John McGahern as the master of the ordinary or the deceptively dark, and to the brilliantly consistent William Trevor; while there is also the European stylist John Banville, with his subversive humour. Even so, Irish literature continues to depend on its stalwart A-Team, the great Ulster poets Longley, Mahon and Heaney.

There are many difficulties – but perhaps the main one is we don't like criticism. That, and the fact that we don't really have literary criticism as such – though, of course, there are newspaper reviews, arts show discussions, and serious pieces written in university reviews that tend to appear years after publication for a limited readership. Criticising Irish writers in Ireland is difficult;

it is viewed as either unsporting or, more seriously, betrayal. Although it is apparently fully acceptable to air one's righteous indignation at Edna O'Brien, she is never afforded the protection given to her countrymen – but that is an essay in itself.

What has happened to thinking, to thought? When considering an artist such as Sebald, there is the very real sensation of engaging with a mind that, in turn, shared so much with the great 18th-century men of ideas. Narrative is now reaction; no thought, no content aside from designer labels and consumerism. Come to think of it, perhaps that's where the me-generation of designer novelists want to consign the novel: to consumerist columns.

Considering that story, the origin of fiction, had for so long a subversive role – consider the novels of Eastern Europe and the Soviet Union, or the South African and Latin American writers of protest for whom the novel alone possessed a hugely important voice of subversion – fiction and even criticism have been in large measure hijacked and devalued. Small wonder that Tom Paulin's wonderful book about Hazlitt, *The Day-Star of Liberty* (1998), reads as a passionate cry from the heart as much as a dazzling exploration of style and purpose.

Eileen Battersby is an Irish Times *staff journalist as well as its literary correspondent.*

INTERRUPTION

—

Martin Earl

—

—

The Samizdat of the small.

Visiting scholars, students on foreign exchange, the odd tourist are invariably taken aback to learn – when our paths cross, and the inevitable queries are made – that I have lived these last seventeen years in Coimbra, Portugal.

It's almost as though I'd exposed some too sordid secret. My interlocutor is suddenly offended. Coimbra is a city one passes through; but it is decidedly beyond the pale. In these moments I wonder if something in me is, well, off. Have I lost track of the difference between here and there, fallen out of step? Mind you, *The New York Times*, *The Washington Post*, *The Guardian*, *Le Monde*, *El Pais* are all within a mouse-flick, and even my daily newspaper, *Público*, has garnered international awards and reviews more poetry in a week than *Nytimes.com* does in a season.

Something else to confess: I often feel isolated from the world as I sit through air-conditioned afternoons on upper Broadway where I have spent many a summer since moving to Europe. And Duxbury, my parent's tiny village on Plymouth Bay, is radically removed from time and relevance in comparison to where I live. Once in America, the whole country begins to close in around me, like a large garbage compressor. Western Europe, for all its bloody history, is more porous, open, and refreshingly vulnerable, flanked by Africa on the one hand, and a newly constituted *Mitteleuropa*, Russia, the Mid-East and Asia on the other. The effect on its urban centers is vivid, a perfect Babel. American multiculturalism is academic in comparison. The difference is that Europe keeps absorbing without swallowing. America swallows.

Nevertheless, it is true that the optics are different here. There is something hampering one from becoming fully contemporary; I think it's the taste of wild olives at lunchtime that drags one back, though it could just as well be the hapless collapse of an old bridge sending a busload of villagers to a watery conclusion. Or maybe it's the quiddity of a piece of cured goat's cheese being unlike that of the next piece; at any rate, living in a small country like Portugal is particular. Though I read the same papers here, I read them differently. And there,

I don't even bother to eat goat's cheese and olives, where they all have the taste of pilfered contexts.

I like to think that after all these years I have become a capable student of quiddities, a restorer of contexts, and, maybe, even a competent reader. But more often than not the world seems to conspire against these achievements. Had I spent, as I set out to do, my life in New York, instead of becoming just a sojourner there (and everywhere else) I'd have a different attitude to the world's inclination to interrupt itself.

When I first began spending time in Berlin, shortly after 1989, I was something of a Wall nut. I'd patrol for hours this vivid nullity splicing through two distinct cities. It was a zone; charged with that annihilation which is poetry's ground; out of the haunted aftermath a new life was already suggesting itself. What would Walter Benjamin, had he survived the War, have thought of the Berlin Wall? His brother's wife, Hilde Benjamin, later became – as Peter Demetz tells us – a "fierce state prosecutor" for the German Democratic Republic, appearing as a character in Le Carré's *Spy Who Came in from the Cold*. I suspect that Walter, had he made it across the Pyrenees and eventually to Lisbon, would have been inclined differently. Inevitably the Berlin Wall would have marked the author of the 1934 essay on Brecht, "The Author as Producer," if not materially, then philosophically.

Benjamin tells us that Brecht's "epic" theatre – which for Brecht was a purging of the dramatic claptrap of 19th century theatrical traditions – "had to portray situations, rather than develop plots. It obtains such situations ... by interrupting the plot." Life's "plot" would soon be interrupted by the War. For Benjamin the interruption was fatal, which only underlines his amazing prescience in this essay.

> Here – in the principal of interruption – epic theatre, as you can see, takes up a procedure that has become familiar to you in recent years from film and radio, press and photography. I am speaking of the procedure of montage: the superimposed element disrupts the context in which it is inserted ... The interruption of action, on account of which Brecht described the theatre as epic, constantly counteracts an illusion in the audience. For such illusion is a hindrance to a theatre that proposes to make use of elements of reality in experimental rearrangements ... Epic theatre, therefore, does not reproduce situations: rather, it discovers them. This discovery is accomplished by means of the interruption of sequences. Only interruption here has not the character of a stimulant but an organising function. It arrests the

action in its course, and thereby compels the listener to adopt an attitude *vis-à-vis* the process, the actor *vis-à-vis* his role.

How would Benjamin have reacted to Khrushchev and his East German
clients, who adopted a Brechtian strategy for the purposes of containment? The
wall was both an interruption in the narrative of city life, and served as an
"organising function". A statement he makes a few lines after the passage just
quoted seems to anticipate things: "At the center of his experiment is man.
Present-day man; a reduced man, therefore, chilled in a chilly environment."

Major interruptions have a way of unveiling the real prescience of certain
neglected authors, how their styles and what they had to say has embedded
itself in our contemporary modes of reaction, often without our even being
aware of it. Like spies, they spend their years mapping the blind spots, the gaps
in the official versions. By uncovering the secrets of their own history, they tell
us something about ours. Hubert Butler combined uncommon prescience with
a prose style that is born of the need to tell things as they are:

> Ignorance rampaging with such assurance and harnessed to religious
> enthusiasm is like a runaway horse and cart. It must be stopped before
> serious mischief results.

That Butler is prescient, that Butler's description of Balkan bellicosity and
religious blindness does, inevitably, hold a mirror up to Ireland's own, that
Butler is Orwell's heir to clear-speaking prose are all truisms which, simply for
being such, must necessarily inform our initial understanding of this writer.
However, beyond the surface felicities lies a subtlety of thought that surpasses
Orwell's. Butler, as a writer of firm Christianity, had the more difficult balancing of paradox, and must have been challenged every step of the way to reconcile his belief with the evidence. The result is an urgency and modernity that
sets him apart from Orwell. Humility and maybe a certain diffidence moved
him to take on subjects which, precisely because they were of a less obvious and
more intricate scale than, say, The Empire, the Spanish Civil War, and
Totalitarianism, resulted in the written record of a consciousness closer to our
own, a less deliberate, less monumental ego, a kind of wandering archivist who
is in it for the long run.

Here, in a statement from his afterword to Butler's *In The Land of Nod*, published by The Lilliput Press in 1996, Joseph Brodsky hits the mark in one sense,
but misapprehends Butler's native circumspection:

A man of immense learning, he was interested in this borderline zone, with its fusion of Latin and Slavic cultures, presumably because he sensed in their interplay the future of European civilisation.

Intimate with the porosity of borders, and the often-cryptic motives underlying cultural and religious life, Butler never would have summed things so categorically. Brodsky's hearkening after an aesthetic "future of European civilisation" recalls Gorbachov's cry, at the peak of Perestroika, for a political version of the same, the building of a "common European home". They are fine words, but are they accurate ones?

In our world the ground is shifting constantly. Geopolitics has, in a sense, caught up with technology. The name of the game is flux, innovation, contingency, and dispersion, Benjamin's "interruption" codified. Eliot Weinberger – in one of the more cogent commentaries published in the first days after September 11th – begins by wondering, almost out loud, that

> It is, of course, impossible to know what the effects of yesterday's horror will be; whether it will permanently alter the national psyche (if there is one) or merely recede as yet another bundle of images from yet another media spectacle. This is clearly the first event since the rise of the omnipotence of mass media that is larger than the media, that the media cannot easily absorb and tame. If the media do succeed, national life, beyond the personal tragedies, will continue in its semi-hallucinatory state of continual manufactured imagery. If they fail, something profound may indeed change.

Butler, in the passage below might even be speaking to Weinberger's Americans – a generalised entity, a television audience:

> I hope I have not appeared to diagnose in my Catholic countrymen a unique susceptibility to a disease with which we are all of us more or less infected. Speed of communications has increased, and we are expected to have strong feelings about an infinite series of remote events. But our powers of understanding and sympathy have not correspondingly increased. In an atmosphere of artificially heated emotionalism, truth simply dissolves into expediency.
>
> Looking for a reason, I can only conclude that science has enormously extended the sphere of our responsibilities, while our consciences have remained the same size. Parochially minded people neglect their parishes to pronounce ignorantly about the universe, while the uni-

versalists are so conscious of the world-wide struggles of opposing philosophies that the rights and wrongs of any regional conflict dwindle to insignificance against a cosmic panorama. They feel that truth is in some way relative to orientation, and falsehood no more than a wrong adjustment, so that they can never say unequivocally "that is a lie!" Like the needle of a compass at the North Pole, their moral judgment spins round and round, overwhelming them with information, and telling them nothing at all.

Slowly, almost by design, everything has come together. The pieces have again been fit into their slots. Names have been assigned, information packages coordinated, themes, derived from the usual sources (God, country, and market health), have again reasserted themselves in symbiotic linkages, dovetailing seamlessly with "the latest information" to rise from the smoldering front. If the President, with his cabal of ex-cold warriors, has not mastered the medium of catastrophe completely, at least CNN has. Commercials for tech-companies, and multi-national telecoms, were discreetly slotted back in sometime around day twelve of the new world order, and the weather has again taken up its non-ideological role as global buffer. One has the eerie sense that the media is one step ahead of us; while we are still in a state of numbed shock, they are already, ever so slightly, bored. Or were until, inevitably, new events animated our world. Some weeks after the 11th of September a growing apprehension, that the ratio between new news and endless spin had reached a kind of journalistic threshold in which the event itself no longer sustained the coverage allotted to it, could be seen etched in the tired faces of the commentators. The innocuous nullity of a media-manufactured sense of the real had been entirely restored, the stakes successfully raised, but the mode itself, gloriously unchanged.

Seen by modernists like Eliot and Brecht as a strategy to de-familiarise the literary subject, and so the subjectivity of the reader, Benjamin's notion of Brechtian montage and interruption has continuously evolved in Media methodology. Even as early as Brecht these strategies were not seen as native to the literary arts, but rather as something that was borrowed from "film and radio, press and photography." As literary strategy they worked marvelously, especially when this alien provenance was recognised, and the methods were combined and defused with traditional ones. Who could imagine the artistry of Delillo without its command of montage; or the surrealist segues and mastery of contextual interruption in Ashbery? However, carried out programmatically (unmediated, as it were, by the non-ideological happiness of the artist), they were as much a disaster for American writers, as social realism was for Soviet ones. If the Language poets dug their own grave by following early postmodernist theory to the letter, the techniques that Benjamin theorised are still very much alive in the Media.

Two days after the event, Eliot Weinberger would of course not attempt to close the case. And yet, one suspects that his conclusions were already there in nascent form, and that he would be unsurprised at how quickly, in subsequent days, the media did begin, as he implied they would, to "absorb and tame" the event. But this could not happen without the collusion of an audience. Hubert Butler's words seem as apt as ever more than half a century on.

> Speed of communications has increased, and we are expected to have strong feelings about an infinite series of events. But our powers of understanding and sympathy have not correspondingly increased. In an atmosphere of artificially heated emotionalism truth simply dissolves in expediency.

Expedient is the relation to the profit motive that underlies the coverage of tragedies, especially when, with a certain collaboration by the media itself, the tragedy is the endlessly ramifying variety. In Benjamin's reading of Brecht, the "interruption of action ... constantly counteracts an illusion in the audience." But what happens when life itself begins to behave according to the patterns of postmodern theory; when the masters of interruption, the global terrorist who inserts himself anywhere and uses the materials at hand to spectacular effect, an effect that is planned to play to, and through, the media, and which the media pick up with unfeigned relish; what happens when this is formatted with a simplified and formulaic discourse, endlessly repeatable in the form of sound bites and catch-phrases, and crafted by spin doctors to combine with a "state of continual manufactured imagery", a brutal montage of endless interruption, endless repetition, to enforce the party line, and coordinate a mass emotional response – out of which all moral discussion has long been bleached; what happens when what is created in the viewer is a muddled and superficial familiarity with everything? And a knowledge of nothing?

It would seem normal – even acceptable – to ask what a little magazine, and, by extension, literature in general, can do in days like these. The answer is no doubt to simply be itself, to not try in the bad times any harder that it might try in the good times to do the job it has always done. This is a job that simply refuses to be categorised, that has no "job description", no hiring policy, no stated aims, and no ambitions save its own survival, and that survival is predicated upon an exception. Literature exists outside the rules we apply to, and by which we condition, the survival of every other social artifact, in that it does not have to be useful. In fact its uselessness is its chief cunning. The closest we can get to knowing what it should do is to quote it, as though some sublime tautology were interpolating between it and us. As Shakespeare has it in his famous 18th sonnet: as long as we continue, poetry itself will continue, even though it is precisely poetry that causes us to continue. His whole argument in 18 is against comparing the elective subject to a summer's day, or anything else under the sun. Poetry is not a reflection of nature. It is another nature altogether. It does not think about the world, but re-invents it in the form of tone, of wit, and metonymy. That is why events such as the one that occurred on September 11th, for whatever else they might do, also end up reaffirming the primacy of literature *vis-à-vis* the world. And by "primacy" we do not mean superiority, or even independence. In fact literature needs the world more than the world needs literature. The world could indeed get by without great books, as it seems increasingly to be doing. We refer more to a modality, a form of operating. The world does not invent literature; it is literature that invents the world. Even terrible events like September 11th will eventually be invented – transfigured might be a better word – by the literary imagination.

As it invents the world, it also invents its own modes of survival, its authors, its critics, its editors, and all the technologies which enforce its material existence: publishing houses, little magazines, literary web-sites, broadsheets. In Soviet Russia – where writing things down on paper was often too dangerous – ways of thinking about, and storing poetry in the mind grew into an almost Augustinian sophistication in some, as when Nadezhda Mandelstam memorised all of her husband – Osip's – poems so that they would not be lost. Who knows to what extent this was an act of altruism, preserving her husband's poetic legacy, or if it was her special way of surviving, of girding her psyche against interruption?

Martin Earl lives in Portugal. He is the author of two books of poems.

THIS ISSUE

The Editors would like to thank the following organisations for their assistance and support in the preparation of this inaugural issue.

Imagine Belfast 2008 is the body organising Belfast's bid to become European Capital of Culture in 2008. It may be contacted at 109/113 Royal Avenue, Belfast BT1 (Tel: 028 9032 2008).

The New Belfast Community Arts Initiative specialises in innovative cross-community arts projects. It seeks to contribute to the peace-making process through the social, economic and cultural regeneration of the Belfast community. It may be contacted at the Clanmil Arts and Business Centre, Northern Whig House, Bridge Street, Belfast BT1 1LU (Tel: 028 90 923493).

Since 1982, *The Orion Society* in the United States has been working to increase awareness of – and responsibility to – human and natural communities through grassroots educational programmes and two award-winning quarterly journals, *Orion* and *Orion Afield*. It may be contacted at 187 Main Street, Great Barrington, MA 01230, USA (Tel: 413 528-4422), or through its website (www.oriononline.org).

The Linen Hall Library, founded in 1788 and located in the centre of Belfast, is the oldest subscription library in the British Isles. Besides its distinguished collections, it organises a range of cultural activities and events. Its address is 17 Donegall Square North, Belfast BT1 5GB.

Nicholson & Bass is the North's leading printer of quality books, catalogues and other publications.

Tonic Design is located in the Cathdral Quarter district of Belfast and can be contacted at Unit 7, Northern Whig House, 3 Bridge Street, Belfast BT1 1LU (Tel: 028 90 439505).

SUBSCRIBE NOW

£16stg/€26/$24 *(for one year)*   £24/€39/$36 *(for two years)*

(For postage outside Ireland and Britain, add £4/€6/$5 per year for Europe or £6/€9/$8 for the rest of the world)

NAME:	
ADDRESS:	
TOWN OR CITY:	
COUNTY OR STATE:	POSTAL CODE:
COUNTRY:	
EMAIL:	

Send as gift (*with card from*   ) to above address.

Enclosed is my cheque or money order to
IRISH PAGES for the amount of £stg   or €
(Cheques in US, Canadian or other currencies cannot be accepted)

Please charge my ☐ Visa   ☐ Mastercard   ☐ American Express

Card number ☐☐☐☐ ☐☐☐☐ ☐☐☐☐   Expiry date ☐☐ ☐☐

Signature

Subscribe now by posting a copy of this form to:

IRISH PAGES
The Linen Hall Library
17 Donegall Square North
Belfast BT1 5GB

LIMITED EDITIONS

The frontispiece has been made by the printmaker and painter Alfonso Monreal, who divides his time between Mexico and Ireland. It is the first of a series of four entitled *Disasters No 1-4*. Each print has been produced in a limited artist's edition of 50 for sale through IRISH PAGES at a price of £200 each.

Carolyn Mulholland's bronze, bearing Seamus Heaney's *A Keen for the Coins*, may also be purchased through IRISH PAGES, at a price of €1100.

A proportion of the sales will go towards the costs of the magazine. Inquiries should be made through our postal address.